VITAL RECORDS

OF

PELHAM,

MASSACHUSETTS,

TO THE YEAR 1850.

PUBLISHED BY THE
NEW-ENGLAND HISTORIC GENEALOGICAL SOCIETY,
AT THE CHARGE OF
THE EDDY TOWN-RECORD FUND.

BOSTON, MASS.,

1902.

THIS publication is issued under the authority of a vote passed by the NEW ENGLAND HISTORIC GENEALOGICAL SOCIETY, 6 November, 1901, as follows:

Voted: That the sum of $2000, from the bequest of the late Robert Henry Eddy, be set aside as a special fund to be called the Eddy Town-Record Fund, for the sole purpose of publishing the Vital Records of the towns of Massachusetts, and that the Council be authorized and instructed to make such arrangements as may be necessary for such publication. And the treasurer is hereby instructed to honor such drafts as shall be authorized by the Council for this purpose.

Committee on Publications.

C. B. TILLINGHAST,   FRANCIS EVERETT BLAKE,
CHARLES KNOWLES BOLTON,   DON GLEASON HILL
            EDMUND DANA BARBOUR.

Editor.
HENRY ERNEST WOODS.

Stanhope Press
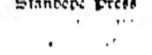

THE TOWN OF PELHAM, Hampshire County, was established January 15, 1743, prior to which time it was the common land called New Lisburne.

June 16, 1788, a part of Belchertown was annexed to Pelham.

January 28, 1822, a part of Pelham was included in the new town of Prescott.

———

Population by Census: 1765 (Prov.), 371; 1776 (Prov.), 729; 1790 (U. S.), 1040; 1800 (U. S.), 1144; 1810 (U. S.), 1185; 1820 (U. S.), 1278; 1830 (U. S.), 904; 1840 (U. S.), 956; 1850 (U. S.), 983; 1855 (State), 789; 1860 (U. S.), 748; 1865 (State), 737; 1870 (U. S.), 673; 1875 (State), 633; 1880 (U. S.), 614; 1885 (State), 549; 1890 (U. S.), 486; 1895 (State), 486; 1900 (U. S.), 462.

EXPLANATIONS.

1. WHEN places other than Pelham and Massachusetts are named in the original records, they are given in the printed copy.

2. In all records the original spelling is followed.

3. The various spellings of a name should be examined, as items about the same family or individual might be found under different spellings of that name.

4. Marriages and intentions of marriages are printed under the names of both parties, but the full information concerning each party is given only in the entry under his or her name. When both the marriage and intention of marriage are recorded, only a marriage record is printed, with an asterisk.

5. Additional information which does not appear in the original text of an item, i.e. any explanation, query, inference, or data shown in other entries of a record is bracketed. Parentheses are used only when they occur in the original text, or to separate clauses found there, such as the last place of parents in the marriage records.

ABBREVIATIONS.

a. — age
b. — born
ch. — child
chn. — children
Co. — county
d. — daughter; died; day
Dea. — deacon
dup. — duplicate entry
f. — female
h. — husband
inf. — infant
int. — publishment of intention of marriage
Jr. — junior
m. — married; male; month
prob. — probably
rec. — recorded
s. — son
Sr. — senior
w. — wife; week
wid. — widow
widr. — widower
y. — year
2d. — second
3d. — third

PELHAM BIRTHS.

PELHAM BIRTHS.

To the year 1850.

ABBOT (see Abbott), ———, ch. Cheney and Pamelia, May 22, •
[18]49.

ABBOTT (see Abbot), Luther Cheney, s. Cheney and Rachael,
May 11, 1831.
Milo Wells, s. Cheney (Abbot) and Rachel, Feb. 15, 1833.
Rachel Ellen, d. Cheney and Rachel, May 27, 1839.
Zilphia S., d. Cheney and Pamelia, Aug. 26, [18]47.

ABERCROMBIE (see Abercrombiee), Ashel, s. Isaac and Mar-
tha, Oct. 21, 1807.
Austin, s. David and Mary, June 18, 1818.
Clarisa, d. Rob[er]t and Mary, July 30, 1800.
David, s. James and Margrey, Apr. 4, 1788.
Elijah Billings (Abercrombies), twin ch. William and Abigail,
Apr. 15, 1818.
Emerson, s. David and Mary, Sept. 7, 1823.
Fanny, d. David and Mary, July 3, 1821.
George B., s. Hiram and Betsy, Mar. 23, 1841.
George Frederick, s. Hiram and Elizabeth, Mar. 23, 1841.
Hiram, s. James and Margerey, Mar. 9, 1807.
Horace, s. David and Mary, Nov. 4, 1827.
Ira, s. Isaac and Marthew, Sept. 25, 1797.
Ira, s. Isaac and Martha, Jan. 28, 1805.
Isaac, s. Isaac and Marthew, July 20, 1793.
James, s. James and Margrey, Apr. 18, 1790.
Jemima Darling, d. William and Jemima, Jan. 4, 1808.
Joel, s. William and Abigail, Jan. 17, 1815.
Lucinda Castle, twin ch. William and Abigail, Apr. 15, 1818.
Margaret Stephenson, d. William and Jemima, Nov. 24, 1805.
Margret, d. James and Margrey, Oct. 11, 1781.
Mary Fields Billing, d. William and Abigail, June 22, 1813.
Mehetebel, d. James and Margrey, Jan. 31, 1786.
Rachel, d. James and Margrey, Mar. 25, 1792.
Rebekah, d. James and Margrey, Feb. 4, 1784.

9

ABERCROMBIE, Sally, d. Isaac and Marthew, May 11, 1798.
Sarah, d. Rev. Robert and Margaret, Oct. 11, 1756.
Sarah, d. James and Margrey, Oct. 17, 1794.
Sunday, d. Isaac and Marthew, May 14, 18 5.
Solmon, s. David and Mary, Apr. 11, 183 .
Sumner, s. James and Margrey, Jan. 8, 1799.
Warren B., s. Hiram and Betsy, Nov. 2, 1! 16.
William Hyslop, s. Isaac and Marthew, Aug. 4, 1791.
Wyman, s. David and Mary, June 24, 1816

ABERCROMBIEE (see Abercrombie) Lucindia, d. Isaac and
Martha, Apr. 20, 18 9.

ADAMS, Avery Ward, ch. Francis and Naomi, Oct. 28, 1826, in
New Bra⁻in]tree.
Elizabeth Jane, ch. Francis and Naomi, June 16, 1829.
Francis Fisk, ch. Francis and Naomi, Sept. 24, 1833.
John Gray, ch. Francis and Naomi, Oct. 13, 1819, in New
Bra⁻in]tree.
Nancy Park, ch. Francis and Naomi, July 22, 1821, in New
Bra⁻in]tree.
Salina, ch. Francis and Naomi, Apr. 15, 1818, in New Bra⁻in⁻tree.
Samuel Holten, ch. Francis and Naomi, Dec. 29, 1823, in New
Bra⁻in]tree.

AIKENS (see Akens), Annis, d. Joseph and Hannah, Nov. 5,
1806.
Daniel [dup. Akens], s. Joseph and Hannah, Aug. 3 [dup. 5],
1792.
Sally, d. Joseph and Hannah, July 25, 1804.

AIRS, Nancy, d. Buenos and Rachel Dec. 26, 1799.

AKENS (see Aikens), Hannah, d. Joseph and Hannah, June 7,
1796.
Joseph, s Joseph and Hannah, June 17, 1795.
Poley, d. Joseph and Hannah, Apr. 23, 1798.

ALBE (see Albee, Albia, Alby), Clecy, d. Laben and Jenna,
May 7 1798.
Nancy, d. Laben and Jenna, Feb. 23, 1 1.

ALBEE (see Albe, Albia, Alby) Barman, s. Laben and Jenna,
May 13, 1 1
George Lewis, s Arta and Sally Aug. 4, 1821.
Lucinda, d. Laben and Johannah Aug. 5, 1816.

ALBEE, Rebeca, d. Laben and Jonah, May 26, 1792, in Milford.
Warren, s. Laban and Joanna [dup. Susanna], Sept. 16, 1808.

ALBIA (see Albe, Albee, Alby), Arba, s. Laben (Albee) and
Jonnah, Mar. 22, 1794.

ALBY (see Albe, Albee, Albia), Rarcy [?], d. Alexander and
Mairy, May 20, 1811.

ALDRICH, Adeline, d. Nathaniel and Nancy, July 14, 1837.
Charles Phelps, s. Nehemiah and Diana, Dec. 2, 1832.
Eliza, d. Nathaniel and w., Mar. 2, 1835.
Martin Grovner, s. Nathaniel and Nancy S., May 25, 1839.
Only, s. Asel and Olive, Aug. 1, 1815.
Orinda F., d. Nathaniel and Nancy, Oct. 1, 1844.
Reuben K., s. Artemas K. and Hannah, Sept. 9, 1849.
Sarah, d. Asel and Olive, June 9, 1819.
Sarah J., d. Nathaniel and Nancy, July 25, 1845.
———, s. Artemas and Hannah, —— 18, 1842.

ALLEN, Anna Caroline, d. Jesse and Anna, Jan. 25, 1812.
Charles Medcaff, s. Jess and Anna, Oct. 28, 1807.
David Houston, s. Sam[ue]l and Elisabath, Oct. 11, 1816.
Debenport, s. Sam[ue]l and Elizabeth, Dec. 11, 1809.
Erastus Willard, ch. Welcome and Anna M., Feb. 8, 1827.
Joseph, s. Samuel and Elisabeth, May 21, 1813.
Joseph D., s. David and Hannah, Dec. 20, 1847.
Martha, d. Sam[ue]l and Elisabath, Sept. 16, 1819.
Martha E., d. David and Hannah, Aug. 3, 1844, in Deerfield.
Nancy, d. Jesse and Anna, Sept. 3, 1814.
Nathaniel, s. Jesse and Anna, Aug. 23, 1817.
Parces, d. Samuel and Elizabeth, May 19, 1803.
Phines, s. Samuel and Elizabeth, Mar. 21, 1801.
Richard Montgomery, s. Jesse and Anna, Dec. 15, 1809.
Sally, d. Samuel and Elizabeth, July 3, 1805.
Sarah Maria, ch. Welcome and Anna M., July 29, 1831.
Silas, s. Polly, Apr. 3, 1799.
Susan A., d. David and Hannah, Sept. 29, 1845.
W[illia]m M., s. Welcom and Anna M., Mar. 24, 1823.

AMSDALE (see Amsdill), Abigal, d. Abner and Susan[torn],
Sept. 16, 1784.
Robert Sekene, s. Abner and Susannah, May 10, 1789.

AMSDILL (see Amsdale), Lydia, d. Abner and Susannah, Jan.
2, 1787.

ANDRESS (see Andrews), Asa, s. Stephen (Andrews) and
  Bridget, Apr. 5, 1787.

ANDREWS (see Andr— Chaster, s. Stephen and Bridget,
  Apr. 9, 17
Joel, s. Steven and Bridget, June 15, 1785.
Leonard, s. Stephen and Bridget, Feb. 19, 1793.

ARNOLD, Samuel Franklin, s. Savanah and Emeline, Nov. 7,
  1828.
Saphronia, d. Savanah and Emaline, Mar. 19, 1827.

ASHLEY, Joel, s. James and Rebecah, Jan. 30, 1805.
William, s. William and Nancy, May 28, 1787.

AUSTIN, Charles, s. Ebenezer and Mary, Nov. 1, 1826.
Joel, s. Ebenezer and Mary, June 16, 1825.
Mary Gage, d. Ebenezer and Mary, Sept. 3, 1835.

AYERS, see Airs.

BABBET (see Babbit), John, s. Sanford and Nancy, Aug. 17,
  1801.

BABBIT (see Babbet, Ezra, s. Silas and Sarah, Oct. 13, 1794,
  in Barry.
Irena, d. Silas and Sarah, Sept. 30, 1791, in Petersham.
Juda, d. Silas and Sarah, Apr. 13, 179-, in Petersham.
Samuel, s. Silas and Sarah, July 21, 1797, in Greenwich.
Silas, s. Silas and Sarah, Aug. 7, 1801.

BAILEY, Elisabeth Lee, d. Rev. Winthrop and Hannah, Nov.
  21, 1822.
Francis Parkman, s. Rev. Winthrop and Martha, Nov. 26, 1820.
Hannah Stanwood, d. Rev. Winthrop and Martha, June 8, 1817.
Idellia M., d. Sidney and Marsha, July 9, 1846.
Levi N., s. Sidney and Marsha, Jan. 18, 1848.
Martha Gray, d. Rev. Winthrop and Martha, Feb. 19, 1819.
Niman Wesly, s. Sidney A. and Marsha S., Sept. 2, 184-.
Sarah Crosbey, d. Winthrop and Martha, Apr. 4, 1845
- —, d. Sidney and Marsha, Sept. 15, 1844. [Rec. May 21,
  1844, prob. b. 1843.]

BAKER, Anna, d. John and Hannah, June 26, 1847.
Anson, s. Ezkiel and Hannah, Aug. 7, 181.
Banjman, s. Isaac and Rebecah, Oct. 26, 1778.
Bratn s. John and Hann Feb. 8, 181.

BAKER, Davis, s. John and Hannah, Mar. 11, 1799.
Elisha, s. James and Sally, Dec. 21, 1790.
Eliza, d. John and Hannah, Apr. 18, 1809.
Ezkiel, s. Ezkiel and Hannah, Feb. 20, 1802.
Hannah Smith, d. John and Hannah, July 2, 1805.
Isaac, s. Ezekiel and Hannah, June 17, 1788.
James, s. James and Sally, July 31, 1788.
John, s. Ezkiel and Hannah, June 25, 1799.
Jonathen, s. John and Hannah, Apr. 20, 1795.
Joseph, s. Ezkiel and Hannah, Feb. 8, 1792.
Joshua, s. Ezekeil and Hannah, Oct. 8, 1786.
Moses, s. Ezkiel and Hannah, Aug. 17, 1796.
Rachel, d. Ezkiel and Hannah, May 29, 1794.
Rebeckah, d. James and Sally, Mar. 1, 1797.
Samuel, s. James and Sally, July 20, 1793.
William, s. John and Hannah, Dec. 17, 1796.

BALLARD, Aurila, d. Joshua and Polly, Mar. 13, 1808, in New
Salem.

BALLOU, Abinem, s. Stephen and Alsa, Sept. 19, 1823.
Adaline Aldridg, d. Leonard and Pheebe, Sept. 26, 1826.
Alonzo, s. Leonard and Phebe, Jan. 22, 1820.
Alonzo, ch. Stephen and Elsa, Nov. 24, 1825.
Angeline Elisebeth B., d. Leonard and Phebe, Nov. 12, 1830.
Barton, s. Stephen, June 22, 1813.
Bethany, d. Stephen and Alise, June 1, 1811.
Emory, s. Stephen and Alice, Sept. 6, 1818.
George, ch. Leonard and Phebe, Nov. 25, 1833.
Hiram, ch. Stephen and Elsa, Sept. 19, 1823.
John Braley, s. Learned and Pheebe, Oct. 28, 1823.
Lillis, d. Stephen and Allice, Jan. 25, 1809.
Live H., s. Learned and Pheebe, Sept. 12, 1821.
Martin Lyman, s. Emery and Mariah, May 7, 1838.
Mary A., d. Hyram and Elizabeth, Oct. 18, 1849.
Orson M., s. Emery and Maria, Dec. 23, 1843.
Rozina, d. Leonard and Phebe, Sept. 23, 1817.
Theadore Sanpson, s. Leonard and Phebe, July 30, 1829.
Welcome, s. Stephen and Allice, Sept. 7, 1805, in Cumberland.

BANET, Elizebeth, d. Isaac Banet and Rebecah Baker, Aug. 17,
1791.

BANISTER, Betheiah, [twin] d. Andrew and Betheiah, Feb. 22,
1796.

BANISTER, William [twin s. Andrew and Bethiah, Feb. 22, 1796.

BARBER, As... John and Azubah, June 17, 18...
Binjebin, s. R... and Sarah, Nov. 23, 1751.
Chester, s. John and Azubah, Dec. 11, 17...
[twin], s. R... and Sarah, Sept. 19 1757.
John, s. John and Azubah, June 15, 1762.
Marg..., R... and [torn] Feb. 22, 1755.
Matthew, s. Robert and Sargent, Apr. 8, 1753.
Nancy, d. John and Azubah, June 3, 18...
Parmer, d. John and Azubah, May 22, 1797.
Rebecca, d. John and Azubah, Mar. 6, 179...
Sarah, d. John and Azubah, Jan. 6, 1788.
Selina, d. John and Azubah, Sept. 5, 1 7.
Warren, s. John and Azubah, Dec. 6, 1785.

BARNES (see Barns), Dexter R. s. Ansel and Deborah, Oct. 8, 1842.
Harriett L., d. Ansel and Deborah, Oct. 20, 1846.
Lewis C., s. Ansel and Deborah, Apr. 9, 1855, in Hardwick.
Louis M., d. Ansel and Deborah, A... 24, 18...
Martha A., d. Ansel and Deborah, F... 27, 184 in Hardwick.
Susan E., d. Ansel and Deborah, Ma... 6, 183 in Hardwick.

BARNS (see Barnes), Estes, ch. ... s. Dwight and L...
[dup. Vol.], Ma. 27, 183 .
James Dwight, ch. Dwight and L..., Aug. 27, 1827.
Joseph M'Ellen, ch. Dwight and Lo... Oct. 6, 1820.

BARROWS, Isaac, ch. Joseph and Patience Nov. 24, 1811, Attleborough.
Joseph, ch. Joseph and Patience, Dec. 29, 1812 in Attleboro.
Laura Ann, ch. Joseph and Patience, Apr. 8, 1827.
Mary Carroll, d. Joseph and Patience, Nov. 18, 1820.
William, ch. Joseph and Patience, Aug. 26, 1819, in Attleboro.

BARRY (see Berry, Berry), Allexander, s. Allexander and Martha, Apr. 2 1791.
Pattsey, d. Robert and Parley, Sept. 8, 1805.
J..., s. Allexander and Matthew, June 15, 1788.
R... d. Alexander and Matthew, Dec. 9, 1784.

BARTLET (see Bartlet, Bartlett), Martha Anne, d. Alexander and Deborah Ju... 1844. Rec. May 21, 1844, prob. b. 1843.

BARTLETT (see Bartlet, Barttlett), Adelia A., d. Philander and Susanna, Feb. 9, 1839, in Enfield.

Alexander, ch. Alexander and Lucy, Aug. 11, 1816, [in] Enfield.

Almaria, ch. Avery and Hannah, June 5, 1833.

Almira, d. Luther and Olive, Nov. 24, 1805.

Alvin, s. Lucas and Lorancy, Oct. 28, 1829, in Enfield.

Avery Franklin, ch. Avery and Hannah, July 5, 1836.

Chester, ch. Alexander and Lucy, Sept. 3, 1826, [in] Shutesbury.

David, s. Lucas and Lorancy, Oct. 23, 1827, in Enfield.

Eliza Maria, d. Horace and Sarah, July 21, 1835.

Ellen M., d. Philander and Susanna, Apr. 4, 1847.

Frances M., d. Philander and Susanna, Feb. 2, 1837, in Enfield.

Henrietta, d. Marshall J. and Abigail, Jan. 5, 1848.

Hiram, s. Luther and Olive, Jan. 13, 1804, in Brookfield.

James Emerson, s. Alexander and Deborah, Sept. 19, 1839.

Liberty, s. Luther and Olive, Apr. 8, 1807.

Lucy, d. Alexander and Lucy, Dec. 5, 1818.

Mariva, d. Lucas and Lorancy, Oct. 12, 1831, in Enfield.

Mirian E., d. Philander and Susanna, Apr. 2, 1843, in Belchertown.

Ocran H., s. Lucas and Lorancy, May 13, 1828, in Shutesbury.

Oliver W., s. Philander (b. Enfield) and Susanna (b. Belchertown), June 20 [dup. 19], 1849.

Paulina H. [dup. Perlina Hunter], d. Lucas and Lorancy, Oct. 3, 1836.

Sally, ch. Alexander and Lucy, Jan. 19, 1829, [in] Shutesbury.

Sally E., d. Lucas and Lorancy, Dec. 31, 1825.

Samuel Baxter, s. Horace and Sarah, Mar. 27, 1837.

Susannah, d. Alexander and Lucy, Sept. 5, 1821.

Sylvenus, ch. Alexander and Lucy, Dec. 21, 1823, [in] Shutesbury.

BARTON, Benjamin Franklin, s. Robert and Elinor [dup. Elenor], July 22, 1820.

Isaac, s. Robert and Elenor, Jan. 15, 1824.

John Leason, s. Samuel and Polly, May 13, 1826, in Enfield.

Lydia, d. Robert and Elenor, Oct. 25, 1822.

BARTTLETT (see Bartlet, Bartlett), Eliza Earle, d. Luther and Olive, Dec. 15, 1808.

BATS, Lydia, d. Eli and Abigal, Aug. 17, 1802.

BENNET (see Banet).

BENSON, Adalaide, d. Danford and Content, Sept. 21, 1844.
Cornelia N., d. Danford Jr. and Frinda, July 18, 1844.

BERREY (see Barry, Berry), James, s. Allax[an]d[e]r (Berry)
and Martha, Mar. 10, 1777, in New Salem.
Molley, d. Alax[an]d[e]r and Martha, Dec. 9, 1784.

BERRY (see Barry, Berrey), Axy, d. John and Betsey, Dec. 29,
1810.
Betsey, d. John and Dorcas, Oct. 24, 1813.
John, s. John and Dorcas, Feb. 27, 1818.
Locket, s. Allax[an]d[e]r (Berrey) and Martha, Oct. 23, 1778,
in New Salem.
W[illia]m Alexander, s. John and Betsey, Sept. 18, 1809.
[torn]er, s. James and Jean, Feb. 5, 1747.
[torn] s. James and Jean, Oct. - , 1749.
[torn] s. James and Jean, June 18, 1751.
[torn] d. James and Jean, June 18, 1753.
[torn] d. James and Jean, June 25, 1755.
[torn] s. James and Jean, May 26, 1758.

BIDWELL, Charles Elliot, s. William F. (b. Malborough) and
Sarah (b. Monson), July 17, 1847, in Springfield.
Jane Hellen, [twin] d. William F. (b. Malborough) and Sarah (b.
Monson), Apr. 10, 1845, in Springfield.
Sarah Ellen, [twin] d. William F. (b. Malborough) and Sarah b.
Monson), Apr. 10, 1845, in Springfield.

BILLING, Melinda Bell, d. Abigail (Billng), May 26, 1808, in
Amhest.

BLACKMER (see Blackmor, Blackmore), William Hack, s.
Amos and Margret, Apr. 14, 1814.

BLACKMOR (see Blackmer, Blackmore), Amos Harvey, s.
Amos (Blackmer) and Margaret, Nov. 12, 1817.

BLACKMORE (see Blackmer, Blackmor), Peter, s. David and
Margeret, Oct. 31, 1811.

BLAIR, Annace Mahala, d. Samuel and Ruba, Aug. 28, 1814,
in Ware.
Calvin Danforth, s. Samuel and Ruba, Nov. 12, 1827.
Calvin Du , s. Samuel and Ruba, Mar. 6, 1817, in Ware.
Caris a Dorna, d. Samuel and Ruba, Mar. 23, 1823, in Ware.
Lui na Sh m , d. Sam and R J t, May 14, 1 , in Ware.
Sally Car line, d. Sam el and Rub a, June 11 1812, in Ware.

BLAIR, William Strong, s. Samuel and Ruba, Mar. 9, 1820, in
 Ware.
[torn]m, s. John and Sarah, Nov. 12, 1744.
[torn]beth, d. John and Sarah, Jan. 26, 1745.
[torn]l, d. John and Sarah, Sept. 17, 1746.
[torn]na, d. John and Sarah, Apr. 22, 1748.
[torn] Kelso, s. John and Sarah, Apr. 21, 1750.
[torn] d. John and Sarah, Apr. 10, 1752.
[torn] s. John and Sarah, Feb. 25, 1754.
[torn] d. John and Sarah, Nov. 15, 1755.
[torn]h, d. John and Sarah, Oct 3, 1757.
[torn] d. John and Sarah, Aug. 21, 1760.

BOSSWORTH (see Bosworth), Ruth, d. Rufus and Mary, May
 7, 1823.

BOSWORTH (see Bossworth), Julia Ann, d. Rufus and Mary,
 Apr. 20, 1825.
Nathaniel, s. Rufus and Mary, Aug. 17, 1827.

BOYDEN, Albert C., s. Sanford [dup. Sandford] and Mary,
 May 1, 1847.
Clara E., d. Erastus P. and Mary R. (b. Belchertown), Nov. 10,
 1845, in Belchertown.
John D., s. Erastus P. and Mary, Feb. 23, 1848.
Lydia Ann, d. Pliny and w., Oct. 26, 1831.

BOYINGTON (see Boynton, Byingtown), Caroline Frances, d.
 Emery and Mary Ann, Aug. 6, 1839.
Hannah Herington, d. Silas and Olive, Apr. 27, 1813.
Jeremiah, s. Silas and Olive, Dec. 9, 1802, in Prexton.
Lucey, d. Silas and Olive, Aug. 20, 1805.
Phebe Maria, d. Silas and Eliza, Nov. 17, 1846.

BOYNTON (see Boyington, Byingtown), Alpha, s. Eben[eze]r
 and Mary, Oct. 3, 1803.
Anna, d. Eben[eze]r and Mary, Oct. 5, 1811.
Asa Jr., s. Asa and Persi[s], Jan. 7, 1825.
Betseyann, d. Alfred and Sarahann, Nov. 16, 1844, in Palmer.
Ebenezar, s. Eben[eze]r and Mary, Oct. 30, 1806.
Ebenezer, s. Asa and Persis, Mar. 3, 1817, in Va.
Emory, s. Eben[eze]r and Mary, Mar. 1, 1809.
Hannah, d. Asa and Perses, Dec. 26, 1814.
Jane Augusta, d. Emery and Maryann, Aug. 13, 1837.
Joseph Elehu, s. Silas and Eliza, Nov. 16, 1844.
Loren Sargent, s. Silas Jr. and Almira, May 11, 1837.

BANXTON, Maria, d. Asa and Persis Nov. 23, 1818, in Va.
Martha Ann, d. Silas and E ta, Jan. 17, 1 45.
Mary, d. Ebenezar and Mary Apr. 13, 1 1.
Mary Ann, d. Asa and Persis July 3   1 1   n N. Y.
M   la, d. Asa and Per   Oct. 19, 132   a Va.
Ph   d. Asa and Pers. Oct. 26, 18 3, in Pexton.
Rut Sumner, s. Sil   al O   Nov. 6, 1816.
Sally Harington, d. Silas and Olive, Aug. 4, 18 ,
Saran, d. Ebenezar and Mary Jan. 1, 1798, in Me rd.
Semantha Jane, d. Silas and Eliza, May 27 1 42.
Silas (dup. B vingto   s. Silas and Olive Jan 21, 1 7.
Silas 2d, s. Asa and Persis Jan. 28, 18 , in Pexton.

BRAILEY see Braily Bridev John Qu nc , ch. John and
     Almira, May 23, 1 7.
Laura Ann, d. John and Almira, N   r 1 25.
Manly, ch. John and Almira, Mar. 11 1 35.

BRAILY (see Brailey, Braley) Atford, s. John and Almira,
     Apr. 3 , 1833.

BRAINARD, Joseph, s. Elijah and Parthina Oct. 4 , 181 .
Mary Marsh, d. Elijah and Parthina, May 16 1   ,

BRALEY (see Brailey, Braily) Amos, s. Solomon and Esther,
     July 19, 1803, in Mendon.
Collins, s. Solomon and Esther, June 3 , 17   Frank's.
Deborah, d. Solomon and Esther Jan. 28, 17 , i Mendon.
George, s. Solomon and Esther, Apr. 10, 1796 " Mend n
Isaac, s. Solomon and Esther, Sept. 14, 18   i Mendon.
Lidia, d. Solomon and Esther, Feb. 3, 1791, i Cumberl d.
Martha, d. Solomon and Esther June 11 17   n Me Cn.
Nancy, d. Solomon and Esther, Nov. 8, 18 7.
Sally, d. Solomon and Esther, June 2, 18 5, in   i d n.

BRIGGS, Betsey Andrews, d. Isaac and Betse De   11 1 25
Charlotte Dutton, d. Aseph (Bri) and Lilly J 1 7 1
I   t Andrews, s. Isaac and Betsey, Aug. 29 1 19.
E   y L., d. Joseph and Emily June 2, 1844.
F   Ell rt, s. Isaac and Betse Jr, Dec 13 1   .
I   W fred, s. Isaac and Betsey, Jul 22 1   3.
I a Francis, s. Isaac and Betse May 25 1   8.
R   I n   d. Isaac and Betsey, June 2, 1   .
W   A , d. Isaac and Betse , Feb. 1   1

BRIGHAM, Barr a Leverin,   Iurt   d M   k, Feb. 2, 1813.

BRIGHAM, Bashua Hamilton, d. Barna and Anna, Sept. 18, 1805.
Benjman Fay, s. Lyscom and Marthew, Aug. 25, 1800.
Charles Fredrick [dup. Fredic], s. Barna and Anna [dup. Anne],
    Jan. 19, 1807.
Curtius, s. Lyscom and Marthew, May 21, 1793, in Wastborough.
Ebenezer Lyscom, s. Lyscom and Marthew, Nov. 13, 1797.
Henry, s. Barna and Anna, Mar. 25, 1815.
Martha, d. Lyscom and Marthew, May 7, 1795, in Hopkintown.
Martia Ann, d. Barna and Anna, Oct. 14, 1817.
Nehemiah Hinds, s. Barna and Anna, Mar. 13, 1809.
Stilmon, s. Lyscob and Martha, Jan. 19, 1808.
Tilly, s. Barna and Anna, Nov. 4, 1810.
Vesta Conkey, d. Barna and Anna, Apr. 10, 1819.

BROWN, Caroline, ch. Robert Jr. and Eliza, June 20, 1823, [in]
    Belchertown.
Charles, ch. Robert Jr. and Eliza, Sept. 30, 1821, [in] Belcher-
    town.
Deborough, [twin] d. William and Alse, Aug. 17, 1803, in Cum-
    berland.
Dexter, s. William and Alse, Aug. 11, 1809.
Eliza, d. William and Alse, Mar. 9, 1808.
Isaac Lincoln, s. Ezra and Polly, Dec. 17, 1810.
John, s. William and Alse, Sept. 15, 1805, in Cumberland.
Louisa, d. Esra and Polley, Nov. 1, 1812.
Lucy Ann, ch. Robert Jr. and Eliza, Jan. 12, 1825, [in] Belcher-
    town.
Lucy Ann, ch. Robert Jr. and Eliza, Feb. 13, 1829, [in] Belcher-
    town.
Lydia, ch. Robert Jr. and Eliza, Dec. 5, 1827, [in] Belchertown.
Mary, [twin] d. William and Alse, Aug. 17, 1803, in Cumberland.
Milton, s. Ezra and Polly, Nov. 9, 1816.
Saloma Wright, d. Ezra and Polly, May 16, 1822.
William, s. Elizebath, Jan. 17, 1824.

BRUCE, Diana, ch. Abijah and Rizpah, Apr. 3, 1799, in Milford.
Edee, ch. Abijah and Rizpah, June 24, 1811, in Dover, Vt.
Elisha, ch. Abijah and Rizpah, Jan. 2, 1804, in Milford.
Ellis Whelock, ch. Abijah and Rizpah, Apr. 27, 1801, in Milford.
Lendol, ch. Abijah and Rizpah, May 3, 1797, in Milford.
Rizpah Maria, d. Ellis and Melinda, Mar. 18, 1826.
Sabra, ch. Abijah and Rizpah, Jan. 27, 1794, in Milford.
Smith, ch. Abijah and Rizpah, Aug. 22, 1814, in Dover, Vt.
Willard, ch. Abijah and Rizpah, Apr. 2, 1806, in Dover, Vt.

BROWE, Winsor, ch. Abijah and Rizpah, June 7, 1808, in Dover, Vt.
— , s. Abijah and Rizpah, Apr. 11, 1811.

BRYANT (see Bryent), Caroline, d. Ichabod and Silance, Sept.
20, 1817.
Elizabeth, d. Ichabod and Silance, Feb. 11, 1808.
Laura Nancy, d. Ichabod and Silance, Dec. 1, 1814.
Samuel Conkey, s. Ichabod and Silance, Sept. 17, 1810.
Sibbel, d. Ichabod and Silance, Feb. , 181 .

BRYENT (see Bryant), Anna, d. Ichabod and Tyla, Sept. 12,
1795, in Amherst.
Charles Gustavus, s. Ichabod and Tyla, June 27, 18 .
Edwin, s. Ichabod and Silance, Aug. 1, 18 .
Mary, d. Ichabod and Tyla, Feb. 26, 1798, in Amherst.
Oliver, s. Ichabod and Tyla, Dec. 23, 18 .
Philip, s. Ichabod and Tita, Sept. 5, 1793, in Bridgwater.

BUFFUM, Angeline Amanda, ch. Thomas and Betsey Ju 23,
1828.
David, ch. Thomas and Petsey, Oct. 1, 1829
Eliza Ann, ch. Thomas and Betsey, Feb. 8, 183 .
George Henry, s. Thomas and Betsey, Jan. 2 , 1831.
John Pratt, s. Thomas and Betsy, Feb. 4, 1837.
Joseph Calhoun, s. Thomas and Betsey B., July 11, 1839.
Mary, s. Thomas and Petsey, Sept. 11, 1841.
William Foster, ch. Thomas and Betsey, Jan. 4, 1815.

BUMP, Olive, d. Znus and Bridget, Jan. 31, 18 7, 1 Bo r
town.

BUNCE, Abagale Aldrich, d. Ellis W. and Melinda, Mar. 11, 182 .

BUTTLER, Battsey, s. of Moses and Abigal, Sept. 1 , 17 2.
Ephraim, s. Moses and Abigal, June 12, 17 7, in Barre.
Jo , d. Moses and Abigal, Feb. 28, 178 , in Hardwick.
S , of Moses and Abagal, Mar. 8, 179 .

BYINGTOWN (see Byington, Byanton), Laiza, d. S and
Olive, Apr. 11, 184.

CABBOT, Calvin, Caroline Matilla, d. Sebastin Columbus
and L N , 1817.
Cordelia C d Sebestin Columbus and El May 181 .
D L S Columbus and El 181
in Bellon r w

CABBOT, William Horrace, s. Sebestin Columbus and Electy, Feb. 12, 1810, in Belchertown.

CABOTT (see Cabbot), Columbus Dwight, ch. Sebastian C. and Electa, Feb. 15, 1819.
Erastus Elbridge, ch. Sebastian C. and Electa, Feb. 18, 1821, [in] Enfield.
Mary Emma, ch. Sebastian C. and Electa, Dec. 14, 1824, [in] Enfield.

CARPENTER, Billenda, d. Daniel and Olive, May 15, 1809.

CARTER, Elisabeth Wharton, d. John and Jarusha P., Jan. 28, 1840.

CHADWICK, Eliza Mason, ch. Harvey and Mary, Sept. 15, 1833.
Harriet Amanda, ch. Harvey and Mary, Mar. 2, 1827, in Waldoboro.
John Harvey, s. Harvey and Mary, Apr. 14, 1831.
Mary, ch. Harvey and Mary, Jan. 20, 1829.
Sarah Jane, ch. Harvey and Mary, Apr. 9, 1822, in Waldoborough.

CHAMBERLIN, Emela (Chambrlin), d. Freedon and Precila, June 27, 1803.

CHAPEN (see Chapens, Chapin), Battsey, d. Luther and Polly, May 17, 1800.
———, ch. Alanson and Amy, Feb. 7, 1835.

CHAPENS (see Chapen, Chapin), Emma, d. Seth and Mary, Mar. 26, 1805.
Luther, s. Luther and Mary, Oct. 19, 1805.

CHAPIN (see Chapen, Chapens), Alanson Lyman, s. Alanson and Amy, Nov. 27, 1830.
Albert Newell, s. Lt. Alanson, June 25, 1828.
Cynthia [dup. Synthia], d. Seth and Mary, Oct. 13, 1807.
Daniel Webster, s. Alanson and Amy, Sept. 25, 1836.
Eli Wedge, s. Luther and Mary, Dec. 13, 1811, in Shutesbury.
Ester, d. Luther and Mary, Apr. 29, 1802.
Frances A., d. Calvin and Amy, May 31, 1843.
Hiran Johnson, s. Alanson and Amy, Apr. 23, 1833.
Lemuel Russel, twin s. Lt. Alanson and Amy, May 13, 1826.
Lovilla Amanda, d. Alanson and Amy, Feb. 9, 1840.
Luther Rawson, twin s. Lt. Alanson and Amy, May 13, 1826.
Mary A., d. Calvin and Amy, July 10, 1844.

CHAPIN, Miranda Emeline, d. Eli W. and Martha, Feb. 16, 1833.
Osmyn W., s. Calvin and Amey, Sept. 24, 1841.
Otis Harrington, s. Eno. Alanson and Almira, May 1, 1833.
— —, d. C— on and Amy, July 16, 1844.
— — C. A.— and Amy Nov. 5, 1844. [Rec. M.— — 14
  Feb. b. 14.

CHASE, Clarinda, d. Robert and Clarissy, Oct. 15, 1816.
Emeline, R. bert and Olive, Feb. 22, 1833.
Louisa, Robert, ch. Robert S. and Clarissy, June 26, 1835.
Mary Ann, ch. Robert S. and Clarissy, Dec. 5, 1827.
Stephen Joseph, s. Robert and Clarissa, Apr. 2, 1822.
Tryphena Jones, d. Robert and Clarissy, Sept. 3, 1819.

CHENEY, Abel Martha, d. Asa F. and Saphrona, Apr. —
Mary Adelia, d. Asa F. and Sophrony, Nov. 19, 1844. [Rec.
  May 21, 1844, prob. b. 1843.]

CHILSON see Jilson, Jilson, Almira, d. Luther C. and
  Olive Montgomery, Dec. 8, 1835.

CHOAT, Maximilian, s. William and Mary, Jan. — 1755.
Roeseeny, d. William and Polly, Feb. 14, 1791.

CLARK, Adam, s. John and — Jan. 16, 1779.
Adam, s. Adam and Jane, Feb. 23, 1750. New born.
  Worcester Co.
Amanda, d. Matthew and Hannah July 23, 1811.
Benjamin, s. Adam and Jean, Dec. 24, 1777.
Charles, s. Samuel and Susanna Jr., July 5, 1801.
Calvin, s. Matthew and Hannah, May 16, 1808.
Charles Hinckley [dup. Hinkley], s. Samuel Jr. [dup. omit Jr.]
  and Susanna [dup. Susanah], Aug. 29, 1811.
C— d. Adam and Jean, Jan 24, 1779.
C— Samuel and Mary "New Mary F.—
  1, 1717, in Hardwick.
Dan, Matthew and Hannah, Apr. 12, 1794.
F— Samuel and Susanna Feb. 1, 1807.
I— Matthew and Hannah Dec. 8, 1817.
Harriet, d. Matthew and Hannah Dec. 27, 1791.
H— Samuel Jr. and S— — h, June 2, 1818.
I— Samuel and Susanna Oct. 1, 1818.
[Jilson — d. Sarah, Sept. 1791.
J— Adam and — Nov. 1755.

CLARK, Joel Warner, s. Samuel Jr. [dup. omits Jr.] and Susanna [dup. Susana], May 19, 1818.
John, s. Matthew and Hannah, Apr. 13, 1789.
Joseph Steward, s. Adam and Jane, Mar. —, 1782, in New Brantry.
Katrien, d. John and Anne, Sept. 4, 1766.
Levi, s. Adam and Jennet, Mar. 30, 1790.
Lucy, d. Matthew and Hanah, Aug. 2, 1776.
Lydie, d. Matt[he]w and Hannah, Apr. 14, 1787.
Mary Nye, ch. Samuel and Mary "Now Mary Fales" [rec. 1831–2], Nov. 18, 1819, at Hardwick.
Matthew, s. Adam and Jane, Dec. 7, 178[torn. Rec. after Joseph b. 1782], in New Brantry.
Molley, d. Adam and Jane, Nov. 6, 1774.
Samuel Wild, s. Samuel and Susannah, Apr. 30, 1824.
Sarah Robinson, ch. Samuel and Mary "Now Mary Fales" [rec. 1831–2], May 10, 1822, at Hardwick.
Silas, s. Matthew and Hanah, May 9, 1784.
Susanah, d. Matthew and Hanah, Feb. 6, 1779.
[torn] d. John and Mary, Jan. 22, 1743.
[torn] d. John and Sarah, Feb. 15, 174[torn].
[torn]rat, d. John [torn], Feb. 26, 1750.
[torn] d. John [torn], Nov. 2, 1752.
[torn] s. John [torn], Aug. 14, 1754.

COCHRAN, John, s. Tho[ma]s and Margaret, Aug. 5, 1759.
Patince, d. Tho[ma]s and Margaret, Jan. 25, 1762.
[torn] s. Tho[ma]s and Margret, Feb. 1, 1741.
[torn] d. Tho[ma]s and Margret, June 9, 1744.
[torn] s. Tho[ma]s and Margret, July 8, 1746.
[torn] d. Tho[ma]s and Margret, Aug. 17, 1748.
[torn] d. Tho[ma]s and Margret, Feb. 8, 1752.
[torn] d. Tho[ma]s and Margret, Aug. 24, 1754.
[torn]el, s. Tho[ma]s and Margaret, July 1, 1764.

COMSTOCK (see Cumstock), Leonard D., s. William [and] Almira, Jan. 14, 1841.
Lucy Draper [dup. Lucy D. Cumstock], d. William and Elmira, Oct. 1, 1843.

CONKEY (see Conky), Achsy, d. Will[ia]m and Mary, Jan. 22, 1796.
Allexander, s. Elisha and Susanah, Apr. 10, 1785.
Anna, d. John and Margret, Apr. 26, 1786.

CONKEY, Ansel, s. William and Mary, June 23, 1799.

A., s. Asa and Mary, 22, 1 4.

Amos, s. Asa and Nancy, Jan. 4, 1 12.

Aaron, William, Dec. and 1 ..., t.

Benjamin, ... and Rebecca, Jan. ..., 7.

E... F., A W. Oct. 10, 1 9.

B., 1. Le... d. Esther and Susanna, Jan ..1 2.

B. W. ... d P J Ju.. , 7

B. 1 E., I F. ..., 1 7 ..

C. E.kel and Frances, M. 1 17 ...

Chloe Watts, ch. Warren and P..., ., 19, 1817, at Green-
     h.

D... ... Ichabod Mar. , S... 27, 1778.

D... d. E... and Susanna, Ap. 1, 1744.

F... r s. John and Margaret, Feb. 7, 1784.

F... d. Thomas and Fidelia, Jan. 14, 1798.

F... d. E... and Susanah, Apr. 13, 17 3.

F... s. E... Isaac and Susanah, Apr. 1, 1717.

F... n. d. Isaac and Rebecca, Oct. 7, 1732.

E... h, d. Thomas and Elizabeth, Nov. 26, 1784.

F... Martha, ch. Warren and P..., Aug. 25, 1821. ... Hard-
     wick.

F...k's s. William and Rebekah, June 15, 1761.

F.k..., Ezekiel and Esther, Aug. 25, 17 7.

G..., ch. Austin and Charlotte, June 27, 1834.

G... Washington, s. Israel and Hannah, Nov. 15, 1 7.

Ha... d. Thomas and Elizabeth, Apr. 23, 1794.

Ha... h, d. Israel and Hannah, Mar. 9, 1 3.

Henry Martin, ch. Austin and Charlotte, Aug. 7, 1832.

Hy... r Abercrombie, s. Alexander and Lucy, Sept. 12, 1811.

Je... Jo... and Margaret, Aug. 7, 17 .

Je... G. ... lep. G... Warren and Mar..., lip. W... and
     P... Jan. 15, ...

Le... a and Margaret, Apr. 15, 1774, in Be... ...

Le... Jo... and H... Sept. 2 1 3.

F... m. and Margaret, May 7, 17 8.

Ja... s. A. and Mary, Apr. 7, 17 .

Lu... Israel and Anna Nov. 29, 1773, in "Hamrix Brush
     ..."

J... E... and Su... Mar. 6, 1 2.

W... RK Oct. 1773.

I... M... Dec. ...

I... I F... Feb. 1787.

D... ... Apr. ...

CONKEY, John M[c]Crelles, s.W[illia]m and Rebakh, May 27, 1767.
John Quincy Adams, s. Israel and Hannah, Mar. 4, 1811.
John Thompson, s. Elisha and Susanah, Apr. 23, 1790.
Joshua, s. John and Margret, Feb. 10, 1777.
Joshua, s. David and Eunice, Feb. 26, 1804.
Lazetta Hinds, d. Isaac A. and Vesta, Aug. 23, 1809.
Levi Washburn, s. David and Patty, Oct. 26, 1802.
Linus Staphenson [dup. S.], s. Warren and Mary [dup. Polly],
    Dec. 1, 1806.
Livy, d. David Jr. and Patty, Feb. 20, 1809.
Lucindia, d. Isaac and Rebecah, Dec. 28, 1791.
Lucy, d. James and Batty, Sept. 22, 1804.
Margret, d. Asa and Margret, Feb. 12, 1780.
Margrey, d. W[illia]m and Rebakh, D[e]c. 6, 1756.
Marindy, d. David and Eunice, Aug. 31, 1799.
Martha, d. W[illia]m and Rebakh, Apr. 1, 1764.
Martha Ann, d. Austin W. and Charlotte, Nov. 11, 1836.
Mary, d. Isaac and Rebecah, May 7, 1786.
Mary, d. James and Betsey, Aug. 8, 1813.
Mary, d. David and Patty, Aug. 11, 1814.
Mary Rebakh, d. W[illia]m and Rebakh, Feb. 28, 1771.
Mehitable, d. Maj. John and Margarett, Feb. 27, 1791.
Meriam, d. Asa and Margret, Apr. 29, 1775.
[Miran‡]day, d. David and Eunice, Aug. 31, 1899 [prob. 1799].
Molly, d. William and Mary, Jan. 13, 1787.
Nancy, d. David and Eunice, Sept. 1, 1797.
Nehemiah, s. Allex[ande]r and Mary, June 15, 1792.
Nehemiah, s. James and Batty, Aug. 25, 1806.
Otis McColough, s. Alexander and Lucy, Dec. —, 1808.
Oran Sidney, s. James and Betsey, Feb. 28, 1811.
Pattey, d. David Jr. and Patty, May 5, 1811.
Polly, d. William and Mary, Jan. 13, 1787.
Prudence, d. Elisha and Susanah, Oct. 2, 1786.
Rebakah, d. Asa and Margret, Jan. 9, 1778.
Rebecah, d. Isaac and Rebecah, Apr. 25, 1788.
Rebekah, d. Ezkiel and Elisebith, Apr. 29, 1789.
Robert, s. Will[ia]m and Mary, Sept. 21, 1792.
Ruben, s. Elisha and Susannah, Sept. 3, 1788.
Salley, d. David and Sarah, Jan. 16, 1794.
Samuel, s. Isaac and Rebecah, Mar. 16, 1783.
Sarah, d. John and Margret, May 8, 1782.
Sarah, d. Elisha and Susanah, Apr. 4, 1792.
Silas, s. Isaac and Rebecah, Mar. 29, 1790.

‡ Torn in original record; supplied from town copy.

CONKEY, Silvia Maria, d. Warren and Mary (dau. Warren and
    Polly) Jan. 19, 1811.
Sophia, d. Irial and Hannah, Sept. 14, 1794.
Susanah, d. Elisha and Susanah, Apr. 22, 1791.
Thomas, s. William and Rebakh, Mar. 20, 1775.
Thomas, s. Asa and Margret, Sept. 22, 1755.
Thomas, s. Thomas and Elizabeth, Dec. 25, 1758.
Thos., s. Ezra and Rebecah, Aug. 5, 1795.
Wm., s. David and Sarah, May 21, 1788.
Ward, s. James and Betty, June 14, 1816.
William, s. Thomas and Elizabeth, Mar. 29, 1791.
William, s. Allex and[er] and Eliner, Apr. 7, 1814.
William, s. James and Betsy, Nov. 6, 1818.
William, ch. Warren and Polly, July 13, 1823, s. Hezekiah, s.
William Hunter, s. David and Sarah, July 26, 1720.

CONKY (see Cakey) Alfbert, s. Alexander and Sa[rah] Oct.
    29, 1761.
Andrew, s. Allexander and Sarah, Dec. 4, 1749.
[H]arriot, d. Alexander and Sarah, Jan. 29, 1758.
Jathned, d. Allexander and Sarah, June 7, 1752.
Jerusha, d. William and Mary, Apr. 3, 1742.
Tertha, d. William (born), Feb. 14, 1743.
Terr[y], l. William, born April 25, 1746.
torn d. James and Isabel, April (born) 1748.
torn s. William, born Sept. 11, 1745.
torr James and Esabel, born 19, 1739.
torn Jaines and Esabel, May 9, 1753.
torr Wm., born Feb. 1, 1751.
torn William, born May 17, 175 torn following 1751.
torr James and Esebel, July 13, 1754.
s. Alexander and Sarah, May 24, 1756.
torn James and Isabel, Dec. 27, 1756.
torn Allexander and Sarah, July 2, 1764.

COOK, Abigail, d. Whipple and Asenath, July 24, 1773.
Adaline d. Lewis and Nancy, June 17, 1827.
Alan, s. Levi and Amy, Apr. 22, 1815.
An s. Levi and Nancy, July 12, 1826.
And[rew] Aaron and Harriet, Oct. 20, 1825.
An s. ... Livi, May 24, 1792.
An... s. ... and S ... Dec. 16, 1816.
An. Wm. Aaron and H ... Aug. 15, 18 ...

Cook, Benjamin Olney, ch. Simon and Loiza, June 23, 1835.
Betsy, ch. Lewis and Nancy, Dec. 2, 1839.
Charles D., s. Aaron and Clarisa, Aug. 31, 1845.
Clara A., d. Amasa and Mehitable, Sept. 14, 1848.
Daniel, s. Lewis and Nancy, May 17, 1830.
David, s. Presorved and Phebe, Feb. 3, 1802.
Dexter B., s. Dana and Betsey, Aug. 9, 1823.
Dwight Madison, s. Olney and Emily, May 23, 1837.
Elias Smith, s. Adanis and Susanna, June 4, 1809.
Eliza Ann, d. Whipple and Asenath, Mar. 12, 1831.
Ellis Arnold, s. Levi and Rachel, May 2, 1821.
Emaline, d. Whipple and Aseneth, Sept. 12, 1817.
Femer, D., s. Nathaniel and Bethiah, Dec. 30, 1845.
Fenner, ch. Ziba and Sally, Mar. 31, 1832.
Frances Wallice, ch. Ziba and Sally, May 26, 1830.
Francis Olney, ch. Olney and Emily, Apr. 21, 1829, [in] Mal-
    bury, Vt.
Hannah, d. Aidnus and Susannah, June 8, 1804.
Harriet E., d. Olney and Emily, July 23, 1844.
Harriet M., d. Olney and Emily, May 2, 1842.
Horace W., s. Nathaniel and Bethiah, Sept. 19, 1836.
Ira Gray, s. Zebina and Mary, June 10, 1818.
James Monroe, s. Ziba and Sally, Feb. 7, 1822.
James O., ch. Simon and Loiza, Apr. 14, 1831.
Jane Warner, d. Lewis and Nancy, Aug. 5, 1832.
Jason W., s. Whipple and Aseaneth, May 12, 1821.
Julia Caraline [dup. C.], d. Olney and Emily, Jan. 2, 1840.
Juliet, d. Elias and Jane, Jan. 10, 1842.
Lavina, ch. Ziba and Sally, Sept. 26, 1827.
Lillis, d. Ammon and Harriet, July 7, 1828.
Lois Thurston, d. Lewis and Nancy, July 21, 1834.
Lucius Webster, s. Olney and Emily, Oct. 20, 1832.
Lucy, ch. Lewis and Nancy, May 3, 1829.
Lycurgus Van Buren, ch. Olney and Emily, Dec. 7, 1830, [in]
    Malbury, Vt.
Lyman, s. Ziba and Sally, Sept. 12, 1825.
Marcelia, d. Simon and Louisa, Jan. 23, 1842.
Marcus Draper [dup. D.], s. Olney and Emily, Jan. 18, 1835.
Marianna, d. Silas and Sina, Apr. 4, 1819.
Mary, d. Adanis and Susanna, May 5, 1793, in Smithfield.
Mary, d. Whipple and Aseanath, Aug. 28, 1823.
Mary Ann, d. Simon and Loiza, Jan. 8, 1833.
Martha, d. Lewis and Nancy, Nov. 24, 1836.
Martha, ch. Lewis and Nancy, Nov. 3, 1837.

Co k, Martin Great, ch. W..ple a... A enath, Apr. 6, 1829.
N...y d. Lewis and N ncy Jan. 1 ...
Nathan, s. Amm n and H.. t, Ma 4 1837.
Nathaniel Henry, s. Nathar st and Beth ah, Apr. 25, 1 .8.
Rh la W 4 , ca. Whig .. d Asenath, Sept. 17, 1 .
Ro dend Be h.., ch. N hanier and Bethia, Oct. 7, 1
R   i, d. Amm n and Harriet, Dec. 12, 1831.
Sa y d. H nnah, Jan. 6 dup. 31, 1 23.
Sar h Maria, d. Nathenie and w., July 20, 1835.
Ser ra W. phi, d. Sim n and L   Jun: 15, 1827.
S ..., s. Zib and Sally, Sept. 27, 1823.
S. v d r,   Simon and L usa, Dec. 21, 1839.
Smith Mon e, s. Nathaniel and L eliah, July 8, 1842.
Th nk ull, ch. Lewis a d N me, Oct. 20, 1823.
The db Frederick, ch. Nath ie nd Be hia Jan. 6, 1842.
Vien .. d. Whip and Asenath Apr. 21, 181.
Wa hing n, s. Simon and L usa Jan. 13, 1 .

COOLEY, Anna, d. Obediah a d L   N v. 10   1
Benjamin Walker s. Ob di h and Lu. Apr. 23 . . .
Obe-E.h, s. Obediah and Lucy May . 18 5.

CORBET (see C rbit), Geo r W shing n up Geo r W.
    Corbit s. Ja n and Mary an, Feb. 21, 1837.

CORBIT (e Corb t Albina A.. d. Sumner and Diana, May ,
    1843, i. Palmer.
Charles E., s. Jas n and Maryann Apr. 24, 1848.
E ma E., d. Sumner and Diana, June 6, 1 4
Harriet E. d. Jason and Maryann, M. 23, 1823, in Palmer.
S rah E. d. Jas and Maryann, Aug 23, 1824 in Palmer.
W an H., s. Jas n and Maryann, Oct. 28, 1841 in Palmer.

CORRUTH, Ja me n, s. Sumner and Susannah, July 2, 1 6.

COWAN (see Cow n, Co wen, Ambr se, s. James and Mary,
    Feb. 11 17 .
Betsey, l. James and M ll   J   o, 1   i. Wo che ter.
F r Page s John Jr   f M il Nov. 8 1757
Ge   ... Jam   nd M rg a Nov. 13, 1757.
G   L. n d M ry, A . . 1
1.   1   M n   M   1761.
1   f   d Mars A   /
Jam Mon k l   Jan . 1   . A   . 1827

Cowan, [John ‡] s. James and Margaret, Aug. 3, 1759.
John, s. James and Mary, Apr. 27, 1786.
Justice, s. James and Mary, July 14, 1794.
Lucy, d. James and Mo[torn], Apr. 1, 1784.
Lucy Conkey, ch. John and Susannah, Aug. 16, 1829.
Marrick, s. James and Mary, Dec. 14, 1803.
Mary, d. James and Mary, Jan. 22, 1801.
Mary M., d. Preston and Lorana S., Oct. 12, 1849.
Presson, s. John and Susannah, Feb. 22, 1824.
Sila, d. John and Susannah, Nov. 12, 1821.
Silence, d. James and Mary, May 18, 1792.
Silvey, d. James and Marcy, Mar. 30, 1797.
Willard, s. James and Mary, Feb. 5, 1788.
[torn] d. Jam[es] and Marg[are]t, April 22 [? ; torn], 1763.

COWDAN, Elisabeth, d. David and [torn], Jan. 25, 1754.
Jam[e]s, s. David and Frain[torn], Feb. 15, 1745.
Jennet, d. David [torn], Aug. 16, 1'749.
Martha, d. David and [torn], Jan. 27, 1752.
[Susanna ‡] d. John and Moly, Sept. 7, 1763.
Tho[ma]s, s. David and Frank, Mar. 13, 1762.
Will[ia]m, s. David and Fr[torn], May 28, 1747.
[torn] d. David and Frank, Feb. 10, 1756.
[torn] s. David and Frank (Cowdin), Jan. 21, 1758.
[torn]e Simson, s. Ja[torn]es and [torn], Sept. 27, 1762.

COWEN (see Cowan, Cowin), Cyrus, s. John and Susannah, Aug. 28, 1816.
Fordyce, s. John and Susannah, Sept. 23, 1819.
John Jr., s. John and Susannah, Jan. 25, 1813.
Mary, d. John and Susanah, Sept. 11, 1814.

COWIN (see Cowan, Cowen), Ambrose B., s. Cyrus and Mary-ann, Aug. 31, 1844, at Prescott.

CRAWFORD, Anne, d. John and Susannah, Apr. 1, 1772.
Chester, s. Levi and Patty, Apr. 30, 1809.
Daniel, s. Levi and Marthew, April 3, 1804.
Eli, s. Levi and Marthew, Oct. 15, 1799.
Hannah, d. John and Susanna, Aug. 29, 1762.
Harvey, s. Levi and Marthew, Nov. 18, 1806.
Ira, s. Levi and Martha, Aug. 22, 1801.
Isreal, s. John and Susannah, Aug. 21, 1775.
Joel, s. John and Susannah, Mar. 2, 1767.

‡ Torn in original record ; supplied from town copy.

Crawford, John, s. John ... ... June 11, 1761.
... ...
... ...
... ...
... ...
... ... M... 1, 1773.
... ... July ... 1754
... ...
... ... M... ... 17...
..., Levi and Martha, July 14, 17.?.

CROSET see Crosett, Cr... ... Iser... s. Ar... ... ...,
    Mar. 5 17...
John Swift, s. Ar... ... ... July 24, 1769.
... ... Arch... d Sa... Jan. 21, 17...
Sarah, d. Archibald and S... n, June 5 1767
... ... s. W... am and Elizabeth, Jan. 6, 1745
... ... y, d. W... m and Elizabeth, J... ... 174...
... beth, d. W... m and Elizabeth, M... 17...
... gr..., d. Wi... ... am and Elizabeth, Dec. 2 17...
... rn] s. Archabald and Sarah, Dec. 19, 174...
... ... s. W... am and Eli... th Sep... ... 17...
... ... d. Arch... d and ... rn 175...
... ...bert s. W... am and E... ... h, Nov. ... 175...
... ... J. Ar... and ... 17 54.
... rn s. W... ... d Eli... ... Nov. 3 1758.
... d. A... ... and S... May 13 17...
... ... Archbald and Sarah, M... 1763.
... d. Ar... ... M... 19, 1765.

CROSETT see Cr... Crosett, Anna d. R... and Nancy,
    June 26 1794.
Betsy, d. R... er and Nancy, Nov. 24, 1792.
... ... d. I... d and Matthew July 22, 1745.
... ... R... ... and Nan... Dec. 4, 175...
... ... d. I... and Matthew, May 22, 1743.
... ... R... and Nancy, June 26, 1797.
James Lemon s. James and P... ... ... 15 1816.
L... ... d. R... ... and Nancy, A... ... 17...
R... ... s. R... ... and Nan... M... 18 17...
S... ... d. Is... ... and Martha, N... 17...
... ... d. Israel and Mart... N... 9, 17...
W... m, s. R... t... and Na... J... ... 175...
W... key ... James and I... ... Nov. 17 1818.

CROSSET (see Croset, Crosett), [torn], s. William (Crosett) and Elisabeth, Feb. 13, 1743.

CROZIER, Caroline Eastman, d. Arther and Submit, Nov. 12, 1822.

CUMSTOCK (see Comstock), Lorenzo B., s. William and Elmira, Apr. 14, 1842.

CUTTING, Clarisa L., d. Joseph and Patience L., Oct. 20, 1844, in Ware.
Stephen M., s. Joseph and Patience L., Oct. 19, 1849.

DANFORTH, Abigail Stimson, d. Samuel and Mehitable, Nov. 14, 1811.
Appleton Howe, s. Samuel and Mehitable, July 8, 1817.
Benjamin, s. Samuel and Mehitable, Jan. 24, 1814.
Henry, s. Samuel and Mehitable, Aug. 6, 1810.
Nancy Marshal, d. Samuel and Mehitable, Jan. 24, 1815.
Richard Sears, s. Samuel and Mehitable, Jan. 26, 1809.
Richard Sears, s. Samuel and Mehitable, June 26, 1819.

DANIELS, Abigal, d. Joseph and Lucy, June 17, 1799, in Mendon.
Anna, d. Joseph and Lucy, Feb. 10, 1802, in Mendon.
David Haris, s. Joseph and Lucy, Feb. 10, 1805, in Worcester.
Lucy, d. Joseph and Lucy, Feb. 16, 1809, in Worcester.
Ruth, d. Joseph and Lucy, Nov. 15, 1797, in Mendon.

DAVIS, Albert, ch. Samuel and Marilla, Jan. 28, 1834.
Henry, s. Samuel and Martha, Sept. 11, 1844.
Jane M., d. Moses and Sally, Mar. 27, 1836.
John Barton [dup. B.], s. Samuel and Marilla, Oct. 2, 1838.
Maria Jane, ch. Moses and Sarah, Mar. 27, 1836.
Ruth Elizabeth, ch. Samuel and Marilla, Apr. 20, 1837.
Samuel Benjamin, ch. Samuel and Marilla, June 1, 1835.
Sarah Ann, d. Moses and Sally, Apr. 11, 1831.
Seth N., s. Moses and Sally [dup. Sarah], Dec. 26, 1833.
Seth Nehan, s. Moses and Sally, Dec. 26, 1834.

DEAN, Harriet Adalaide, d. Laprelate and Harriet E., July 22, 1844.
Hurburt A., s. Laprelate and w., June 24, 1847.
Minerva A., d. Laprelate and w., Oct. 26, 1845.

DICK, Ann, d. John and Jean, July 14, 1763.
Cattran, d. Thomas and Mary, Jan. 15, 1781.

D k, David, s. Thomas and Mary Jan. 17, 1787.
J   s, Thomas and Mary, Sept. 2, 175?
I   , Th   s   M s   25, 178
t   , Th   and Mary   Dec   , 38
   d, Th   and M   e Jan   y
   , Th   as   and Margaret An   y, 17
   r   Th   as   and Ma   e, Oct. 7, 1745
   n a. Th   ary   and Ma   e, Ma. 4, 1743
   i, Th   as   and Margaret Mar. 31, 1
      L. Th   and J   rn   J.   17, 1747.
      d, Th   as   d Ma   et, Sept. 17, 1745
   as   Th   as and Marg   t Mar. 12, 175
   D   t   d J   rn   rn
   s, L   ra   d Margaret Jan.   1755
   D   t   d J   rn   Sept.   1755
   s   Th   as   and Margaret Dec. 14, 1754.
   s   Jo be   and Jea   July   17-4
   t   a   n   nd Ma   ne   July 12, 1756.
   t   s, J   and Jea   Dec.   1756.
   s, J   h   Jea   N   175
   r, Th   and Margaret Aug. 12, 175

DICKENSON (see Dickins   Charles s. Th   and Louisa Sept.
    23, 1805.
Eli   a, Ch   I. L   sa, Mar. 11, 1813.

DICKERSON,   a.   shea Smith s. Obed and Experance July
    14, 1815.

DICKINSON (se   Dickens on, Esther Maria, d. Henry and
    Esther M. M.   14, 1833.
Henry Wil   n h. Henry B. and Esther M., Oct.   1835.
Mary Ann, d. Henry B. and Esther M. Jan. 1, 1829.

DILLON, L   a Elisabeth, d. Sidney and Hannah, Jan. 4, 1845

DODGE, Ab   Da   d and Esther, Nov.   1823.
Achsah, d. Da   and Esther, Jan. 14, 1816
A   s Mar   Chester L. and Levi   a, Mar. 29, 1834.
Ar   n   s D   id and Est   r, Dec. 16, 1817.
C   s   Da   l and Esther, Apr. 23, 1821.
J   C   nd L   sa Sept   21, 1839.
J   s   C   and Louisa Dec. 12, 184
H   L   1   h Est   a Feb. 27, 1813.
H   J   J   h   Sept.   1831.

DODGE, Lewis, ch. Elison and Esther, Oct. 12, 1829.
Lorinda, d. John C. and Lovicia, Sept. 6, 1837.
Mary, d. Chester and Lovica, Sept. 19, 1827.
Nancy, d. Eleson [dup. Alason] and Esther, Nov. 12, 1820.
Ora, ch. John Chester and Lovisa, Jan. 31, 1832.
Otis, ch. John Chester and Lovisa, Nov. 23, 1829.
Pelina, d. Daniel and Esther, July 16, 1831.
Philo T., s. Ralph K. and Susan J., Aug. 26, 1849.
Ralph Kellogg, s. Daniel and Esther, June 14, 1827.
Sarah Ann, d. Elison and Esther, Nov. 27, 1824.

DRAPER, Adeline Orne, d. Mary Ann and Lyman, Oct. 2, 1832.
Albert Lyman, s. Lyman and Sally, Apr. 18, 1826.
Alonso O., s. Learned and Anna, Jan. 23, 1824.
Angeline Maria, d. Learned and Anna, Feb. 25, 1830.
Cordelia Emily, d. Learned and Anna, June 11, 1826.
Edgar Leroi, s. Lyman and Mary Anne, Feb. 15, 1843.
Emelia, d. Lewis and Lucy, Feb. 1, 1806, in Attleborough.
Emeline, d. Lewis L. and Margret, Oct. 25, 1828.
Henry Emerson, s. Lewis L. and Margret, Nov. 2, 1831.
Henry Oscar, s. Lyman and Maryann, Jan. 19, 1836.
Larnard Orne, s. Lewis and Lucy, Sept. 10, 1793, in Attle-
    bourough.
Lewis, s. Learned and Anna, Aug. 14, 1822.
Lewis Le Prelite, s. Lewis and Lucy, Mar. 28, 1801, in Attle-
    borough.
Lucy, d. Lewis and Lucy, Jan. 21, 1790, in Attleborough.
Lyman, s. Lewis and Lucy, Mar. 9, 1799, in Attlebourough.
Maria, d. Lewis and Lucy, Feb. 3, 1809.
Mary Ann, d. Learned and Anna, Feb. 5, 1825.
Miranda Philena, d. Larnard O. and Anne, June 17, 1831.
Sarah Ann, d. Lyman and Sally, Feb. 20, 1821.

DUNBAR, Chester, s. Josiah and Patty, Oct. 16, 1796.
Eunice, d. Josiah and Marthew, Mar. 26, 1799.
Josiah, s. Josiah and Patty, Sept. 2, 1794.
Stephen, s. Josiah and Patty, June 11, 1804.

DUNLAP, James, s. James and Margaret, Mar. 8, 1772.
James, s. John and Mary, Feb. 13, 1819.
Jane, ch. John and Mary, Sept. 25, 1824.
Margarett, d. John and Mary, June 19, 1810.
Mary Ann, ch. John and Mary, May 19, 1828.
Nancy, d. John and Mary, June 8, 1815.
Sarah, d. John and Mary, Oct. 12, 1808.

Dunlap, William 2d, s. J   M   June 29, 17

Y   C   g   Mar Ma   9, 1

p   C   &   1

DWALLEY , D   1   1   r   , Aaron
     (Dwal)   Al   C   1.

DWELLEY , Dw   N   S
    and Abi   Oct.

Rebek h K   4   d. A   D

DWELLY   Dwel , Dw   N   A
    Nov. ,

Prin B   A   V   O

Silas Ela   Tho   r   A   Ac   , O

EATON, Am   M   M   a   t   Int   O
Calvin Du   p D   M   d C a   O
C   tte   w. Ma   A   t   Jo
Jon   Mar n ard Char   t   Se   1   8   L
         C

E   s A   d N in J   and D   N   18

Is   Eiq   s   M nr e and C   a Ma   1 43.

Hon   d. Ma   and Ch r tte Sept 25. 1

H   n D s, Ca n D   d H   t E   La   1 42.

H   er, s C   D   d H   t E   Ma   t

Jen   s S   M rs n and Ch   , June   Ar   r

      Eme   y d. Calv n D   nd H   t E S   8.

Ja   nl   Walter and L   an M r 15, 1 7.

L   u Mars n and Ch   t, June 2 1   l

M   , s M   d C   tte Au   p

M   , Charl tte A   m T

M   tt, Ma   d Ch   M   2

M   d M   n and Ch   tte D   2   17

M   s M   d C   4   1 17   8

M   M rs   M   C   A

F   M   d C   M

I   t   e   M   t   E   N

A   M   C   C   4   b

          N   d C   N

EDSON, o   t   N   17

J   s E   N   M   2

G   D   I

H   a   d I   A

EDSON, Irene, d. Banj[a]m[in] and Anne, Sept. 26, 1791.
Luther, s. Seth and Desire, May 8, 1805.
Martin, s. Banj[a]m[in] and Anna, Mar. 11, 1794.
Olive, d. [Jacob and w.‡], June 12, 1783.
Phebe, d. Seth and Desire, Sept. 3, 1802.
Rufus, s. Seth and Desire, Aug. 27, 1809.

FAIRBANKS, Alonzo, s. Stephen and Nancy, Mar. 7, 1817.
Banjamin, s. Stephen and Nancy, Mar. 26, 1823.
Esther Sophi, d. Stephen and Nancy, Dec. 16, 1833.
Hannah Graves, d. Stephen and Nancy, Apr. 27, 1821.
Isaac, s. Stephen and Nancy, Nov. 10, 1818.
Nancy, d. Stephen and Nancy, Apr. 23, 1815.
Nancy, d. Stephen and Nancy, Jan. 26, 1825.
Polly Briggs, d. Stephin and Nancy, Sept. 1, 1813.
Steven Stratton, s. Steven and Nancy, Jan. 16, 1831.

FAILES (see Fails, Fales), Oliver, s. Sewel and Lowis, Feb. 24, 1811.

FAILS (see Failes, Fales), Caroline Amelia, d. Abijah and Mary, Apr. 10, 1840.

FALES (see Failes, Fails), Abijah Thurston, s. Sewal and Lois, Dec. 25, 1801, in Holden.
Adaline, ch. Daniel and Elizabeth, Aug. 3, 1834.
Almira, d. Sewal and Lois, Feb. 10, 1800, in Walpole.
Anthea Hunter, d. Abijah and Polly, Jan. 19, 1837.
Caroline Augusta, d. Daniel and Elizabeth Sophia, Sept. 12, 1831.
Charles, s. Sewal and Lois, July 10, 1807.
Daniel, s. Sewell and Lois, Nov. 29, 1803, in Holden.
Edward A., ch. Daniel and Elizabeth, Apr. 30, 1840.
Edwin Augustus, ch. Daniel and Elizabeth, Jan. 17, 1838.
Emma J., d. Daniel and Elisabeth, Jan. 27, 1845.
Emoline, d. Daniel and Lucy, Mar. 27, 1819.
Eunice, d. Amos and Mille, Feb. 7, 1822.
Frances Sophia, ch. Daniel and Elizabeth, Apr. 7, 1836.
Francis Edwin, s. Daniel and Elizabeth, Dec. 29, 1828.
George Lyman, s. Abijah and Polly, Nov. 1, 1831.
Henry, s. Daniel and Lucy, Sept. 28, 1821.
Joseph, s. Amos and Milla, May 23, 1817.
Juliet Maria, ch. Daniel and Elizabeth, Jan. 12, 1833.
Lois, d. Sewal and Lois, Feb. 28, 1809.
Louis, d. Abijah and Mary, Dec. 28, 1829.

‡ Torn in original record; supplied from town copy.

FAIRS, Madison, s. Daniel and Elisabeth, Jan. 6, 1846.
Mary Ann Andrews, d. Daniel and L.. y, Oct. 15, 1814.
Nancy, d. Sewal and L. is, Mar. 22, 1793, in Wrentham.
Norman, Dan. l and Elisabeth, May 19, 1848.
Pedee B. ke, d. Sewal and L. is, Mar. 29, 1816.
Perm.. R., ch. Daniel and Elisabeth, Sept. 4, 1841.
Sarah K. g. ary. d. Daniel and Lucy, 24 1817.
S. n. Elik. d. Ames and Millev, Au. 13, 1814.
S. w. ... Sawd and Lois, Aug. 9, 1805.
S. as s. Sewal and L. is, June 2. 1811.
W. an Albert, s. Al. m and Mary July 5, 1828.
Wi. an Baxter, s. Daniel and Elisabeth, May 16, 1830.

FALTEN (see Fulton, Felton), Mary Powers, d. Nathen and
    Mary, Dec. 16, 1811.

FALTON (see Falten, Felton), Nathen, s. Nathen and Mary
    Oct. 5. 18 5.

FELTON (see Falten, Falton), Augustus Wales, s. Nathan and
    Mary, Oct. 26, 18 7.
Catharine, d. Nathan and Mary May 1 1816.
Ch.. Shephard, s. Nathan and Ma. Aug. 11 1810.
I. .. Hf. ls d. Nathan and Mary, June 5, 1817
K. H. r. .. d. Nathan and Mary May 4, 1818.
W. G. H. .. wn, s. Nathan and Mary, May 12 1813.

FERGESON, A. one, d. Wi. .am and Jane torn, Oct. 9, 1749.
Jannet, d. W... a and Jane sorn, Apr. 4, 1752.
.. .. W... . and Jane't in, Mar. 25, 1755.
S. .. .. W. .. am and Jane torn, Apr. 26, 1736.
W. .. s. W. am and Jane torn, Apr. 2, 1748.

FILSON, D. .. Henry, s. Zebin and Pr. .. and S. .. th
    d. M. .. wn, N. g Oct. 8 1845 in E. .
H. .. M. .. d. Z. .. and Pr. .. am i S. .. k. .. M. ..
    N. , Oct. 1. 1746 in E. .. d.

FIRMAN, D. .. H. d. Albert and P. .. E. Oct. 12 1845.
Jennatte, d. A. .. .. P. .. E. N. .. c
M. .. .. A. .. d. P. .. E, N. 27 1849.

FISH, N. .. J. .. C. .. H. .. 1. c 2 1847
F. s. c. .. .. P. .. I. .. 44.
I. .. A. .. .. F. .. 1. .. 1849.

Fish, Francis Wesley, s. Cummings and Esther, Nov. 23, 1831.
Leroy Franklin, s. Cummings and Esther, Aug. 13, 1830.
Mary Angeline, d. Cummings and Esther, Aug. 14, 1827, in Casenvia, N. Y.

FLACHER (see Flatcher), Solomon, s. Solomon and Dorkes, Dec. 29, 1801.

FLATCHER (see Flacher), Alvin, s. Solomon (Flacher) and Dorces, May 19, 1805.

FLINN, Ellen Matilda, d. Samuel and Sarah Ann, May 15, 1846.

FREEMAN, Hiram A., s. Hiram and Charlotte, Aug. 25, 1844.
Mabel A., s. [*sic*] Hiram and Charlott, Aug. 19, 1845.
Maryett T., d. Hiram and Charlott, May 24, [18]43.
W[illia]m H., s. Hiram and Charlott, Nov. 19, 1846.

FRY, Bathsheba, d. Benjamin and Siene, Feb. 6, 1828.
Betsey, d. Benjamin and Siene, Apr. 3, 1826.
Washington, s. Benjamin, Apr. 5, 1822, at Winchindon.

GAMWELL, Julia Maria, d. Sarah, Dec. 30, 1840. "Illegetimate."

GARDNER, Lydia B., ch. Jonathan and Abigail, Feb. 19, 1827, in Levert.
Senaca R., ch. Jonathan and Abigail, Dec. 14, 1828, in Shutesbury.

GASKELL, Philena S., d. Chester and Mary, Dec. 26, 1848 [changed to 1847 in pencil].

GASKIN, Chester, s. W[illia]m and Phebe, Oct. 8, 1817.
Joanna, d. W[illia]m and Phebe, Feb. 12, 1815.
Lucy, d. W[illia]m and Phebe, Dec. 13, 1812.
Lybbeus Cook, s. W[illia]m and Phebe, July 23, 1808.
Lyman, s. William and Phebe, Jan. 7, 1806.
Madison Garry, s. W[illia]m and Phebe, Sept. 21, 1810.
Phila Cook, d. W[illia]m and Phebe, Jan. 11, 1820.

GATES, Asahel Aldrich, ch. Levi and Anne, Aug. 24, 1827.
Lamsford, ch. Levi and Anne, Apr. 2, 1829.
Margret, ch. Levi and Anne, Apr. 13, 1825, in Wendell.
Sarah Ann, d. Levi and Anna, July 27, 1835.
Sarah Ann, d. Levi and Ann, July 28, 1836.
Wealthy, ch. Levi and Anne, Nov. 6, 1823.

GIBBS, _____

Ameline Art _____ H. _____ 1825.

Elb____ _____ H. _____ P____ W _____

Gra___ _____ H _____ W. W__,

GILLMORE. _____

David's W____ _____ N____

F__ W____ _____ 17__

I____ d, J____ Ma____ ____ 11, 17____

H____s, s. W____ ____ M v 14, 171__

L____ Berry ____ Margaret ____ 17__

Jenney, d. J____ ____ Mar, M_ 1, 1771.

Mar d. W____ ____ 1743.

Sar n, d. W____ ____ May 7 1758.

____ s, W____ ____ E__ May____ 17__

____ s, I____ Margaret ____ 1, __

GILMORE ____ Gilmor__ _____ M

Dec. 5, 17__.

GOLD, ____ M____ M____ ____

F____ C____ M____ ____

I____ W____ s. M____ S____ De____

L____ W____ M____ ____ M____

____ b M____ d S____ by ____ I__

GOODIEL, ____ I____ M____

David, s. ____ M____ Oct. 28 __

S____ ____ M____ Au____ 17_4

Z____ ____ M____ Oc____ 1706

GOOLD G____ J____ H____ d b____

GOULD G____ H____ M____

GRAHAM, I____ ____ M____

M____ I____ ____ M____

N____ ____ M____

W____ I. ____ M____

GRAY, ____

____ W____ ____ M____

GRAY, Amos, s. Eben[e]z[e]r and Agness, Sept. 8, 1792.
Andrew, s. Jacob and Jennet, Apr. 19, 1781.
Anne, d. Jacob and Jennet, Mar. 23, 1784.
Anson, s. Calester and Phebe, Aug. 21, 1799.
Apeltown, s. John and Susanah, Jan. 18, 1797.
Archabeld, s. Matthew and Sarah, Jan. 12, 1787.
Calister, s. Calister and Pheebe, Oct. 4, 1800.
Calister, s. Calister and Hannah, Aug. 20, 1805.
Chester, s. Moses and Marcy, Sept. 1, 1794.
Chester [dup. Chaster], s. Levi and Abigal, Nov. 13, 1802.
Chester Harrison, s. Chester and Lydia, Dec. 28, 1818.
Clerecy, d. Eben[e]z[e]r and Agness, June 25, 1795.
Collester, s. John and Susanah, Nov. 29, 1795.
Daniel, s. Lamon and Isabel, Feb. 5, 1787.
David, s. Adam C. and Eunice, Oct. 20, 1780.
David, s. Justice and Lucy, June 24, 1802.
Daxter, s. Moses and Marcey, Dec. 13, 1801.
Deidemiah, d. Dea. Matth[torn], July 11, 1769.
Edwin Calvin, s. Horace and Louisa, Sept. 2, 1837.
Eli, s. Jonathen and Elizabeth, Dec. 8, 1781.
Eliza, d. Jerimiah and Margarett, Apr. 10, 1810.
Elizabeth, d. Jonathen and Elizabeth, May 20, 1779.
Elizabith Allexander, d. Eben[e]z[e]r and Agnos, Feb. 10, 1802.
Elizebeth, d. Lamond and Isable, July 16, 1779.
Ephriam, s. Adam C. and Eunice, Apr. 28, 1783.
Eri, s. Eliot and Hannah, May 21, 1803.
Ester, d. Jonathen and Margaret, Mar. 5, 1754.
Eunice, d. Levi and Abigal, Apr. 15, 1799.
Hapy Nelson, d. Patrick Jr. and Sally, Jan. 10, 1814.
Harriot, d. Chester and Lydia, Dec. 28, 1818.
Hinckley Rankin, s. John and Betsey, Apr. 16, 1818.
Horis, s. John and Betsey, Mar. 16, 1811.
Ira, s. John and Battsey, Oct. 19, 1800.
Isabel, d. Jeramiah and Margaret, July 23, 1804, in Salem, N.Y.
Isebal, d. Nathaniel [torn], Nov. 22, 1771.
Isriel, s. Eliot and Hannah, Nov. 2, 1797.
Jabel, s. Moses and Mercy, Aug. 22, 1796.
Jacob, s. Jacob and Jennet, Nov. 3, 1787.
James, s. Jonathan and Margaret, Jan. 23, 1766.
Jeremiah, s. Tho[ma]s and Lydia, Aug. 12, 1786.
Jerimiah, s. Jeramiah and Margaret, Jan. 8, 1803, in Greenwich.
Joel, s. Lamond and Isable, Oct. 20, 1784.
Joel, s. Justice and Lucy, Apr. 21, 1792.
John, s. Nathaniel [torn], Mar. 20, 1773.

Gray, John, s. Ebenezer and Anna, Jan. 8, 1788.
Jonathan, s. Jonathan and Margaret, Mar. 27, 177.
Jonathan, s. Jonathan and Margaret, May 2, 1782.
Joseph P., s. Patrick Jr. and Sally, s. 18.1.1.
J...n W..., s. Jonathan and Elizabeth, Feb. 20...
J..a Ann, d. He..., Jan. 14, 1855.
h..., d. Matthew and Sarah, A.. 16, 1797.
L..., s. Adam C. and F... e June 8, 1778.
L..., Jesse and Lucy, Dec. 8, 1785.
L...a, d. J...n and Betsey, July 23, 1776.
L..., d. Patrick and Lewey, Apr. 13, 1778.
Margret, d. Robert and Hannah, June 1., 1778.
Mar., s. Patrick and Battsey, N... 25, 1...
Mar., d. L... d a...Hsde, N... 16, 17...
Mar., d. John and Battsey, Oct. 5, 1798.
Mary, d. Eben... and Ann, Feb. 3, 18...
Mary Peirce, d. Patrick Jr. and Sally, March 2...14.
Matthew, s. Jacob and Jennet, Aug. 1, 1791.
Melinda, d. J... s and Lydia, Nov. 22, 175...
Mercy, d. Che... r and Lydia, Mar. 4, 1811.
M...., d. Jonathan and Elizabeth, Feb. 25, 1...
M... d. Dea. Med... and ... h ... Oct 20, 7...
N... y, d. Jesse and Lucy, Feb. 1, 18...
N.... d. J... en and M... gt, Dec. 1771
Nathaniel, s. John and Betsy, July 2, 178.
N...m., d. E... and A... N...v. 17, 17...
O... d. Dea. Matthew and Jes... Sept. 1, 17...
O... , d. Dea. Matthew and J... June 1, 177...
Oliver, s. Patrick ... June ... Feb. 17, 1803.
Polly d. Jos... and Hannah, June 11, 1792. Vol...
Patrick, s. Patrick and Alice d, Jan. 28, 17...
Pe... d. Jonathan and Margaret, Sept 14, 17..7.
P...y, d. Ebenezer and Hannah, Apr. 6, 1794.
P... d. Peter and Lucy, Aug. 17, 1796.
P...y, Jeremiah and Margaret, May 23, 1...
Roxy, d. Patrick and Abigail, Jan. 2, 179...
R... d. Jeremiah and Margaret, Aug. 23, 1795.
S... d. Jesse and Abigail, Aug. 2, 1794.
S... d. Matthew and Sarah, May 24, 1789.
Sarah, d. Dea. Matthew and Jane, Apr. 25, 1771.
Sarah, d. Edward H... Mar. 24, 1...
Saran Harkness, d. E... and Betsey, Mar. 1, 1803.

GRAY, Silas, s. Justice and Lucy, Dec. 25, 1793.
Silva, d. Jeremiah and Margret, Mar. 3, 1794.
Simeon, s. Jonathen and Elizabeth, Aug. 19, 1785.
Simon, s. Levi and Abigal, Jan. 21, 1801.
꙯ Sinthey, d. Matthew and Sarah, Mar. 9, 1793.
Susanah, d. John and Susanah, Apr. 12, 1793.
Susannah, d. Eliot and Hannah, May 8, 1790, in Ashfild.
Whetcomb, s. Moses and Marcy, July 7, 1798.
W[h]itcomb, s. Jarimiah and Margart, Aug. 6, 1807.
Willard, s. Eliot and Hannah, Feb. 17, 1806.
William, s. Jonathan and Margaret, May 23, 1770.
Will[ia]m, s. Jacob and Jenne[t], Sept. 21, 1782.
William Dexter, s. John and Betsey, July 7, 1814.
Zebina, s. Justice and Lucy, Jan. 19, 1798.
[torn] s. John and Isabel, July 1, 1743.
[torn] s. John [torn], Feb. 1, 1747.
[torn] s. Jonathan and Ma[rg]aret, July 14, 1757.
[torn] s. J[ona]th[an] [torn] [rec. after son b. 1757].
[torn]iel, [torn] and Isebel [torn].

GRIFFIN, Daniel, s. Jonathan and Lydia, Aug. 14, 1814.
George A., s. Johnethan and Eunice, May 4, 1841.
Hannah, d. Jonathan and Lydia, Jan. 25, 1800.
Jonathan Jr., s. Jonathan and Lydia, July —, 1811.
Lydia, d. Jonathan and Jane, Nov. 10, 1818.
Nancy, d. David and Betsey, Oct. 13, 1809.
Orlando N., s. Jonathan and Unis, July 25, 1847.
Otis Bradford, s. Johnathan and Eunice, Oct. 8, 1838.
Silas, s. Jonathan and Lydia, Nov. 10, 1802.
Sumner, s. Jonathan and Lydia, Oct. 12, 1809.
Susannah, d. Jonathan and Lydia, Aug. 13, 1797.

GROUT, Albert Adison, ch. Orra and Melinda, June 13, 1833.
Alden, s. Joel and Asenath, Sept. 2, 1803.
Anice, d. Joel and Asenath, Mar. 4, 1813.
Asenath, d. Joel and Asenath, Mar. 17, 1796.
Austian, s. Joel and Asneth, Nov. 26, 1805.
Austin Osgood, s. Austin and Susan, Nov. 17, 1840.
Clarrissa Hall, ch. Rufus and Clarrissa, June 15, 1834.
Edwin Augustus, s. Rufus and Clarisa, July 6, 1826.
Elizabeth Walker, d. Austin and Susanah, Jan. 9, 1830.
Francis Emerson, s. Orra and Melinda, Dec. 9, 1831.
Hannah Davis, d. Austin and Susan, —— [rec. between Jane
    b. 1832, and Vienne b. 1838].

Grover, Henry Martin, s. Rufus and Clarisa, July 4, 1828.
Jane Ballou, d. Asa and Sarah, Dec. 11, 1792.
Josiah W. Morse, s. Joel and Azubath, Jan. ..., ...
Lyman M. ... Orra and Melinda, J... 2 ... ...
Martin Curt... Rufus and Clarisa, Jan. 3, 1832.
Ma... ... Azubath, May 2, 176..., in Gr...
M. ... Rufus, d. Orra and Melinda, Apr. 3, 1837.
M. ... d. Rufus and Huldah, Sept. 27, 1...
Na... H. d. Rufus and Clarisa, Dec. 27, 1829.
O... , d. Joel and Azubath, July 5, 1798.
Orra, s. Joel and Azubath, Oct. 17, 18...
Rufus, s. Joel and Azubath, Mar. 1..., 1792, in Garry.
Vienne Elizabeth, d. Asa and Susan, Apr. 14, 1835.

HACH, Maria, d. Harris and Deborah, Sept. 6, 18...
Nancy Harris, d. Harris and Deb..., ..., Nov. 22, 1...

HADEN (see Hayden, Hayden, Hoyt), A, Phebe ... and Molly, Mar. 31, 1795.
Sarah, d. Thomas and Molly, Oct. 6, 1797.

HALBERT, [Jat]mes, s. James and Jannett, May 25, 176...
Nathanjiel, s. James and Jennet, Mar. 5, 1767.
Sarah, d. James and Jennet, Oct. 23, 1769.
William, s. James and Jannet, Jan. 4, 1763.
[tern]h, d. James and Jennet, June 9, 1765.

HALL, Amelia, d. Lemard and Milla, Mar. 26, 1818.
Caroline, d. Levi and Mariah, May 16, 1828.
Clarisa, d. Lemard and Milley, Jan. 3, 1814, in Cumberland.
Elizebeth Dean, d. Levi B. and Mariah, Mar. 2..., 1839.
Jean Born, d. Levi B. and Maria, Oct. 2, 1836.
Henry Clay, ch. Levi B. and Mariah, Mar. 12, 1822.
Lewis, Lemard and Milley, July 18, 1815, in Cumberland.
Levene, ch. Levi B. and Mariah, Aug. 30, 1834.
M... Anna, d. Lemard and w., May 2, 18...
Sis... Tom, ch. Lemard and Milla, Sept. 11, 182...
Seth Bart..., ch. Levi B. and Mariah, Jan. 6, 18...
Seth A...ll, ch. Lemard and Milla, Nov. 4, 1822.
Sophia, d. Lemard and Milley, July 10, 1827.
Vienna, d. Lemard and Milla, Apr. 13, 18...

HAMILTON, M... d. Thomas and Ernest, Aug. 9, 1765.
A... e, d. Joseph and Anne, Feb. 1..., 1775.
Anne, d. Oliver and Hannah, ..., ..., 1783.

HAMILTON, Augustus, s. Joseph and Silvia, Dec. 4, 1821 [dup. 1820].
Bathshua, d. Barna and Anne, Sept. 18, 1805.
Betsy, d. Oliver and Betsy, July 22, 1807.
Charlottee, d. Isaac and Rachel, Apr. 7, 1816.
Cynthy Westley, d. Oliver and Betsey, Dec. 9, 1819.
Elizebath, d. Joseph and Anne, Dec. 1, 1781.
Emily, d. Isaac and Rachel, Feb. 9, 1822.
Enock Clinton [dup. omits Clinton], s. Isaac and Rachel, Jan. 4, 1814.
Frances Jannet, d. Joseph and Sylvia, Apr. 30, 1836.
George Judson, ch. Joseph and Silva, Jan. 23, 1825.
George Whitfield, s. Oliver and Betsey, Apr. 4, 1816.
Hannah Emeline, ch. Joseph and Silva, Mar. 13, 1827.
Harriet Augusta, d. Joseph and Silvia, Jan. 20, 1823.
Henry Clay, ch. Joseph and Silvia, Apr. 9, 1834.
Hiram [dup. Hirum] Sumner, s. Isaac and Rachel, Oct. 3, 1811.
Homer, s. Joseph and Silvia, Mar. 23, 1821.
Horrace Milton, s. Joel and Abigal, Dec. 31, 1818.
Isaac, s. Joseph and Anne, Dec. 5, 1786.
Jacob, s. Joseph and Anne, Jan. 21, 1777.
James, s. James and Sarah, Dec. 20, 1758.
James, s. Thomas and Jannet, May 23, 1767.
Joel, s. Joseph and Anne, June 29, 1784.
John, s. James and Sarah, Nov. 18, 1760.
John Allexander, s. Thomas and [J]annet, May 13, 1764.
Joseph, s. Thomas and Margrey, Aug. 17, 1750.
Joseph, s. Joseph and Anne, Mar. 15, 1789.
Joseph Warren, s. Joel and Abigal, June 8, 1816.
Julian, d. [sic] Joel and Abigal, Feb. 5, 1813.
Margret, d. Tho[ma]s and Margret, Feb. 2, 1754.
Maria Augustia, d. Joseph W. and Bathua, July 25, 1804.
Marietta, ch. Joseph and Silvia, May 3, 1832.
Mary Ann, d. Isaac and Rachel, July 12, 1819.
Oliver, s. Joseph and Anne, Oct. 1, 1774.
Polley, d. Joseph and Anne, July 11, 1794.
Reuben, s. Joseph and Anne, Nov. 1, 1791.
[Rober‡]t, [torn] Oct. 26, 1772.
Rosette Ann, ch. Joseph and Silva, May 13, 1829.
Silvia, d. Oliver and Betsey, Sept. 2, 1811.
Susannah, d. Jam[e]s and Sarah, Feb. 8, 1763.
Thomas, s. James and Sarah, Oct. 8, 1765.

‡ Torn in original record ; supplied from town copy.

HAMILTON, Thoma., s. Th n Jr. and Jannet, May 14, 1769.

HANKS, Adah , ch. I   A' . Nov. 1   .
Alfred [dup. A. rd], s. h   and I   r   A   M. 1.
    1, 1 31.
Jam , s. J hn H. k   H oct. F S. 12. .
John M., s. J hn and F th   A   19,
N   ch R   ', s. John   d ther I
Pe   nn, ch. W   m and N   N   ,
R   ett, ch. W   and N   Apr. 3 1837.
W. r   r, s. J hn a l Esther, Dec. 22,
Zi a Ambr se, s. J hn and Est r, Sept 16 1 2

HANNAM   H   N thenial Lud e s. D   and I
    beth, J   1

HANNUM   H   Ame ia Mariah, ch. Gr   W.
    Ame   B. Jan. 1
Arn   s. P   O   11 181
D   F   . s. D   Sept 1
          G   W   L June   , 1827.
          D id   F   16 17 1, in B chel
          r, s. H r   Apr 14 1 1.
H   A   , d. Gr   W. an   An   B. Dec 5, 1831
H   Da   and E   eth, S t 9, 17 5   town
Hen   C   Gr   W. and An   B. Jun 10, 1
J n   Ad m   Gr   W. and Am   ia, Ju   25, 1823.
J   W   H   ry and Mi   Oct. 16.
I   and A   d   L   l   F   h, Dec. 19, 1807.
I   d. P   n l P   A
Mar a A   Arth   d Gr   W. and Amelia [dup. M.
    9 , O   1   r   err r].
Mes s, s. D id a l F   12, 18 3.

HANNUM, Moses, s. Pliny and Polly, Oct. 9, 1818.
Pathania, d. Pliney and Polly, June 4, 1809.
Sidney, s. David and Elizabeth, June 10, 1796, in Belchertown.
William, s. Grove W. and Amelia, Dec. 12, 1821.
[torn]ny Jr., s. Pliny and Polly, Apr. 3, 1815.

HARKNESS, Abigail H., ch. John and Esther, Feb. 8, 1828.
Adaline, d. John and Esther, Mar. 21, 1813.
Ambrose, s. John and Kesiah, Feb. 15, 1801.
Ambrose, s. John Jr. and Esther, Nov. 10, 1811.
Anna, d. David and Sarah, Oct. 24, 1782.
Anna, d. John Jr. and Esther, Oct. 2, 1819.
Anne, d. Daniel and Battsey, June 29, 1805.
Betsy, d. Daniel and Lyda, Oct. 23, 1788.
[B]ettey, d. John and Keziah, Apr. 16, 1786.
Cloe, d. Daniel and Lydia, Sept. 23, 1790.
Daniel, s. Daniel and Lyda, June 5, 1796.
Dexter Right, s. Daniel and Betsey, May 26, 1807.
Edward, s. William and Abigal, Sept. 9, 1817.
Edwin Oliver, s. Daniel and Betsey, June 7, 1811.
Grove, s. William and Abigal, Oct. 25, 1818.
Harriot B., ch. William and Abigail, Feb. 21, 1827.
Harvy, s. John and Esther, May 25, 1821.
Henry, s. John and Esther, Feb. 25, 1833.
Huldah, d. Daniel and Batsey, Dec. 6, 1803.
Isaac, s. John and Keziah, Sept. 27, 1782.
Isaac, s. W[illia]m and Abigail, Feb. 1, 1822.
Joel, s. Daniel and Lyda, Aug. 25, 1786.
John Jr., s. John and Keziah, Mar. 31, 1788.
John R., ch. William and Abigail, Mar. 26, 1830.
Joseph S., s. Sumner and Mary A., Jan. 26, 1848.
Lonzo Oliver, d. [*sic*] Daniel and Betsey, Aug. 5, 1809.
Lovicy, d. Daniel and Lyda, June 23, 1794.
Lyda, d. Daniel and Lyda, Mar. 13, 1800.
Martin H., ch. John and Esther, Nov. 19, 1830.
Nancy, d. Daniel and Lyda, Sept. 1, 1792.
Patte, d. John and Keziah, — 16, 1786.
Polly [dup. Polley], d. John and Keziah, July 14, 1784.
Prisilla, d. Daniel and Lyda, May 19, 1798.
Sarah, d. David and Sarah, Oct. 19, 1784.
Sumner, s. John Jr. and Esther, Nov. 17, 1817.
Susanah, d. David and Sarah, Jan. 8, 1789.
Veste, d. John and Keziah, July 29, 1790.
William, s. John and Keziah, Jan. 12, 1793.

HARKNESS, William Jr. s. W... ...m... N... 9, June 1... ...31.

HARLOW, Lew... s. H... ... ... A... 76
Sa'v, d. Th... ...a... at i... N...

HASKEL, J... s. D... ... H... ... ... N... ... ...

HASTINGS, M... ... H... a Ch... ter and Mary, m. A... ...

HATCH (see H...

HATHAWAY, B... ... ...na...tion... and Catharin... ... ...
   in Brookfield.

David, s. J... ...n... ...C...hari...e, June... 17... ... ... d
Dexter, ...s...ith... a... Ch...rine, De... ... 176... ... ... .u...
Jam... ... ...ath...n a... C...r... ...S...p...e...t...,... ... .k...
Jonathan ... ...n... ...natha... and C...r... S...... ...5..17...,... I... .fied

HAYDEN ... H... P... ... H... ... C... ... ... C...o.
   Th... m... and Ch...r... ... ...7..756...

HAYWARD, C...o...d... I... ... ... K... a M... ...g... 17...6
Jonathen, s. S... ...al P... I... ... ...
K... ... Ichab...d and R... A... ...1...17...
s... ... d. Ichab...d an... R... a M... 1... 17...
s... ... d. Ichab...d and R... tu... ... ...
Z... ...g, s. Ich... ...d and R... Ch... N... ... ...t...

HEADEN ... H... a Hay...en Ho... ... Syl... ... Th...m...
   and M... ... Oc... ...,... 18...

HEYDON ...ee H...den Hayden Hey...en Charles Caro..., s...
   Capt. Th...mas and Chloe, Feb. 13, 1829.

Jose...h... ...e C...l... ...d. Ca...t. Th...mas and Chl...e, Apr... ...1831.
M... ...s Th...m...a...d Chloe. Oct. 25, 1833.

HIDE ...ee Hi...de. Hyde... Lydi... d. Andrew and M...ry, Jan... ...
   17...4.

HILL, E...r...am... ...s... m...,... ... P...deri...e F... ...c...17...2.

HINCH, I...h... s... ...e... ...Pa... ...N... ... 17...1
R...turn, d. J...h... ...d Pa... ...S...p... ...1... 17... &
N... ...s... ...n... ...d Pare... A... ... ...

HINDS, A... ... N...b... ...a... ... d. A... ...M... 14, 17...
Hannah, ... N... ... ... A... ... N... ...,... 17...0
I... ... N... ... ... A... ...I... ... ...
...s... ...d, s... N... ... ... Abe...t, Sep... 13, 17...1

HINDS, Luzetta, d. Neh[emia]h and Anne, Feb. 9, 1794.
Mary, d. Neh[emia]h and Anne, Jan. 25, 1777.
Sarah, d. Neh[emia]h and Anne, Oct. 5, 1782.
Vesta, d. Neh[emia]h and Anne, May 10, 1787.

HIYDE (see Hide, Hyde), ———, s. Sam[ue]ll (Hyde) and
Hanah, Sept. 17, 1766.

HOAR (see Hore, Horr), Adah, d. John and Abigal, Feb. 4,
1806.
Edmund, s. John and Abigal, Jan. 9, 1811.
Evelina, d. John and Abigal, May 5, 1809.
Hapy, d. Jonathan and Pricilly, Sept. 4, 1811.
Harit, d. John and Abigal, Apr. 11, 1804.
Judah, d. John and Abigal, Jan. 5, 1797.
Loiza Jane, d. Phillip and Harriet, May 23, 1831.
Marcy, d. John and Abigal, Sept. 20, 1802.
Nelson, s. John and Abigal, Oct. 23, 1807.
Sarah, d. John and Abigal, May 1, 1795.
William Godfrey, s. John and Abigal, Oct. 14, 1813.
[torn]abath, d. Calvin and Betsey, Apr. 22, 1813.
[torn]in Jr., s. Calvin and Betsey, May 29, 1814.
[torn]al, s. Calvin and Betsey, Jan. 15, 1817.

HODGKIN, Charles Wedge, s. Joseph and Roxey, Feb. 10, 1822.

HOLLAND, [torn]en, s. Hugh and Elisabeth, Sept. 3, 1759.

HOOD, Austin Harkness, s. James and Nancy, Sept. 26, 1816.
Dexter Wright, s. James and Nancy, Sept. 13, 1818.
Edwin Holland, s. James and Nancy, Sept. 16, 1814.
Lovicy Smith, d. James and Nancy, Oct. 20, 1822.
Sally, d. Daniel and Battsey, Mar. 10, 1802.
Sally Ann, d. James and Nancy, Oct. 19, 1820.
[torn] s. James and Ester, March —, 1748.
[torn] d. James and Easter, Oct. 18, 1749.
[torn] d. James and Easter, Feb. 2, 1752.
[torn] s. James and Easter, Mar. 10, 1754.

HOOKER, Austin, s. Nathen and Betsey, June 1, 1811.
Luther, s. Nathan and Betsey, Nov. 22, 1813.
Lydia, d. Nathan and Betsey, Aug. 5, 1817.

HORE (see Hoar, Horr), Harmon Parce, s. John (Hoar) and
Martha, Abigal, Jan. 29, 1799.
Rachel, d. John (Hoar) and Abigal, Feb. 15, 1793.

HORR (see Hoar, Hore, Charles Henry, ch. Harmon and
Mar... , O... 2..., 1 ...

Elbrid... S. N... in a... Ma... L... 22, 184...

F... M... H...d, d. Harm... ..., M...., Aug. 21, 1838
...

L... ..A... Pie ce, ch. Phi... and Har... Sept. 21, 18...5
, Pres... t

M... ia An... s Harmon and Mart... May 1... 1... 3.

... n A... Hu ter, ch. Ph... p... a... i Har... Mar. 27, 1829,
n Pres... 6.

S... Piece... 6. E... d. Nel... n and M... Apr. 2... 1838.

... ... , d. Hamm... P. and Martha, O... .... 1... 44.

HOUSTEN see H... sten, H... st... ... ..., D... 'd... 1 Mary,
Mar. 6, 17... 8.

HOUSTON ... H... t... , H... t... A... nt L... r s. ... hn O.
and Lu... , Feb. 1..., 1828.

Lyman Ar... ... John O. and L... July 1..., 1...

M... h... Jan... d. J... n O. and Lu... , Fe... 14, 1831.

M... d J... O... and Lu..., De... 5, 1...

Os... d N... ..., s. J... n O. and Lu... M... 2, 1...

E... s S. ... "Se... ," C. John O... n H... J... 6, 1823.

S... h L. David and Martha Aug... 1... 7.

Sara... d. John O. and J... , Ma... 6, 1... 6.

W... n... O... s. Jo... O. and Lu... De... 1..., 1841.

Wa... r... n F... ... s. J... n O... ... d Lu... , In... 8, 1825.

... n... s. David ... d M... ry, J... e... 1..., 175...

HOW   H... e..., Abra... s. 1... 1... G... L... y. Jan. 6, 1... 54.

HOWARD, L... h Ar... 1... 1... h... Hu... lah, Apr. 26, 18... 9.

L... w, d. L... ... d L... w O... 25, 1...

s... c. J... h... 1 H... n M... 14, 1... 7.

HOWE   H... v... Mary d... t... r... O... 2, 17... 3.

HUBBARD, L... ... d. 1... ... d N... J... 7, 1...

Nan... , d. F... ... 1 A... M... 17... 6.

HUMPHIRES ... Hum... br... H... ... ... 1... ... I... nk... r...
s. N... h... Mar. S... t. ... 1

HUMPHREY ... H... ... H... ... H... ... Noah
... d M... ... ... 1...

Mar... N... ... M... 1... ... ...

HUMPHRIES (see Humphires, Humphrey), Noah Jr., s. Noah and Mary, Nov. 19, 1820.

HUNT, Huldah, d. Sam[ue]ll and Sarah, F[e]b. 2, 1768.
Joshua Osgood, s. Sam[ue]ll and Sarah, July 6, 1770.

HUNTER, Anna, d. W[illia]m and Nabby, May 18, 1812.
Anne, d. James and Susanah, May 7, 1778.
Clarinda, d. William and Abigal, Nov. 18, 1809.
Ebenezer D., s. Stephen (b. Hadley) and Hannah, May 2, 1840.
Fanna, d. William and Abigal, July 21, 1814.
George Stephen, s. Stephen (b. Hadley) and Hannah, Oct. 23, 1843, in Hatfield.
James, s. James and Susanah, Nov. 11, 1780.
James William, s. William and Abigail, June 5, 1817.
John, s. James and Susanah, July 12, 1773.
John Lyman, s. William and Abigail, Mar. 13, 1821.
Lorenzo L., s. Stephen (b. Hadley) and Hannah, Mar. 11, 1838, in Hadley.
Maria P., d. Stephen (b. Hadley) and Hannah, Oct. 28, 1841, in Hatfield.
Mary Elisabeth, d. Stephen (b. Hadley) and Hannah, Nov. 18, 1836, in Hadley.
Nabby, d. William and Nabby, Sept. 4, 1807.
Sally, d. William and Nabby, Feb. 24, 1803, in Greenwich.
[Sarah‡] d. James and Susanah [dup. Susanna], Feb. 24, 1769 [dup. 1768].
[Susannah‡] d. James and Susanah, Dec. 10, 1771.
Syrena, d. William and Nabby, Feb. 12, 1805, in Greenwich.
Thomas M., s. Stephen (b. Hadley) and Hannah, Jan. 25, 1846, in Hatfield.
William, s. James and Susanah, Oct. 5, 1775.

HUSTEN (see Housten, Houston), Anne, d. David [and] Marthew, Mar. 1, 1799.
David, s. Robert and Katrinen, Oct. 3, 1784.
David, s. David and Marthew, July 3, 1793.
Elizabeth, d. Rob[er]t and Caturen, Nov. 10, 1787.
James, s. Robert and Cataren, July 24, 1786.
John, s. Robert and Caturen, May 17, 1789.
John Orr, s. David and Marthew, Mar. 21, 1797.
Mary, d. David and Sarah, Sept. 13, 1785.
Pattrick, s. Rob[er]t and Caturen, Aug. 17, 1798.
Robert, s. David and Marthew, Mar. 24, 1795.

‡ Torn in original record; supplied from town copy.

Hosmer, Samuel, s. David and Martha, Feb. 17, 1792.
Sarah, d. David and Catharine, Apr. 27, 17..
William, s. David and Cathern, Nov. 18, 1794.

HYDE (see H. H. Hyde), (Andrew, s. Samuel), Feb. 1, 1765.
Andrew, s. James and Martha, Nov. 3, 17..
Charles Austin, s. James and Martha, Apr. ..
Chester, s. James and Marthew, Feb. 13, 17..
June, d. James and Marthew, Oct. 3, 1788.
Har. d. Samuel born March 177..
Hannah, d. Archa and Mary March 8, 1801.
Ira, s. Andrew and Mary, Oct. 28, 1795.
Ira, d. Samuel. David, Henry, June 2, 179..
Isaac, s. Samuel and Hariton, June 17, 2.
Lee, d. Andrew and Mary Sept. 8, 17..
Martha, d. James and Martha, Aug. 24, 17
Mary, d. James and Matthew, Dec. 13, 17..
Hartton, s. Chester and Chester, ..
in Ohio.
Reuben, s. James and M.... Dec. 29, 17 7.
Richard, s. Andrew and ..., Feb. 10, 18..
R..., James and Matthew Oct. 3, 1790.
Samuel, s. Samuel and Henry, Nov. 27, 179..
Susan (Gil. Mc Herard), s. Andrew and Ma. No. .. 6
Sally Gil... and Marthew June 18, 18 4.
Sybil C. James and Marthew, July 4, 18 2.

INGALS, Augustus Everett, s. Augustus and w... Dec. 21, 1834.

INMAN, Huldah, d. William and Polly, June 25, 18 .
Nancy, d. William and Polly, Feb. 2, 18 7.

JENCKS (see Jenks. Lyman Franklin, s. Dr ... March, Aug. 3, 18..

JENKS (see back. David Jr., Dec. 1 and L.... Dec. 27, 1823.
Elijah D. ..., s. Elisha, J... M... M.....
.... J... ... M.... Oct. ....
L... ... David and Lu... Dec. 27, ... Lee, town.
M... L.... s. Lyman and M... Mar....
R.... ... s. David and Lu... Aug. 10, 1817,
...
S.... ... David and Lu... Oct. 1, 18 1.

JENKS, William Clark, s. David and Lucinda, May 12, 1815 [dup. 1821 *sic*], in Belchertown.
——, s. Lyman and Maria, Mar. 24, 1847.

JENINGS (see Jennings, Jinnins), Cyrus, s. Rowswel and Nancy, May 29, 1810.

JENNINGS (see Jenings, Jinnins), Leretta, d. Roswell and Nancy, Apr. 15, 1813.
Lovisa, d. Roswell and Nancy, May 3, 1815.

JEWET (see Jewett), Cretia, d. Banjman and Cretia, Apr. 20, 1796.
Hariot, d. Banjman and Cretia, June 13, 1798.

JEWETT (see Jewet), Laury, d. Benj[ami]n and Cretia, Oct. 8, 1800.

JILLSON (see Chilson, Jilson), Albert Lyman, ch. Amasa and Esther, Aug. 28, 1823.
Eunice Hannum, d. Riley and Sylvia, June 14, 1816.
Loiza Minerva, ch. Amasa and Esther, Apr. 1, 1814, at Amherst.
Olive, ch. Amasa and Esther, Feb. 14, 1817.

JILSON (see Chilson, Jillson), Charles W., s. Manly and Maria, May 4, 1848.
Edwin M., s. Manly and Maria, Mar. 10, 1839.
Lucy Capron, d. Peleg and Silvey, Jan. 11, 1809.
Marinda, d. Peleg and Silvey, Dec. 6, 1805, in Cumberland, R. [I.]
Otis Capron, s. Peleg and Silvey, June 2, 1810.
Salla M., d. Manly and Maria, Feb. 22, 1841.

JINNINS (see Jenings, Jennings), Georg, s. Roswell and Nancy, Mar. 15, 1804.

JOHNSON (see Johnston), Andrew Henry, s. Joel and Maria, July 17, 1847.
Ann Janette, d. Joel and Maria, July 16, 1845.
Franklin S., s. Joel and Maria, Sept. 12, 1842.
Joel, s. Andr[e]w and Judith, Aug. 25, 1813.
Rosalyn, d. Andrew and Judith, Dec. 6, 1815.
[torn] d. Jam[e]s and Elisabeth, Apr. 3, 1749.
[torn] s. Hugh [torn], June 30, 1749.
[torn] s. James and Elisabeth, Aug. 26, 1750.
[torn] d. Jam[e]s and Elisabeth, Dec. 18, 1751.
[torn] s. Hugh [torn], Mar. 8, 1752.

JOHNSON, ... James ...

JOHNSTON, ...

Adam, s. A... ... 17.

Ardrew, W... ... and Margret Mar. 11, 1, 81.

Ar... W... ... and Marg... Nov. 17, 1783.

A... M. d. Andrew ... Jun. May 1, 181...

Da... H... and E... Apr. 14, 1763.

F... d. He... and E... Jan., Sept. 4, 177

... G. W... ... M... ... Au...

[H]... M. r. ... and E... th M... 1...

H... W... ... and Margret Nov. 17, 17...

[H]... s. H... and E... dear Oct. 2, 17...

J... s. W... ... and Mar... Jan. 12, 17...

J... s. W... ... and M. r... Mar. 1, 177...

Levi ... J... s. W... and Ma... M...
   M... 3, 1756 [dup. Ma, 11, 1... si

Levi S... s. Andrew and E... Ma...

La... Andrew and Jud... Oct. 4, 1...

[M... ... d. H... ... A...

[S... e. Hugh and E... M... ...

W... W... and M... D...

... Hugh ... E... Mar. 11, 175...

JONES, ... Presbyterian d. Ir... and Pr...
   1. 37.

KEEP, M... d. Ch... and K... F...
W... S... ... G... and Cath... A...

KEITH, ... J... C. M... M...

KELLY, ... L. W... and J... ...
D... W... C. W... L D..., Oct. 14, ...
... D... Dec. 1, 18...
... W... n D... Dec. 11, 17...
N... d. W... D... N... 22, ...
O... d. W... and D... D... 11, 18
R... W... d D... N...

KIMBALL, A... Sophia E... S... H
   ... 3, 1842
Alonza F... s...] Jr and Han... th Dec 9, 1841
   ...

KIMBALL, Charles, twin ch. Samuel and Hannah, Dec. 22, 1836.
Clarissa, twin ch. Samuel and Hannah, Dec. 22, 1836.
Edwin T., ch. Samuel Jr. and Hannah, Apr. 8, 1840.
Henry, ch. Samuel and Hannah, July 22, 1834.
Otis, s. William and Sophronia, Feb. 23, 1836.

KING, Abigal, d. Peter and Abigal, May 13, 1792.
Apeltown, s. Peter and Abigal, Oct. 2, 1801.
Charles Thornton, ch. John M. and Lucy, Feb. 10, 1836, in
   Worcester.
Clarrisa A. [dup. Clarrissa Almira], d. Robert and Thedia [dup.
   Theda], Sept. 14, 1829, in Belchertown.
Cloe, d. Peter and Abigal, Nov. 13, 1798.
David, s. James and Elizabeth, Mar. 17, 1791.
Dency, d. Peter and Abigal, Dec. 14, 1795.
Dolley, d. Rob[er]t and Sarah, Mar. 31, 1796.
Eben[e]z[e]r, s. Peter and Abigal, Oct. 7, 1784.
Elizabeth, d. James and Elizabeth, Oct. 27, 1787.
Georg, s. James and Elizabeth, Feb. 13, 1800.
George Walter, ch. John M. and Lucy, May 21, 1830, in Worces-
   ter.
Isabella Jane, d. John M. and Lucy, Apr. 24, 1838.
Isadore J., d. Robert and Thedia, Dec. 14, 1845.
James, s. James and Elizabeth, July 24, 1789.
James Higginson, ch. John M. and Lucy, Feb. 11, 1832, in
   Grafton.
Jennet, d. Robert and Sarah, Jan. 12, 1808.
John M. Jr., s. John M. and Lucy, Apr. 17, 1840.
Jonathen, s. James and Elizabeth, Feb. 25, 1797.
Joseph P., ch. Robert and Theba [sic], Mar. 22, 1841.
Margret, d. Rob[er]t and Sarah, July 13, 1800.
[Mary‡] [torn; prob. d. Starling] Aug. 11, 1774.
Nancy, d. James and Elizebeth, Oct. 16, 1783.
Oliver, s. James and Elizabeth, June 17, 1795.
Perez T., ch. Robert and Theba [sic], Apr. 26, 1839.
Peter, s. Peter and Abigal, July 22, 1788.
Robert, s. Sta[rling] [torn], Sept. 1, 1770.
Robert, s. James and Elizabeth, June 12, 1793.
Robert, s. Robert and Sarah, Jan. 16, 1806.
Rufus Powers [dup. omits Powers], ch. Robert and Theda [dup.
   Thedia], Sept. 21, 1833 [dup. in Belchertown].
Sarah, d. James and Elizabeth, Feb. 16, 1782.
Sarah, d. Robert and Sarah, July 29, 1803.

‡ Torn in original record; supplied from town copy.

K____, Sarah F., d. R____ bert ___ d Thes___ Oct. 17. 184_.
S___pua E., d. p. Se___, ___ ___ d. R_bert and Thedia Sep.
____ Theda__ A_g__, 18__ ___ Lekherttown.
Siras, s. Pe___ and A___, ___ Jar. 10 18_3.
William ___ in; pr_b. Stat__ _, Oct. 16, 1772.
W____'a____ James ___ D___eba___ oct. 19, 1785.
W_____ ___ob ___an, s. R__b__r ____ _s_rah, Oct. 12, 17_5.
W____ m H____, ch. J_hn M. _nd Lucy, Feb. 23, 1834 n W
____ r.

KINGMAN, Abel s. Henry and Sally, Oct. 5, 1812.
Ab___aíl Cobb, d. Martin and Phebe, July 30 1825.
At____ Ma___, d. Henry and An__a, May ___6, 18_5.
Charles, s. Henry and S__ly Apr. 27, 1819.
C_r__, s. Henry and A___, Feb. 23, 17__, in Darkmouth.
E___ n Mary, L. Col. Cyrus and Phebe, May 24, 1833.
F___ er F___, d. Martin and Phebe July __, 1837.
Fr____, s. Cyrus and Phebe, Oct. 14, 18__5.
F____ ___, s. Henry and An__a, M__ 16, 17__, _n Bridgewater
H__nn ___kard, s. Martin and Phebe, Feb. 24, 1834.
H___ _, s. Cyrus and Phebe, A_g. 1, 1807.
Jane L., d. Cyrus and Phebe, June 22, 1823.
J__n H__ar__, s. Martin and Phebe, S__ _ 22, 1821.
Le___der Crosby __p. Crosby?, s. M__ton ___d Phebe Oct
18__13.
L___t B____, d. Martin and Phebe, Mar. 3 __18___.
L__ander He___y, s. C___. Henry and Anna, Ap___, 18_7.
M____a Augusta, d. Col. Cyrus and Phebe, Oct. 6 1842.
M__ A__ ___s, d. Cy___ _nd P___be, Mar. 28, 1828.
M___ H___ L___, d. H___ __d An__ July 12, 18_3.
M___w ___ He___ r_a___ _ S____ Jan. 2_ 1815.
____ d H____ _ F___ d S__ly, M__ 12 18__.

KNIGHT, C____ s S___, F___der S__ and Mar___ A___ 4 18__.
Geor_ W.____ G___ge W_ker N___ ___, Ph___ _ S___q.
____ I____ ___s S____ and Mary Ap___ 18__.
____ W_____ E___bers ___d M__ F__ __ __ 17
M__y C____ L___ der s__ ___v, Mar. __ ___ 1844
Or____ ___ __ ____ Am___h, Sept. 15 __ __.

LATHAM, E___r C____r P T___ ___ P F____ ___ ___ 1751.
Eunice, d. J___ ___ E___ Apr. ___ 1___
Fr___ A__ ___ W___ ___ ___ __ F___ Apr. 1 18_9.
H__ ___, ___ ___ ___ ___ N___ ___

LEACH, Charles, s. Jonathen and Lydia E. Jr., May 12, 1799.

LEE, Aurilla Maria, ch. Ezra and Mary, Dec. 6, 1825.
Eanos, ch. Ezra and Mary, Dec. 27, 1827.
Edward, s. Ezra and Mary, Aug. 2, 1816, in Amherst.
Levonia, d. Ezra and Mary, Aug. 27, 1822.
Loisa, d. Ezra and Mary, Jan. 9, 1821.
Maira, d. Ezra and Mary, Jan. 15, 1824.
Mary, d. Ezra and Mary, Jan. 9, 1819, in Amherst.
Noah, s. Ezra and Mary, June 11, 1815, in Amherst.
Rozilla, ch. Ezra and Mary, Feb. 3, 1830.

LEWIS, Catharine, d. James (Lews) and Rachel, June 15, 1814.

LINCOLN, Almond, s. Luther and Lucy, Jan. 18, 1832.
Appollos, s. Luther and Lucy, Nov. 3, 1826.
Cordilea Jene, d. Marshall and Lucindia, Dec. 16, 1834.
Elisa Ana, d. Luther and Lucy, June 30, 1828.
Emerson M., s. Marshal T. and Lydia J., Oct. 30, 1824.
Horrace, ch. Luther and Lucy, Dec. 10, 1837.
Isabel, ch. Luther and Lucy, Apr. 4, 1841.
Lydia Elizabeth, ch. Marshal T. and Lucinda, Apr. 27, 1830.
Marietta, ch. Marshal T. and Lucinda, Oct. 14, 1827.

LINZIE, Augusta Haley, d. Stacy and Haley, Jan. 8, 1817.
Catharine, d. Stacy and Haley, Apr. 22, 1819.

LIVERMORE (see Livirmore), Daniel, s. Abraham and Hepze-
beth, Sept. 23, 1782.
Hepzebeth, d. Abraham and Hepzebeth, Oct. 11, 1780.
Polley, d. Abraham and Hepzebeth, Sept. 12, 1778.

LIVIRMORE (see Livermore), Abraham, s. Abraham and
Hepzebeth (Livermore), July 10, 1776.
Rebaccah, d. Abraham and Hepizebath, Aug. 18, 1774.

LOTHERIGE, James King, s. John and Nancy, Nov. 11, 1804.
Reuben, s. Reuben and Mary, July 26, 1801.
Roxana Barber, d. Reuben and Mary, Aug. 6, 1803.

LOTHROP, Ira, s. Isaac and Elizabeth, July 25, 1794.
Jared (Lotrop), s. Isaac and Elizabeth, June 10, 1792.

LOVETT, Angeline, ch. Sanford M. and Anne, June 13, 1842.
James Monroe, s. Sanford and Ann, Nov. 26, 1836.
John A., s. Sanford M. and Ann R., Mar. 13, [18]48.
John F., s. Sanford and Anne, Jan. 15, 1843.

Loveys, John H., s. s. of d M. and Ann. R., Feb. 15, 1844.
John M. H., s. Sam... ... Ann. ... S. ..., 184...
    P... ... ... d p... ... w... b...
Esther A... ... ... M. and Ann... Jan. 4 17...
M... A... ... ... d M. and Ann. R., April ... 1846.
Ma... B... s... ... : M. and Ann. R., Apr. 24, 1...

LUCORE, ... d. John (Lucore no M... are, M... ...
tern... d. ... ... and Margaret, N... 1,, 1, 4.
    ... L. J... and Margaret, F... 17, 1737.
    ... L. J... and Margaret, F... ... 174...
    ... s. J... and Margaret, F... ... 1743.
    ... J... and Margaret, Feb. 27, 17 4...
    d. L. John and Margaret, M... 2, 1751.
    ... L. John and Margaret, O... ... 1754.

LYMAN, Lewis s. John and H... ... Oct. 2... 1816.
Malvina C... d... d. John and H... ... Oct. 14, 1843
Mer... ch. John and Hannah, Ap... 7...
Ot... S... s. John and Hannah, Au...
S... S... ch. John and Hannah, May 16, 1821
Walter Scott, ch. John and Hannah, Aug. 2... 1822 ... b...
    t... h.

MACOMBER ... Macumber... Batse L... d. George and Ann...
    May 25, 1...
George Washington, s. George and Anna, Sept. 26, 1837.
Sarah Blair, s. George and Anna, Sept. 15, 1842.

MACUMBER ... Macomber), David W... am, s. George ...
    Anna, Jan. ... 1813.
Esther H... es, d. George and Anna, May 10, 1811.
W... m H... es s. George and Anna, July 11, 18...

MAKLAM ... M... ... K... Mason... d... ... ...
    drew ... H... ... A... ... 17...

MANARD, L... and W... m. ... H... Ag... ...

MANLEY ... M... M... L... ... ... Chimu...
    ... Lew... M... ... ... 3 ...
Sarf... s. C... ... H... ... L... ... 27, 1829

MANLY ... M... ... John M... ... C... ... and Le...
    M... ... 1...
Mart... F... ... C... ... L... ... M... 2, 1838.

MAYNARD (see Manard).

McCOLLAH (see McColloch, McColluch, McColluh, McColoch, McCullah, McCulloh), Alford, s. Hanery and Marthew, Oct. 16, 1797.
All[e]x[ande]r, s. Hanery and Marthew, Apr. 17, 1791.
Amos, s. John and Molly, Aug. 10, 1797.
Anne, d. Hanery and Marthew, Aug. 27, 1799.
Daniel, s. Honary and Marthew, July 18, 1802.
John, s. Hanery and Marthew, Feb. 20, 1794.
Sarah, d. Hanery and Marthew, Nov. 29, 1788.

McCOLLOCH (see McCollah, McColluch, McColluh, McColoch, McCullah, McCulloh), [Ale‡]xander, s. Allexander and Ann, June 7, 1747.
[Alexander‡] s. Robert [torn], Jan. 14, 176[3‡].
Henrey, s. Allex[an]d[e]r and A[torn], Mar. 3, 1751.
[J‡]ames, s. Allex[an]d[e]r and Ann, Apr. 22, 1749.
[Jan‡]net, d. Allex[an]d[e]r and Ann, May 12, 1744.
John, s. Allexander and Ann, July 9, 1742.
[Mar‡]garet, d. Allex[an]d[e]r and Ann, Feb. 19, 1746.
[S‡]arah, d. Allex[an]d[e]r [torn], May 2, 1760.
William, s. Rob[er]t and Sarah, June 10, 1761.
[torn] s. Rob[er]t and Sarah (McColluch), June 4, 1756.
[torn] d. [Ro]bert and Sarah, Dec. 25, 1757.
[torn] s. [Robert] and Sar[ah], O[c]t. 9, 1759.

McCOLLUCH (see McCollah, McColloch, McColluh, McColoch, McCullah, McCulloh), [Margaret‡] d. Rob[er]t (M[c]-Coloch) and Sarah, Nov. 13, 1754.
[torn] s. Rob[er]t and Sarah, May 29, 1766.
[torn]ma, d. Robert and Sarah, Sept. 8, 1770.

McCOLLUH, (see McCollah, McColloch, McColluch, McColoch, McCullah, McCulloh), Melinday, d. John and Moly, May 16, 1788.

McCOLOCH (see McCollah, McColloch, McColluch, McColluh, McCullah, McCulloh), [torn] d. Rob[er]t and Margret, Apr. 24, 1748.
[torn] s. Rob[er]t and [torn], [A]pr. 9, 1751.
[torn] d. Rob[er]t and Sarah, Sept. 3, 1752.

McCULLAH (see McCollah, McColloch, McColluch, McColluh, McColoch, McCulloh), Nathen, s. John and Moly, Jan. 9, 1789.

‡ Torn in original record ; supplied from town copy.

McCULLOH (see McCollah, McC... l, McC...ah, McCollah,
McColloc, McCud.h., Isaac...l...., and M... Oct. 1.., ...

McFARLEN, ...min, s. Ephr.am and F.t., N.v. 17...2.

McKEE, ...t.m; ? Robert and Mar... 1, 174..
...orn s. P... and Mar... Aga 2, 1751.
.. P... and Mar., Mar. 1., 175..
.... R... and Mar... June 7. 17...

McKLIAM (... Mak'im, McK.am, Mckem... John... J.....
Eunice, Mar. 10, 1788, n. P...ford.
Margret, d. Andrew and Lelol, May 1., 17..
Rev. J.., John and Eunice July 7, 17.., n. Enf..
S..m.. s. John and Eu..., Sept. 27, 17...
Sanford, s. John and Eu... May 15, 17..

McKLIEM (... Maklam, McK.am, Moskery, John... ...g..., d. Andrew and Is.el, Mar. 12, 17...

McMILLEN (see McMillin, McMull.. H......... t.......
Mary, Mar. 27, 1791.
James, s. James McM.ll.. and Sara, Mar. 5, 17..
J.., s. James and S.rah, Apr. 2, 1756.
Mart.a, d. Tho.... McMillin, and M.r..a, Oc... 1... 7..
F.. Dec. 11, 1775.
Ru... s. John and Mary, Dec. 22, 1787.

McMILLIN (see McMillen, McMull.n), David... Ir
(McMill.. ..., Martha, Mar. 23, 17...

McMULLEN (... McMillen, McMill.n. [D] avid, s. Patr... d
Mary, Feb. 8, 1762.
David, s. W... ... ... H...h, Aug. 4, 1783.
J.h... Emi... Mar... Aug. 1, 17...
I.... s. Patrick and Mary, Dec. 6, 1764.
[M].. Patrick and Mary, Mar 7, 1...
Ma... Lee and s... Mar. 1. 17...
Mer... l. Th... ... M... Oc... 1778.
M... Th... od Marth. M... 1, ..
N... d. P... Mary, A... ...
S.. .... N... Ju.. ..
S.. Ib ... M.... N.... 8.
T... ... ... M... N.... t.. t
W... W... M... M.... H... D...
... P... 17..

McMULLEN, [torn] Caldwell, s. Patrick and Mary, Jan. 25 [? 21], 1751.
[torn] s. Patrick and Mary, Mar. 23, 1752.
[torn] s. Patrick and Mary, Apr. 26, 1754.
[torn] s. Patrick and Mary, Mar. 29, 1756.
[torn] s. Patrick and Mary, Feb. 7, 1758.

MEKLEM (see Maklam, McKliam, McKliem), [Ro‡]bert, s. Robert and Rebekah, Aug. 15, 1762.
[torn] s. Robert and Rebakah, Aug. 27, 1752.
[torn] d. Rob[er]t and Rebekah, Aug. 21, 1754.
[torn] d. Rob[er]t and Rebekah, July 27, 1756.
[torn] s. Rob[er]t and Rebekah, July 13, 1758.
[torn] s. Rob[er]t and Rebekah, May 28, 1760.
[torn]abeth, d. Robert and Rebekah, Jan. 5, 1765.

MELLEN (see Millan, Millen, Millin), Catherine Elvira, d. Patrick and Judith, Jan. 17, 1832.
Isaac Rowens, s. Patrick and Judith, Apr. 28, 1829.
Patty, d. David [and] Laura H., Oct. 14, 1820.

MILLAN (see Mellen, Millen, Millin), Betsey Elizy, d. Pattrick and Livony, Dec. 15, 1810.

MILLEN (see Mellen, Millan, Millin), Achsah, [twin] d. Wil-l[ia]m and Jean, Mar. 16, 1790.
Amy, d. Jeremiah and Nancy, Sept. 20, 1798.
Anne, d. Jonathen and Sally, May 10, 1790.
Battsey, [twin] d. Will[ia]m and Jean, Mar. 16, 1790.
Betsey, d. Jeremiah and Polly, Aug. 16, 1812, in Brookfield.
Betsey Eliza, d. Pattrick and Lavina, May 11, 1812.
Calister, s. Jonathen and Sally, Mar. 27, 1798.
Charles Witherbee, s. David and Laura, Mar. 29, 1819.
Cloa, d. Jeremiah and Nancy, Jan. 2, 1793.
David, s. Will[ia]m and Jean, Aug. 4, 1783.
David, s. Jonathen and Sally, Sept. 3, 1802.
David Rankin, s. David and Patty, Apr. 2, 1816.
Eliza, d. Jonathan and Sally, Mar. 10, 1812.
Erastus, s. Jeremiah and Nancy, Oct. 13, 1800.
Hannah, d. John and Mary, Mar. 27, 1791.
Hannah, d. Will[ia]m and Jean, Nov. 6, 1794.
Hannah Pach, d. David and Patty, Feb. 20, 1814.
Henry Loring, s. Jeremiah and Polly, July 3, 1819.
Ira, s. John and Mary, Mar. 26, 1799.
James, s. Jonathan and Sally, July 12, 1807.

MILLES, Jeremiah, s. W[m] . . . . 1756.
. . . . s. W[m] . . . . 1793.
. . . . M . . . .
. . . . D . . . . .
. . . . 17 . .
. . . . N . . N . . . 17 . .
M . . . . . . Le . . . . E . . . .
. . . . p. M . . , C . . . . . . W . . . . . and
. . . . . Oct . . . . 16.
N . . . . Oct . . . . 17 . .
P . . . . . Luath . . . . . . Oct . . . . 17 .
P . . . . Dec . . . 17 .
R . . . kiah, d. Je . . h . . . P . . Oct . . . 1816
S . . H . . . . . d. . . . . . P . . . M . y 27 1814.
Samuel Peter, ... M . . . . 14.
S . . . Eliz[a] . . . . D . . . . and L . . . . , Dec 29, 1817.
S . . r . . . Ed . . . , d. L . . . . P . . . M . y 25 1813.
S . . . . h, d. . . . and M . . . . J . . . 1793.
W . . . . . s. W . . . . . . and . . . . Dec 27, 1794.
W . . . P . . . . s. W[m] . . . . and
S . . . . 1814.
————, . . . Patr . . . . J . . . . Dec . . . . 1827.

MILLER . . . . Mi . . . . M . . . ,
Sep[t] . . . .

MILLIN . . . M . . . M . . . . M . . . . d
F . . . . . D . . . . . 1 . . .

MILLS, . . . M . . . . Br . . h . . . . . . V . . . . 1 . .
. . . . G . . . . N . . . M . . . .
M . . . . M . . . .

MONTGOMERY, ... M . . . . M . . . . . .
Anna, d. Th . . . . M . . . . . N . . . . 1777.
. . . . M . . . .
. . . . G . F . . . . . M . . . N . . 14 17 . .
. . . . ar . M . . . . S . . . . . 17 . .
. . . . . T . . . . . . d M . . . . 1 . .
. . . . M . . . . G . . . . .
. . . . M . . . . 17 . . . . . Gre . . .
. . . . M . . . . N . . . . 1 . .
. . . . M . . . . O . . . . . 1 . .
. . . . M . . . . 1 . .
. . . . N . . . . 17 . .

MOWREY (see Mowry), John Osborn, s. Osborn and Elizaann, Feb. 10, 1824.

Lavinia Buffum, d. Osborn (Mowry) and Elizaann, Dec. 20, 1820.

——, ch. Osborn and Eliza Ann, Nov. 10, 1819.

MOWRY (see Mowrey), Alice Chase, d. Osborn and Elizaann, Sept. 7, 1822.

NEWALL (see Newell), Joanna, d. Levi (Newell) and Metilda, Jan. 31, 1804.

NEWELL (see Newall), Ambross, s. Ruben and Sirene, May 13, 1819.

Charles Lyman, ch. Lemuel H. and Charlotte C., Mar. 18, 1837.

Cythia Tilson, d. David and Charlottee, Feb. 11, 1815.

David Emerson, s. Russel and Elizabeth, Nov. 5, 1831, in Franklin, Conn.

Elizabeth M., d. Samuel A. and Rebeca E., Jan. 26, 1849.

Fanny C., ch. Silas C. and ——, Jan. 24, 1834.

George M., s. Lemuel and Charlotte, Aug. 9, 1844.

Hannah Green, d. David and Huldah, May 12, 1840.

Henry F., ch. William and Sarah, June 9, 1824.

Henry Smith, ch. Lemuel H. and Charlotte C., June 19, 1839.

Huldah B., ch. William and Sarah, Feb. 29, 1828.

Job Arnold, s. Samuel A. and Rebekah E., Oct. 22, 1835.

John Willard, s. Samuel A. and Rebekah E., July 5, 1837.

Josiah T., ch. William and Sarah, Jan. 16, 1826.

Katharine, d. Reuben and Syrena, Feb. 25, 1821.

Lemuel Hall, s. David and Charlottee, Mar. 13, 1810.

Lemuel Henry, s. Russel and Elizabeth, Aug. 11, 1834.

Loiza Maria, ch. William and Sarah, Nov. 2, 1834.

Lucy M., d. Samuel A. and Rebeca E. (b. "Mansfield C. T.") of Leverett, Aug. 25, 1846, in Leverett.

Lyman E., ch. Silas and Mary, Sept. 23, 1838.

Mary Adelia [dup. A.], d. Silas C. and Mary, Sept. 30, 1836.

Maryette, ch. William and Sarah, Mar. 16, 1830.

Oliver D., s. David and Huldah, Feb. 12, 1845.

Rufus Dean, s. David and Huldah, Sept. 2, 1837.

Russel, s. David and Charlottee, Oct. 12, 1805.

Sally, d. Levi and Metilda, Sept. 17, 1797.

Samuel Arnold, s. David and Charlottee, Sept. 30, 1810.

Sarah Ann, ch. William and Sarah, Apr. —, 1832.

Seth H., ch. Silas C. and ——, Feb. 24, 1835.

William S., ch. Silas C. and Mary, Apr. 4, 1840.

OLDS, Chester, s. Josiah and Hannah, Dec. 28, 1817.
Harriet, d. Josiah and Hannah, Oct. 17, 1819.
Josiah, s. Josiah and Hannah, Apr. 20, 1814.
Wyer, s. Josiah and Hannah, Feb. 22, 1816.

OLIVER, Andrew William [ ] Mary Ann [ ]

Andrew [ ] Andrew and [ ]
1791, in Londonderry.
Betsey Ormston, d. Rev. Andrew and Battsey [ ]
in Londonderry.
Esther Hannam, d. William and Mary, Aug. [ ]
Francis William, s. William and Lucinda, Sept. 1, [ ]
Jenny Julietton, d. Rev. Andrew and Battsey Jenny [ ],
Londonderry.
Margaret, d. Rev. Andrew and Battsey, Nov. 17 [ ]
Mary, d. William and Mary, Dec. [ ] 1797.
Mary Given, d. Rev. Andrew and Battsey, Feb. 11 [ ]
Bedford.
Nancy, d. Rev. Andrew and Battsey, Nov. [ ]
Robert Ormston, s. Rev. Andrew and Battsey M [ ]
William Morison [twin], s. Rev. Andrew and Battsey, Oct. [ ]
1791, in Londonderry.
William Williams, s. William and Mary, Sept. [ ]

OTIS, Almira, d. Isaac and Betsey [ ]
Eliza, d. Isaac Jr. and Tryphena, Nov. 12, [ ]
Galen, s. Isaac and Betsy, Sept. 10, 1790, in Monson.
William Smith, s. Isaac Jr. and Tryphena, Sept. 20, 1813.

PACK (see Peck), [torn] Jay, s. Jasse Foster and Anna Peck,
16, 1832.

PACKARD (see Packard) Abiel R. s. Isaac and Sophia S.
17, 1823.
Abigail William, d. Davis and Sally [ ] 1814.
A [ ] d. John and Martha Mar. 18, 18 [ ]
Aria Kingman, d. David and Nancy Nov. 6, 18 [ ]
Anna, d. David and Martha Nov. [ ] 17.
Asa [ ] Given [ ] and Polly M. 21, 1795.
Betsy, [ ] wid. d. Timothy and Betsey Mar. 23, 1777, in Brockton
Brad, d. Jacob and Zilah Dec. 16, 1814.
David Bethiah, ch. Solomon and Sally Jan. 16, 1814.
Deborah Given, d. Jonathan and Ann [ ] Apr. 17, 1812.
DeWitt Clinton, s. Ichabod and Sally, Aug. 16, 1836.

PACKARD, Dulceney, d. Jacob and Zebia, Feb. 10, 1794.
Elbridge Gerry, s. Eliphaz and Rebecah, Feb. 15, 1811.
Eliezer, s. Timothy (Pekard) and Betey, Aug. 26, 1784.
Elijah, d. [*sic*] Elijah and Abagal, July 6, 1805, in Bridgwater.
Eliza, d. Elijah and Abagal, June 18, 1803, in Bridgwater.
Harry Augustus, s. Elijah and Abagal, Jan. 17, 1794, in Bridge-
    water.
Hary Augusts, s. Jacob and Zebia, July 17, 1797.
Henry La Fayette, ch. Solomon and Sally, June 7, 1827.
Hollis, ch. Solomon and Sally, Sept. 29, 1825.
Ira, s. Jonathen and Anna, Jan. 26, 1796.
Irene Sophia, d. Justin and Sophia, Mar. 19, 1826.
Jane, d. Daniel and Nancy, Oct. 6, 1813.
Joel Clark [dup. omits Clark], s. Job and Martha, Aug. 31, 1806.
Joel Edson, ch. Solomon and Sally, Feb. 6, 1812.
Jonathan, s. Jonathan and Anna, Dec. 21, 1810.
Jonathen, s. Jonathen and Anne, Aug. 1, 1804.
Joseph, s. Timothy (Pakard) and Betty, Nov. 6, 1774, in Brookfield.
Lyda, d. Jonathen and Anna, Jan. 8, 1800.
Lydia, d. Elijah and Abagial [dup. Abagal], Sept. 12, 1807.
Lymon, s. Jacob and Zebiah, Aug. 2, 1802.
Mary, d. Gooding and May, Jan. 15, 1801.
Mary Howard, d. Daniel and Nancy, Aug. 10, 1818.
Noah Foard, s. Davis and Sally, Dec. 5, 1815, in Abington.
Orrin [dup. Orren], s. Jacob and Zebah [dup. Zebbiah], Jan. 27,
    1800.
Otis, s. Jonathen and Anna, Oct. 2, 1797.
Philena, ch. Solomon and Sally, Mar. 29, 1822.
Polley, [twin] d. Timothy and Bettey, Mar. 22, 1777, in Brook-
    field.
Polly, d. Liab and Hannah, July 9, 1799.
Rhoda, d. Elijah and Abagal, Aug. 7, 1796, in Bridgwater.
Rhoda, d. Liab and Hannah, June 5, 1803.
Rhoda Ayres [dup. Ayrs], d. Jonathan and Anna [dup. Jonathen
    and Anne], July 4, 1806.
Sally, d. Timothy and Betty, June 15, 1779.
Sally, d. Elijah and Abagal, Mar. 18, 1798, in Bridgwater.
Sophronia, d. Gooding and Polly, Sept. 2, 1798.
Thomas, s. Elijah and Abagal, Jan. 14, 1800, in Bridgwater.
William, s. Jonathan and Anna [dup. Jonathen and Anne],
    May 31, 1802.

PACKERD (see Packard), Timothy, s. Timothy and Betty,
    Mar. 12, 1782.

PARK, Jenney, d. Stewart James ... N... M... 1..., 1759.
John, s. Stewart Jam... ... N... A... ...

PARMENTER, Ch... O..., J... b... ... F... 11 ...33.

PATTEN, A..., s Ch... r... ... ... M... ...
Mary, d. Cr... her ... S... an... L... ...

PEBELS (... Pebles Peebles ...t c... d... Patrick ... F... ...
     May 22 17...
[orn] d. John ... d Sarah, b... e 11... 1754.

PEBLES (... Pebles Pe... ... ... Patrick ... t:
     (Pebel ... Apr. 1 ..., 1737.

PECK (see Peck..., Ad... ... d. J... e F... ... Anna J... ...
Harriet, d... Je... F... an... A... a, M... r. ... 3, 1.1..
Livan..., d... J... e F. and Ann... An..., 4...1
Ly... ..., s. J... e F... d Ann..., M... r. 13, 1...

PEEBLES (... Peb... J... N... Fr... k... J... ...
     Sept. 2 ..., 1775.
Jame... s James and R... l... I... 1..., 1772.
J...e-G... y, s. Pett... I... d I... t, Apr... 11 ...
J..., s. Jam... and R... c... M...
Maria d. Pa... k an... G... et, Sep... ..., 1...
McPe... Sup. P... d... y d James... d R... l... I... 1771
P... (... Y..., s. ... me and R... l... M... ... 17...
S... n d Patt... k ad Jaret, July ...
J... d. P b... ... Pe... and Margrat Ma... 17...
... ... s. Patr... k ... d M... g... t Apr. 2 ..., 176...

PEESO ... Pes... P... ly d. Samuel and S... ly Aug. ... ...

PEIRCE ... P... Alb... n Day, ch. Rev. Luther P... o... and
     Mary A... S... ... 1..., 1.45
Cam... A... d. L... h... and Ruth, Mar. 9, 1812.
G... r ... L... L... Luth... (P...) ... d Mary Ann. I... ...
     1...3.
J... n H... w... r... Lather P... a... M... Ann, Jan. 21, 1...
L... ther A., ch. R... L... he... Pe... an... M... A... July 8, 1...
M... y Ann, ch. R... La... P... d M... An... N... 5 1...

PESO ... P... T... d s... ... 1 S... S... 12, 1...

PETINGALE, M... f... N... fr... M... n. Au... 18,
     1845, in H...

PETTESON, Adam, s. George and Margaret, Oct. 27, 1754.
George, s. George and Margaret, July 19, 1756.
James, s. George and Margaret, Nov. 9, 1751.
John, s. George and Margaret, Nov. 18, 1762.
Neamoi, d. George and Margaret, Sept. 16, 1759.

PHELPS, Amy Phebe, d. Noah and Polly, Feb. 8, 1841, in Ware.
James C., s. Noah and Polly, Apr. 14, 1847.

PHILLIPS, Grizel Euing, d. Pattrick and Mary (Given), Mar. 27,
1805.

PIERCE (see Peirce), Foxwell Thomas, s. Rounsivell and Louis,
Apr. 5, 1819.
John, s. Rounsivell and Louis, Dec. 2, 1816.
Maria Diany (Piercee), d. Josiah and Ruth, Apr. 28, 1814.
Rhoda Felton, d. Josiah and Ruth, July 13, 1816.

PITMAN (see Pittman), Phebe Ann, ch. George B. (Pittman)
and Abigail, Mar. 27, 1821.
Sarah Eliza [dup. Elizabeth], d. George B. (Pittmen) and Abigail,
Dec. 3 [dup. 4], 1834.

PITTMAN (see Pitman), Abigail Ann, ch. George B. and Abigail,
Nov. 22, 1823.
John Nichols, ch. George B. and Abigail, May 19, 1828.

POLLEY (see Polly), Abigail Desire, ch. Amos and Jerusha,
Sept. 15, 1823.
Amos Sawyer, ch. Amos and Jerusha, July 16, 1817.
George Proctor, ch. Amos and Jerusha, July 16, 1832.
Hiram, ch. Amos and Jerusha, June 2, 1820.
James, ch. Amos and Jerusha, Sept. 6, 1838.
Jerusha Elizabeth, ch. Amos and Jerusha, June 4, 1827.
Sumner Osgood, ch. Amos and Jerusha, July 12, 1825.

POLLY (see Polley), Anna Willard, ch. Amos (Polley) and Jerusha, Oct. 16, 1815.

POWERS, Anna Maria, d. Dr. Isaac and Anna, July 10, 1808.
Polly Millin, d. Isaac and Anna, Nov. 14, 1810.

PRAT (see Pratt), Margret, d. Micah and Martha, Nov. 17, 1781.
Nathan, s. Micah and Martha, Mar. 16, 1785.
Will[ia]m, s. Micah and Martha, Mar. 18, 1783.

PRATT (see Prat), Amelia Ann, ch. Nathaniel and Mary H.,
Dec. 22, 1827, in Belchertown.

P... , Calvin Dwight, s. ... ... Oct. 19, 1837.
E... ..d, ch. Nath... ... and Mary H. ... ...
E...la C... ch. J... and w. June 1... ...
F... a la..., ch. Nathaniel and Mary H., ... Bethle-
    ... w...
I... ...e s. W... ...lm and Batt... , Jar. 18... ...
J... , ch. I... d w., July ...] ... , ...
M... y A... d. W... ia m and B... ... , A... ... ...
Warner Lysander, s. Nathaniel and M... M... , ...

PRESHO, Betsy, d. Zad... and Be..., J... 14... ... .
Jane, d. Zed... k and Betsy, J... ly 27, 1...
I...a Mal... d. Zad... k and Betsey, A... 3, 1837.
Laraina, d. Ze... k and Betse, A... g. 2..., 1... 4.
R... u...a, ch. Za... e and Betsey, Aug. 15, 1826.
S... , d. Zed... k a... d Pets... J... y 12, 1... 8.
S... n, d. Zad... k and Be... y, A... r. 18, 1822.
Z... e Lym... n, ch. Z... d... e a... d Betsey, May 14, 1829.
Za... k D... , s. Zad... k and Betsey, J... n. — 1... .

RAMSDELL, Horace A... s... , s. Pich... l a... L... ... ... Dec.
    2..., 1836.

RANDAL (see Randall, Rans..., Rand..., Ame..., G... ... and
    Z... kiah, Oct. 17, 181...
Ma... , d. I... ra... ... and Han... ch. Feb. 11... 1811.
S... s, s. Gib... and w., Oct. 24, 1812.

RANDALL (see Rand... , Randell, Rand... Alonz... G... er, ch.
    Benjamin and Lucy, Jan. 1, 1826.
C... arisa A... eline, d. I... st... (Randal) and Bethiah, N... ... 23, 182...
I... ... S., d. Arba and w... A... g. —, 1824.
Ge... rg... N...lson, ch. Benjamin and Lucy, Feb. 1... , 1... .
Th... a ... a, d. Arba and Esther, N... v. 1... , 18... .

RANDELL (see Randal, Rand... , Randle..., Ar... ... ... ch. El...ah
    and Henriet..., A... r. 3..., 18... .
D... n... ...], ch. Arba and Esther, Mar. ..., 1828.
F... ... Jr., s. El... ah and Ho... n... e, S... t... 9, 1833.
I... ... d. J... ph... and S...t... A... g... 14, 182...
E... b... ch. A... ... and F...l... A... g. 9, 1828.
H... ... , J... a... 1 8... w 18... 22, 182...
I... ... F... ... d B...t... ah, S... , ... 1822.
Mary, ch. El... h and Heariet..., Feb. 16... 1818... to Bethlert w...
Ma... y A... n, ... Elij... rim and H... s... ? A... 14, 183...

RANDELL, Nancy, ch. Elijah and Henrietta, Jan. 31, 1816.
Naomi, ch. Elijah and Henrietta, Sept. 21, 1819, in Belchertown.
Octavia, ch. Arba and Esther, Jan. 27, 1831.
Thankfull, d. Gideon and Zeviah, Apr. 8, 1823.
Warren, s. Elisha and Bethiah, Dec. 19, 1817.

RANDLE (see Randal, Randall, Randell), Dexter [dup. Randell],
    s. Ephraham [dup. Ephrian] and Hannah, Mar. 15, 1816.
George Washington, s. Joseph and Sally, Sept. 17, 1819.
Marcy, d. Benjamin and Lucy, Jan. 17, 1813.
Merilla, d. Benjamin and Lucy, May 29, 1818.

RANKIN (see Rinken), Adaline, d. Zebina and Nancy, Oct. 9,
    1821.
Angeline Amanda, d. Abiel and Mary, Oct. 21, 1826.
Ansel Augustus, s. John and Anna, May 9, 1807.
Augustine Hall, s. Ansel and Vienne, Oct. 27, 1835.
Austin Hinkley, s. John Jr. and Anna, July 4, 1813.
Austin Loring, s. Zebina and Nancy, Aug. 30, 1819.
Edwin Harkness, s. Silas and Sally, Nov. 27, 1813, in Belcher-
    town.
Elizabath, d. Silas and Sally, Oct. 23, 1823.
Emeline Diantha, d. Abiel and Mary, Oct. 10, 1823.
Hinkley, s. Silas and Sally, Oct. 2, 1821.
Hiram, s. James and Margaret, Dec. 11, 1817.
Ira Packard, s. Zebina and Nancy, Jan. 10, 1817.
John Gray, s. Silas and Sarah, Dec. 11, 1815.
Julia Green, d. Ansel and Vienne, Aug. 15, 1837.
Mary Carline, d. John Jr. and Anna, Sept. 11, 1810.
Mary Caroline, d. John Esq. and Abigail, Nov. 18, 1834.
Nancy Jane, d. Zebina and Nancy, Jan. 5, 1824.
Patty Millen, d. John and Anna, Dec. 30, 1816.
Sarah Ann, d. Chester and Anthea, Feb. 1, 1838.
, Silas Merton, s. Chester [and] Antha, May 4, 1834.
William Conkey, s. James and Margaret, Sept. 5, 1815.
[torn]y Ann, d. Silas and Sarah, Apr. 16, 1819.

RECKARDS, Nancy Adelia, d. Hosea and Tirzah Mariah, July
    16, 1827.

RENIEFF (see Reniff), Huldah, d. Abisha and Huldah, Mar.
    10, 1800.

RENIFF (see Renieff), Ephriam, d. Morrey and Sally, Sept. 17,
    1812.

Rester, Eunice, d. Abisha and Huldah, Apr. 19, 1794.

Eunice, d. Morrey and Sally, May 19, 1809.

Loren, s. Daniel and Rhoda, July 24, 1819.

Mary, d. Morrey [dup. Mowry, and Sally, June 16, 1827, in Holden.

Nancy, d. Abisha and Huldah, Oct. 13, 1797, in Worcester.

Sarah, twin d. Daniel and Rhoda, Feb. 15, 1815, in Shutsbury.

Susannah, twin d. Daniel and Rhoda, Feb. 15, 1815, in Shutsbury.

RHOADES (see Rhoads, Rhodes, Rodes), Caroline Eunice, ch. Joel and Lucy, July 25, 1829, in Leyden.

Relief, ch. Joel and Lucy, Mar. 25, 1831.

RHOADS (see Rhoades, Rhodes, Rodes), Abigail, d. Solomon and Eliner, May 3, 1802.

Amos, s. Solomon and Eliner, Sept. 16, 1792.

Betsey, d. Solomon and Eliner, Apr. 11, 1801.

Chester, s. Solomon and Eliner, July 1, 1799.

James, s. Solomon and Eliner, May 31, 1789.

Levi, s. Solomon and Eliner, Sept. 6, 1794.

Nancy, d. Solomon and Eliner, Feb. 15, 1796.

Pate, d. Solomon and Eliner, Oct. 18, 1797.

Silas, s. Solomon and Eliner, Mar. 8, 1791.

RHODES (see Rhoades, Rhoads, Rodes), Nancy Maria, ch. and Lucy, May 2, 1835.

RICE, Caroline Flora, d. Moses and Mary, Dec. 24, 1821.

RICHARDSON, Enos S., ch. —— and Hannah, Dec. 28, 1823.

Emma, d. Jonathan and Naby, May 19, 1805.

Henry Irad, s. Henry and Selina, July 31, 1816.

Henry, s. Jonathan and Naby, Oct. 4, 1807.

Martha B., ch. —— and Hannah, Sept. 15, 1831.

Orvil T., ch. —— and Hannah, Nov. 1, 1830.

Royal, s. Wyatt and Hannah, June 4, 1837.

Sarah H., ch. —— and Hannah, Oct. 23, 1826.

William, s. Henry and Salena, May 21, 1813.

RIDER, Ann Maria, twin ch. John and Rebecca, Oct. 28, 1

Betsey Ward, ch. John and Polly, Sept. 1, 1828.

James B., s. and Olive, Nov.

Harriet, s. John and Capt. R., June 12, 1847.

Isaac, s. John and Rebecca, Nov. 2, 1832.

Isaac, s. Daniel and Capt. R., Mar. 21, 1840.

John, twin ch. John and Rebecca, Oct. 31, 1842.

RIDER, Lucinda, ch. John and Rebeca, Mar. 20, 1833.
Marshal, twin ch. John and Rebekah, Oct. 22, 1835.
Martha, twin ch. John and Rebekah, Oct. 22, 1835.
Nancy, d. Isaac and Olive, Dec. 19, 1806.
Nehemiah, twin ch. John and Rebeca, Oct. 28, 1835.

RIGHT (see Wright), Gaius, s. Gaius and Lucy, May 9, 1811.

RINKEN (see Rankin), Abial, s. John and Mary, Apr. 2, 1796.
Amos, s. John and Mary, May 1, 1790.
Betey, d. John and Mary, Apr. 3, 1786.
Chaster, s. James and Sarah, Jan. 21, 1805.
Cinthia, d. John and Anne, Nov. 15, 1803.
Cyntha, d. John and Mary, Jan. 15, 1794.
Esther, d. Matthew [and] Martha, July 29, 1785.
James, s. James and Sarah, Aug. 27, 1795.
Melinda, d. James and Sarah, Sept. 2, 1793.
Otos, s. James and Sarah, Sept. 28, 1802.
Polly, d. John and Mary, July 12, 1788.
Polly, d. James and Sarah, Aug. 23, 1797.
Salley, d. James and Sarah, Oct. 9, 1791.
Susanah, d. James and Sarah, Jan. 31, 1790.
Walthey, d. James and Sarah, Aug. 9, 1800.
Zebina, s. John and Mary, June 5, 1791.
[torn] s. Joseph and Elisabeth, Feb. 12, 1749.
[torn]w, s. Joseph and Elisabeth, Feb. 2, 1751.
[torn] d. Joseph and Elisabeth, Mar. 2, 1755.
[torn] d. Joseph and Elisabeth, Mar. 12, 1758.
[torn] s. Joseph and Elisabeth, July 6, 1760.

ROBERTSON, [John‡] s. Ebenezer and Jean, Aug. 9, 1758.

ROBINSON, Albert Brown, s. Abiel and Mary Ann, Apr. 12, 1835.
Ellen Stone, ch. Abial and Mary Ann, Jan. 7, 1829 [*sic*].
Henry Pond [?], s. Abial and Marian, Oct. 15, 1840.
Sanford Mason, ch. Abial and Mary Ann, Sept. 27, 1829 [*sic*].
Sanford Mason, s. Abiel and Mary Ann, May 30, 1833.

RODES (see Rhoades, Rhoads, Rhodes), Lucyann, d. Joel and
Lucy, Mar. 5, 1845.

RUGGLES, Daniel Dwight, s. Constant and Sarah, Jan. 1, 1812.

RUSSELL, Chloe E., d. John and Mary, July 15, 1836, in
Granby.

‡ Torn in original record ; supplied from town copy.

R..... F.... M., d. J.h. .... M.... M... 17. 1.45.
L.m... L.... .br.... Mar.... ... .
Mar. J. .... Mar.. .... A...... .
Sar... J. ... . Mar.. Ma.. .. ..,
      S.. .. C. .. Ma. ...

SAMSON, ... d. Nat.... and Nat.... ....
Chester, s. N. .... d Nanc.. Jan. .. , 17.. .
C..... N. d... .... N... .... Aug. 14. 17.4
F... N... ... .. and N... . ... , 1797
H..... ., N. .. .... and N... .. N... 12. 17..7.
H... ... No. .. .. Nan.... June 3.., 17...
Me....... d. N.... .... N... .. Oct. 27. 17..5.
N..... .. s. N.... .... N... .. Oc. .. 16. 17.1.
Th... ...s. Nathaniel and N..... J.... 13. 17.1.

SEARS, J.... P.... ... s. J.... .. .. Fr... .. 1.. .. 1.. .

SELFRIDGE, J h.... .. O. .... and Est.. Oct. 12. 17.7.
Margaret, d. O.... .r and L.. .... J.. .. .. 17.1.
O. .... .. O.... and Est.. Sept. 1. 175..
..... G. Edwa.d a.. J.. .... Lee. .. 1746.
.... Edwa.d a.. J.L.. ...th, Fe.. 24. 1748.

SHAW, A.......... ch. J.... and L.... ... De.. 28. 7
Carr.... .. .. L.... J. .. 1.23. .. ..
F.... .... A..... .. I..'s M... .. 1. 2..
F.... .... W.... s. A... .. M... , M.r. 24. 1.... .
E.... .. W.... d. A.. a. d. M.... 1.. ... 1.... .
M...... .. .... and E.... A... 1.. 1.1.. .. ..
N..... .. .. J.... a.. L.... Oc. .. 1.2... .. ....

S... .. .... J..... a. .... 16. 1..5. .. S.. .. ...
S... M.... .... s. a. .... A... M.. 6. 1.. 7

SHIRTLIEFF, A... .. d. J.h. C..... .. 1 J.. .. ..
      .... 1. 17.. .

SIBLEY, L... .... J. M.... .... .
M....., J. ....
M.... J. .... P.... M.... .... 1..
.... .. J. .... P.... ....

SLOAN, ... J.... ....
A... C. J. .... .. A...

SLOAN, Archia, s. Samuel and Eunic, Nov. 11, 1793.
David, s. David and Elisabeth, Jan. 9, 1790.
Dick, s. Samuel and Eunice, Aug. 1, 1784.
Elictia, d. Samuel and Eunic, Aug. 9, 1795.
Eunic, d. Samuel and Eunic, June 12, 1791.
Garner, s. David and Elesibeth, Mar. 1, 1783.
James, s. David and Elisabeth, Nov. 14, 1777.
James Procter, s. George W. and Mary, June 24, 1836.
Jason, s. Samuel and Eunic, Mar. 3, 1789.
John, s. Samuel and Eunice, May 21, 1780.
Jonathen, s. David and Elisabeth, Nov. 14, 1785.
Lois, d. Samuel and Eunic, Sept. 18, 1786.
Samuel, s. Samuel and Eunice, Feb. 9, 1782.
Sarah, d. James and Abigal, Sept. 20, 1754.
[torn]dr, s. James and Abegal, Sept. 17, 1756.

SMITH, Abial, s. Will[ia]m and Rebecah, Nov. 27, 1804.
Betsey Otis, d. James and Betsey, Oct. 25, 1819.
David Fals, s. Oliver and Hannah, Feb. 28, 1798.
Gilbert Pierson, s. David F. and Maria, Jan. 12, 1832.
Hannah, d. Oliver and Hannah, Mar. 5, 1802.
Hannah, d. James and Betsey, Mar. 27, 1822.
Hannah M., d. Job and Martha, Jan. 20, 1842.
Henry B., s. Abiel B. and Hannah, July 24, 1826.
James Napoleon, s. James and Betsy, Mar. 25, 1826.
     " Name canged By Request of his father to this."
John, s. Hugh and Jennet, Apr. 21, 1784.
Joseph Warren Putnam, s. Abial B. and Hannah, Aug. 17, 1828.
Laura C., d. Job and Martha, June 21, 1845.
Lucy Almira, d. James and Betsy, Sept. 27, 1832.
Maria, twin d. James and Betsey, June 2, 1817.
Mary, twin d. James and Betsey, June 2, 1817.
Mary Louisa, d. Job and Patty, Oct. 27, 1834.
Mehitable S., d. Job and Martha, Feb. 15, 1838.
Mittee, d. Abner Smith and Parces Blair, Jan. 5, 1785.
Napolean Bonaparte, s. James and Betsey, Mar. 25, 1826.   [See
     James Napoleon.]
Oliver C., ch. David F. and Mariah, Apr. 19, 1825.
Rachel Cook, ch. David F. and Mariah, Apr. 17, 1820, in Bel-
     chertown.
Sally, d. William and Rebecah, Mar. 18, 1807.
Will[ia]m, s. Oliver and Hannah, Apr. 28, 1800.

SOUTHWARD, Asa, s. Uriah and Patiance, Apr. 14, 1786.

Southward, Elizabeth, d. [...] March, May [...] 1759.
Han[...] a [...] Pa[...] [...] Me-
    [...] Ass[...]
M[...] d. [...] Pa[...], M[...]

SOUTHWICK, G[...] Ch[...] Ame[...] N[...] M[...] 24,
    18[...]

SOUTHWORTH, E[...] d. [...] N[...] a[...] K[...] [...]
Martha, d. A[...] and K[...] Ma[...] [...]
M[...] d. W[...] and K[...] N[...] 6[...]
R[...] [...] N[...] and K[...] F[...]
S[...] [...] N[...] K[...] N[...]
S[...] m[...] N[...] d. K[...] F[...]
W[...] N[...] th[...] K S[...] N[...] 17[...]

SQUIRES, He[...] R[...] [...] [...]22
    in Bel[...]
Jeremiah N[...] Z[...] d. s[...] N[...] [...]
    [...]
La[...] M[...] L[...] G[...] Go[...] [...] f
    Z[...]
Ly[...] [...] Z[...] [...] A[...]
M[...] [...] Z[...] [...] E[...]
    N[...]

STEBBINS [...] S[...] W[...] S[...] J[...] M[...]
    Sept. 23, [...] [...]
Clara E, L D[...] M[...] [...]

STIBBINS [...] S[...] F[...] D[...] [...] M[...]
    Nov. 6, [...] G[...]

STROWBRIDGE, D[...] [...] A[...] [...]
    [...] Car l Ar[...] M[...] [...] 17[...]

TAFT [...] T[...] J[...] [...] [...] [...]
Mary A[...] d E[...] Jac[...] M[...]

TAFTS [...] Ta[...] A[...] Lu[...] M[...] [...]
N[...], d. [...] M[...] A[...] [...]
M[...] [...] M[...] J[...] 7
M[...] [...] d Martha, M[...]

TALOR [...] Lucius C. J[...] [...] Ly[...] d
    Sa[...] C[...] N[...]

TARREL (see Terrel), Noah, s. Noah (Terrel) and Reliance, Apr. 9, 1795, in Bridgwater.

TAYLOR (see Talor), Alford, s. John and Martha, Oct. 20, 1804.
Ann, [————] w. Alfred, June 28, 1812, at Staten Island.
Betsy, d. James and Abiah, July 21, 1780.
Caroline Augusta, ch. Alfred and Ann, Feb. 22, 1837.
Catharine, d. James and Abiah, May 11, 1782.
Ellen Amelia, d. Stewart P. and Sally Rosina, May 22, 1837.
Emeline Eusebia, d. James and Sally C., Oct. 23, 1832.
George Washington, s. James and Sally, Aug. 28, 1837.
Henry, ch. Alfred and Ann, Apr. 29, 1833, in N. Y.
Isaac Newton, s. James and Sally, Nov. 22, 1834.
Israel, s. Alfred and Ame, Mar. 28, 1841.
Israel H., s. John and Martha, Oct. 28, 1811.
Isreal, s. James and Abiah, June 4, 1775.
James, s. John and Martha, June 2, 1802.
Jane Eliza, d. John and Lucy, Oct. 21, 1838.
John, s. John and Martha, Aug. 18, 1809.
John Bailey, s. James and Sarah, Sept. 18, 1839.
Lucy, d. John and Marthew, Apr. 17, 1801.
Lucy Lavina, d. Alfred and Ann, Apr. 26, 1845.
Martha, d. John and Martha, Nov. 17, 1816.
Martha Jane, d. Alford and Ann, Feb. 19, 1839.
Mary Ann, ch. Alfred and Ann, Feb. 15, 1835, in N. Y.
Phebe Marsha, d. Alfred and Anne, Apr. 29, 1843.
William, s. John and Martha, Apr. 13, 1807.
W[illia]m, s. Alfred and Ann, Nov. 5, 1847.
[torn] s. Jam[e]s and Margret, May 4, 1747.
[torn] s. James and Margret, May 11, 1749.
[torn]beth, d. Jam[e]s and Margret, Apr. 2, 1751.
[torn] d. Jam[e]s and Margret, Feb. 2, 1753.

TERREL (see Tarrel), Clarisa, d. Noah and Reliance, Jan. 1, 1800, in Bridgwater.
Deborah, d. Noah and Reliance, July 16, 1805.
Mary, d. Noah and Reliance, May 6, 1803.
Rebecca, d. Noah and Reliance, Dec. 12, 1807.
Thadius, s. Noah and Reliance, Aug. 26, 1798, in Bridgwater.

THIRSTIN (see Thurston, Thustain, Thuston), Nancy, d. Paul and Mary, May 23, 1810.
Thomas, s. Paul and Mary, Dec. 18, 1811.

THOMPSON (see Thomson, Tompson, Tomson), Achsah, d. Joseph and Margret, May 23, 1739.

THOMSON, Albert Porter, s. A... ... ..8, Dec. 4, 182...
Albert Porter, s. ... P... ... ... M... ... ...
Amb... ... ... Pe... ... Sept. ...
[A... ... ... M... ..., Sept. 9, 17...
Ar... ... ... 1 J..., De... 1, 17...
Ar... ... W... s. P... ... Pe... ..., M... ... ...
C... 'n... s. I... ... ... d J... S... ... ...
J... ... b... and Pud... ... M... 4, 17...
J... ... s. ... m... and M. ... ... De... 14, 1...
D... ... s. J... ... and M. ... ... F... 2, 1...
D... s. d. J... ... Ir... d N. ... ... Mar. 4, 1812.
F... n... s. James ... ... Ma... M... 16 1 1...
F... J... ... d. J... ... and Ma... et, Jun 2, 1773.
E... eboth, d. J... ... and Pudl... Apr. 1, 174...
Faustus C... key, s. Is... ... Thomp... n and Rebe... th C...k ...
        8, 18 3.
F... ..., d. ... n... ... Pru... e... O... 1, 17...
G... ..., s. ... n... and Pru... 1... F... 17, 1775.
G... g... s. T... m... and D... ... Sept 1, 1774.
H... ... h, d. Th... ... and J... ... Dec. 22, 1...
Hannah, d. Ar... ... w... d A... d g, N... ... ...
... ... s. T... m... ... J... ... N... 19, 1773.
Is... ... s. Dan'l ... so h M... r 14, 1...
I... l, s. J... ph ... M... et, N... 7, 1774.
J... ..., s. T... ... a... Pru... ... Apr. 1... 17...
J... ... s. J... ... d M... I... ... 17...
... ... d. J... ... an... Mar... N... 17, 1775.
J... s, ... J... ... C... nd s... t. H. M... 28, 1854.
J... l, s. J... ... ... 1 M... ... Apr. ... 179...
J... ... s. J... ... a... Pru... ... N... ... 17...
J... M... ... a... J... ... J... ... Oct. 17, 17...
J... ... s. T... ... ... J... ... 9, 17...
J... ... s. J... ... M... e... J... ... 17 10.
J... ... ... (M... et) M... ... 17...
J... ... ... A... ... Birth O... 14, 1...
L... ..., P... ... ... J... ... June 11, 1791.
L... y, d. J... ... and M... ... N... 1, 18...
L... ... N... ... J... ... J... ... S... ... ...
M... M... ch. J... ... N... ... May ... ... N ch...
     ...
M... ... ... M... ... A... 17 0.
M... ... J... ... ... A... ... 8...
M... ... J... ... P... ... A... ... 17...
[M... ... ... A... ...

THOMPSON, Martha, d. Joseph and Margret, Sept. 11, 1787.
Mary, d. John and Prudance, July 1, 1758.
Mary, d. Tho[ma]s and Marcy, Jan. 3, 1786.
Mary, d. James Jr. and Mettilda, June 30, 1808.
Mary Ann, d. Erastus C. and Sarah H., June 11, 1831.
Mary Esther Hooker, d. Andrew and Almeda, Nov. 29, 1812.
Matilda, d. Tho[ma]s and Marcy, July 9, 1781.
Merrick Monroe, ch. Isaac and Mercia, Dec. 21, 1826.
Metilda, d. James and Metilda, June 22, 1797.
Miriam, d. Joseph and Margret, Apr. 27, 1777.
Molley, d. John and Prudance, Oct. 6, 1770.
Molley, d. Joseph and Margret, Mar. 16, 1785.
Myra Esther, ch. Asa and Ruth, Oct. 24, 1835.
Olive, d. Tho[ma]s and Marcy, May 25, 1788.
Peleg, s. James and Matilda, Dec. 12, 1798.
Peleg Peirce, s. James Jr. and Metilda, Apr. 22, 1810.
Rachel Carroline, ch. Isaac and Mercia, Apr. 18, 1829.
Ruben, s. Tho[ma]s and Jean, Apr. 15, 1797.
Sarah, d. John and Prudance, Jan. 5, 1773.
Sarah, d. Joseph and Margret, May 11, 1793.
Sarah Ann, ch. Asa and Ruth, Mar. 12, 1826.
Sophia Jane, ch. Asa and Ruth, June 19, 1830.
Susanna, d. John and Prudance, Mar. 19, 1762.
Suzannah, d. Daniel and Sarah, Mar. 22, 1807.
Thomas, s. James and Martha, Apr. 15, 1753.
William, s. Joseph and Margret, Sept. 29, 1778.
William, s. Tho[ma]s and Marcy, Aug. 1, 1785.
William Linsey, s. John and Katuien, Feb. 4, 1789.

THOMSON (see Thompson, Tompson, Tomson), Mehitable, d.
    Daniel and Sally, Nov. 4, 1805.

THORNTON, Lucina M., d. Elisha S. and Lovina, Mar. 25, 1843,
    in Belchertown.
Mary H., d. Elisha S. and Lovina, Apr. 5, 1845.
Prudence J., d. Elisha S. and Lovina, Mar. 25, 1847.
Smith, s. Elisha [S.] and Lovina, Dec. 12, 1848.

THURBER (see Thurbur), Charles Wesley, s. William W. and
    Pamilla A., Nov. 6, 1832.
Mary Ellen, d. W[illia]m W. and Permilla, Jan. 10, 1840.
Mary Maria, d. William W. and Permelia, Mar. 23, 1830.
Permelia, d. W[illia]m W. and Pemelia, Oct. 9, 1823.
Susan Hall, d. William W. and Permela, Sept. 17, 1827.
W[illia]m Manda, s. W[illia]m W. and Pemelia, Aug. 31, 1825.

THURBER, Zimri, s. W[illia]m W. and Permilla, Sept. 2, 1837.

THURBUR (see Thurber), Edwin W., s. Whitaker, July 22, 1845.

THURSTON (see Thirstin, Thustain, Thusten, Thuston), Elizabeth, d. Paul and Mary, July 22, 1808.
James Jr. [dup. James Thursten], s. James and Susannah, Apr. 29, 1820 [dup. 1821].
Lydia E. E., d. Thomas and Lydia, Oct. 9, 1849.
Lysander, twin ch. James and Maria, May 25, 1837.
Marrilla, ch. Paul and Mary, May 18, 1823.
Mary, d. Paul and Mary, June 20, 1807.
Olive, d. James and Maria, Nov. 22, 1828.
Philander, twin ch. James and Maria, May 25, 1837.
Stillman, ch. Paul and Mary, Nov. 15, 1820.
Thomas J., s. Thomas and Lydia, June 24, 1848.

THUSTAIN (see Thirstin, Thurston, Thusten, Thuston), Jason, s. James and Maria, Apr. 5, 1840.
Lorenzo E., s. Thomas and Lydia, June 10, 1838.

THUSTEN (see Thirstin, Thurston, Thustain, Thuston), Susan Maria, d. James (Thursten) and Susan, Dec. 16, 1822.

THUSTON (see Thirstin, Thurston, Thustain, Thusten), Elmira, ch. James and Maria, Jan. 21, 1832.
Emoly, d. Paul and Mary, Apr. 20, 1815.
John Thayer, s. James and Susana, Jan. 11, 1818.
Rial Gleason, ch. James and Maria, Sept. 27, 1834.
Rufus, s. Paul and Mary, Apr. 8, 1818.
Susanna, d. Paul and Mary, June 7, 1816.

TILER, Aaron, s. Daniel and Molley, July 23, 1798.
Daniel, [twin] s. Daniel and Molley, Mar. 16, 1788.
Eunice, d. Daniel and Molley, Sept. 8, 1796.
Moses Wilson, s. Daniel and Molley, May —, 1793.
Polley, [twin] d. Daniel and Molley, Mar. 16, 1788.
Sally, d. Daniel and Molley, Mar. —, 1791.

TINKHAM, David, s. Joseph and Mary, Feb. 18, 1789.
Deborah, d. Joseph and Mary, June 12, 1779, in Plymtown.
Hannah, d. Joseph and Mary, Dec. 16, 1792.
Joseph, s. Joseph and Mary, July 21, 1781, in Plymtown.
Molly, d. Joseph and Mary, Aug. 28, 1787.
William, s. Joseph and Mary, Oct. 14, 1784.

TITUS, Almira, d. Sylvester and Nancy, Dec. 18, 1809.

TITUS, Angelina, d. Sylvester and Nancy, Feb. 23, 1812.
Clementine, d. Sylvester and Nancy, July 1, 1818.
Harriot, d. Silvester and Nancy, Sept. 4, 1804.
Liraann, d. Sylvester and Nancy, Feb. 26, 1815.
Lucian, s. Silvester and Nancy, Oct. 11, 1807.
Silas, s. Silvester and Nancy, Oct. 8, 1801.

TOLEMAN, Sarah Jane, ch. John and Sarah Jane, Aug. 31, 1839.
W[illia]m A., ch. John and Sarah Jane, Dec. 19, 1841.

TOMPSON (see Thompson, Thomson, Tomson), Mally, d.
James and Mary, May 17, 1767.
Sarah, d. James and Mary, Dec. 8, 1769.

TOMSON (see Thompson, Thomson, Tompson), Asa C., s.
Asa and Ruth, Jan. 14, 1848.
James, s. Asa and Ruth, Aug. 25, 1843.
Viola T., d. Asa and Ruth, Dec. 18, 1845.

TORNER, [torn] s. Allex[an]d[e]r and Mary, [torn, prob. 174]3.
[torn] s. Allex[an]d[e]r and [torn], [torn]47.
[torn]ll[ia]m, s. Jam[e]s and Susanna, Dec. 26, 1760.
[Sarah ‡] d. James and Susanna, July 11, 1762.

TORRANCE, Levi, s. Alaxander and Priscilla, Dec. 1, 1781.
Sarah, d. Prisilla, Apr. 7, 1779.
Susanna, d. Alax[an]d[e]r and Priscilla, June 11, 1785.

TOWER, David, s. Isaac and Elizabeth, June 12, 1798.
Hepzabeth, d. Isaac and Elizabeth, June 24, 1802.
Samuel, s. Isaac and Elizabeth, Nov. 26, 1796.
Sibal, d. Isaac and Elizabeth, Apr. 15, 1794.

TRASK, Charles Greenlief, s. Porter Trask and Betsy Taylor,
Jan. 1, 1806.

TURNER, Abigal, d. Allice [Ellis] and Thankfull, Aug. 18,
1793, in Tempeltown.
Amelia, d. Alice [Ellis] and Thankful, Jan. 3, 1800.
Caroline, d. Jonathan and Betsy, Oct. 1, 1827.
Daxter, s. Alice [Ellis] and Thankful, Sept. 25, 1802.
Ellinor [dup. Elenor], d. Jonathan and Betsey, of Enfield,
May 27, 1837.
Henry Dutton, ch. Dexter and Poll, Nov. 23, 1827, in Belcher-
town.
Hollis, s. Jonathan and Betsy, Dec. 1, 1829.

‡ Torn in original record ; supplied from town copy.

TURNER, John, ch. Dexter and Poll, Dec. 3, 1829.
Jonathen, s. Allice [Ellis] and Thankfull, Jan. 2, 1791, in
    Tempeltown.
Joseph, s. Allice [Ellis] and Thankfull, Sept. 23, 1795.
Louisa, d. Jonathan and Betsy, Nov. 26, 1825.
Martha Jane, d. Jonathan and Eliza, Sept. 16, 1831.
Mary, d. Ellis and Thankfull, June 25, 1805.
Mary, ch. Dexter and Poll, Nov. 13, 1825, in Belchertown.
Zilphia, d. Allice [Ellis] and Thankfull, Oct. 18, 1797.

TYLER (see Tiler).

VAUGHN, Amanda, d. Thomas Jr. and Loiza, Feb. 12, 1818.
Leretta, d. Thomas Jr. and Loiza, Feb. 28, 1816.
Loiza, d. Thomas Jr. and Loiza, Feb. 12, 1814.
Thomas Warren, s. Thomas Jr. and Loiza, Nov. 10, 1819.

WAGE, Cyntha, d. Naham and Cyntha, May 7, 1801.
Roxeylindia, d. Naham and Cyntha, Feb. 7, 1803.
Samual Chapens, s. Nahum and Cyntha, Dec. 16, 1798.

WALKER, Horac, s. Abel and Mary, Oct. 12, 1799.
Otis, s. Abel and Mary, Dec. 28, 1800.

WALLIS, Francis, ch. Nahum and Zilpha, Jan. 27, 1827.
Franklin, ch. Nahum and Zilpha, Dec. 4, 1828.
Mary, d. Nahum and Zylphia, Nov. 10, 1824.

WARD, Hannah, d. John and Polly, Nov. 14, 1807.
Joseph, s. Joseph and Amanda, Nov. 26, 1847.
Luthera B., d. Moses L. and Sally, May 10, 1846.
Martha, d. John and Polly, July 20, 1821.

WASHBURN, Garner, s. James and Sarah, June 26, 1792.
Hiram, s. James and Sarah, Nov. 9, 1800.
Roxey, d. James and Sarah, Aug. 15, 1795.

WASON, [torn] s. John and Agnes, June 28, 1741.
[torn] s. John and Agness, June 29, 1748.

WEATHERBY (see Wetherby), Ephrayhan Ruggles, ch. Var-
    num G. and Betsy R., Oct. 24, 1836.
Olive Eliza, ch. Varnum G. and Betsy R., Oct. 25, 1841.

WEBSTER, Martha Lucretia, ch. Augustus and Amy, Jan. 4,
    1828 [? in Bolton, Conn.]
Rachael Rebecah, ch. Augustus and Amy, Apr. 12, 1830, in
    Bolton, Conn.

WEBSTER, Sarah Ann Eliza, ch. Augustus and Amy, Jan. 1, 1825
[? in Bolton, Conn.]

WEDG (see Wedge), Ellen Merinda, [twin] d. Lemuel C.
(Wedge) and Lucy, Jan. 5, 1843.

WEDGE (see Wedg), Adaline, d. Lamuel C. and Cynthia, Feb.
16, 1824.
Amy, d. Lemuel and Cynthia, Sept. 7, 1822.
Elizabeth Augusta, [twin] d. Lemuel C. and Lucy, Jan. 5, 1843.
Esther, d. Lamuel C. and Cyntha, Nov. 23, 1825.
Lodicy Ugene, d. Lemuel and Cynthia, Aug. 25, 1829.
Lucy Jane, d. Lemuel C. [and] Cynthia, July 12, 1835.
Warren Chapin, s. Lemuel C. and Cyntha, Dec. 20, 1827.
Zoe Taft, d. Lemuel C. and Cynthia, July 27, 1833.

WELLS, Stilman Plumer, s. Augustus and Rebecah [dup.
Rebekkah], May 22, 1810.

WESCOTT (see Westcott), Hannah Green, d. Ruben and Lucy,
Jan. 3, 1813.
Jered Taft, s. Reuben and Lucy, Oct. 9, 1805.
Lydia, d. Ruben and Lucy, July 12, 1815.
Reuben, s. J. T. and Ann, Sept. 16, 1841.
Walter D., s. J. T. and Ann, May 7, 1848.
Zoe Taft, d. Reuben and Lucy, June 8, 1810.

WESTCOTT (see Wescott), Elisebeth Rebecca, d. Jared T. and
Sarah C., Oct. 21, 1830.
Mary Florett, d. Walter and Harriet, May 18, 1839.
Reuben Arratus, s. Walter and Harriet, Oct. 4, 1835.
Walter, s. Reuben and Lucy, Mar. 23, 1808.
William Smith, s. Jared T. and Sally C., July 5, 1835.

WETHERBY (see Weatherby), Eunice E., d. Varnum and
Betsy, Dec. 9, 1843.
John Rice, s. Varnum (b. Enfield) and Betsy (b. " Somerset,
V. T."), Nov. 25, 1845.

WETHEREL (see Witherel), Emma M., d. Willard and w.,
Nov. 7, 1847.
Emory M., s. Willard and w., Nov. 7, 1847.
George E., s. Willard and w., Apr. 22, 1842.

WHEELER, Abigale Brown, ch. Nathaniel and Faithfull, Jan. 1,
1830.
Chancelor Livingston, s. Nath[anie]l and Faithfull, July 24, 1819.

WHEELER, Eunice, d. Nathaniel and Faithfull, Feb. 9, 1814.
Henry, s. Nathaniel and Faithful, May 5, 1835.
Joseph Marik, s. Joseph and Lois, Nov. 5, 1806.
Joshua Linkorn, s. Joshua and Abigal, Dec. 8, 1797.
Lois Loiza, d. Joseph and Lois, Apr. 11, 1808.
Mariah Jane, ch. Nathaniel and Faithfull, Oct. 6, 1825.
Mary Ann Augusta, d. Nath[anie]l and Faithfull, Apr. 27, 1816.
Sally, d. Edward and Sally, June 1, 1806.
Thomas, s. Edward and Sally, Jan. 6, 1808.

WHIPPLE, Abigail Joslyn, ch. Joseph and Azubah, Jan. 26, 1815.
Ambra Sultina [dup. Saltina], ch. James Greenwood and Ann
    Mariah [dup. James G. and Anne M.], Jan. 27, 1840.
Brooksey Waters, ch. Joseph and Azubah, Dec. 29, 1806, [in]
    Sutton.
Danniel D., s. James G. and Anna M., Dec. 14, 1841.
David, ch. Russel and Mary, Oct. 28, 1826, [in] Enfield.
David Russel, ch. Joseph and Azubah, July 30, 1810, [in] Sutton.
James Greenwood, Mar. 2, 1815, [in] Enfield.
Joseph Jr., ch. Joseph and Azubah, Aug. 16, 1812.
Lucy Maria, d. Russel and Mary, July 30, 1832.
Mary Ann, ch. Russel and Mary, Jan. 21, 1812, [in] Enfield.
Mary E., d. James G. and Anna M., Mar. 10, 1846.
Oliver C., s. James G. and Anna M., Nov. 10, 1843.
Russel, ch. Russel and Mary, Dec. 1, 1823, [in] Enfield.
Sarah Houston, ch. Joseph and Azubah, Mar. 11, 1818.
Sarah Jane, ch. Russel and Mary, Dec. 27, 1820, [in] Enfield.
Solomon, ch. Russel and Mary, Jan. 24, 1810, [in] Enfield.
William Dunlap, ch. James Greenwood and Ann Mariah [dup.
    James G. and Anna M.], Aug. 26, 1838.

WHITE, Josiah, s. S[torn], Nov. 20, 1893 [sic 1793], in Wor-
    cester.
Susanna, d. James White and Miss Abigail Boynton, Sept. 18,
    1830.

WHITEMORE, Levinia, d. Benj[a]m[in] and Hannah, Nov. 7,
    1817.

WILBER, Mary Morell, d. Solomon and Mary Ann, Jan. 13, 1823.

WILLARD, Hannah Aborn, d. Sam[ue]ll and Sally, Mar. 1,
    1819.

WILLIAMS, Anna Mixter, ch. Moses and Ruey, June 5, 1818,
    in Amherst.

WILLIAMS, Hannah Lee, ch. Moses and Ruey, Oct. 5, 1820, in Amherst.

Harriet Newell, ch. Moses and Ruey, Aug. 20, 1816, in Amherst.

James, [twin] s. Silas and Susannah, Oct. 28, 1799.

Jason, [twin] s. Silas and Susannah, Oct. 28, 1799.

Lucy, d. Silas and Susanah, Feb. 2, 1804.

Milicent, d. Silas and Susannah, Feb. 2, 1802.

Polly, d. Silas and Susanah, Apr. 16, 1797.

Sarah, d. Silas and Susanah, Feb. 9, 1795.

WILLSON (see Wilson), Anne Mayo, d. Will[ia]m and Margrit,' Jan. 8, 1804.

Asenath, d. Plinne, Dec. 13, 1813.

WILSON (see Willson), Charles Baker, s. William and Margaret, Nov. 22, 1807.

Elizabeth, d. Will[ia]m and Allice, July 7, 1795.

Harriot Mari, d. William and Margeret, Oct. 12, 1810.

John Shepherd, s. William and Margeret, Aug. 16, 1812.

Joseph Horace, s. William and Margaret, Nov. 16, 1814.

Lousia, d. William and Allice, Feb. 14, 1797.

Otis Emerson, s. William and Margaret, Feb. 23, 1821.

Reuban Sumner, s. William and Margart, Nov. 27, 1805.

WINSLOW, Lucian S., s. Alden S. and Bethia, May 6, 1839, in Belchertown.

Oscar F., s. Alden S. and Bethia, Feb. 26, 1841, in Amherst.

WITHEREL (see Wetherel), Lucinda [dup. W. Wetherel], d. Willard and Sarah [dup. omits Sarah], Aug. 26 [dup. 29], 1844.

WOOD, Daniel, s. Daniel and Susanna, Jan. 7, 1809.

George Nelson, s. Jonathan and Lydia, June 22, 1807.

Lyman Gaskill, s. George N. and Johanna C., Aug. 23, 1834.

Mary, d. Jonathan and Lydia, Apr. 22, 1802.

Sally, d. Daniel and Suzannah, Sept. 9, 1806.

Stephen Taft, s. Jonathan and Lyda, Sept. 18, 1805.

William Augustus, s. Jonathan and Lydia, July 23, 1810.

WOODS, Ancel, s. Ebenezer and Sarah, Mar. 10, 1787.

Catharine Arminda, d. Charles N. and Hepzibah, June 25, 1836.

Ebenezer, s. Ebenezer and Sarah, July 4, 1780.

Elijah Williams, s. Ebenezer and Sarah, Apr. 22, 1782.

Molly, s. Ebenezer and Sarah, Mar. 26, 1784.

WRIGHT (see Right), Ebenezer, s. Gad and Thankfull, Apr. 16,
1802.

Eunice, d. Gaius (Write) and Lucy, Mar. 14, 1805.

Gad [dup. Right], s. Gad and Thankfull [dup. Thankful], May 31,
1810.

Hiram Taylor [dup. Hirum Taylor Right], s. Gad and Thankfull, Oct. 23, 1807.

Lucy, d. Gaus and Lucy, July 3, 1809.

Pearcias, d. Gad and Thankfull, Apr. 21, 1804.

Thankfull, d. Gad and Thankfull, Jan. 1, 1799, in Lonox.

Thomas, s. Gaius and Lucy, Dec. 15, 1806.

PELHAM MARRIAGES.

PELHAM MARRIAGES.

To THE YEAR 1850.

ABBET (see Abbot, Abbott), Squire and Marthew Thompson, int. Oct. 19, 1795.

ABBOT (see Abbet, Abbott), Cheney [int. Chene of Prescott] and Rachel Chapin, Nov. 29, 1827.*

ABBOTT (see Abbet, Abbot), Cheney, widr., 47, b. Prescott, s. Zephaniah and Eunice of Prescott, and Permelia Thompson, wid., Aug. 30, 1846.*

ABELL, Mitty of Goshan, and Henry Hannum, int. Apr. 9, 1820.

ABERCROMBIE, Andrew [int. Ebercrombie] and Mary Conky, Nov. 22, 1773.*
David and Mary Eaton, Jan. 18, 1816.*
Emerson, 25, of Amherst, s. David and Mary, and Lovina [int. Lavinia] S. Lovell, Oct. 23, 1848.*
Hiram [int. Abercrombe] and Betsy [int. Betsey] Babbet, Dec. 26, 1839.*
Isaac, Ens., and Martha McCollah, int. Dec. 5, 1789.
James and Margary Conky, Nov. 15, 1780.*
Mahetable and Job Smith, int. Nov. 11, 1804.
Margaret and John Conky Jr., June 4, 1772.*
Margret and William Wilson Jr., int. Sept. 25, 1803.
Rachel and James Lewis, int. Mar. 5, 1814.
Rebeca and William Smith, int. Nov. 6, 1803.
Robert and Mary Thuston, int. Oct. 7, 1799.
Sally and Waterman Fuller, Apr. 20, 1824.*
Samuel and Lucinda Castle, int. Dec. 12, 1802.
Sarah and Robert Field, Apr. 5, 1832.*
William and Jemima Darling, int. Jan. 1, 1804.
William and Abigial Bell, int. Sept. 26, 1812.

ADAMS, Edward of Greenwich, and Sarah Stanford, int. Dec. 12, 1777.

* Intention also recorded.

85

ADAMS, Francis of New Braintree [int. Worcester Co.], and Naomi Gray, June 10 [1817].*

ALBE, Arba [int. Albee] and Sally Lewis, Dec. 24 [1817].*

ALDRICH, Adaline and John Pratt, Jan. 5, 1826.*
Asahel and Mrs. Margaret Rankin, Nov. 17, 1825.*
Asenath P. of Bernardston, and Warren Randall, int. Mar. 11, 1840.
Rachel and Asa Wilson [int. Willson] Jr., Aug. 27, 1828.*
Relief of New Salem, and Cheney Cooley, int. Jan. 20, 1822.
Saral A. of Uxbridge, and Tyler D. Aldrich, int. Oct. 5, 1843.
Sarah C. and Marcus J. Pease, Sept. 6 [1836].*
Tyler D. and Saral A. Aldrich, int. Oct. 5, 1843.
Wiley, 22, of Ware [int. of Belchertown], b. Belchertown, s. Nehemiah, and Caroline Crosier, Feb. 19, 1846.*

ALLAXANDER (see Allexander), John [int. Allex[an]d[e]r] of Benningtown, and Elisabeth Berry, Feb. 29, 1780.

ALLEN, Anna, Mrs., and Oliver Gleason, Nov. 26, 1826.*
Lucy and Joel Rhodes [int. Rodes], Oct. 2, 1828.*
Persis, 43, d. Samuel and Elizabeth, and Jonathan Turner, widr., Jan. 29, 1846.*
Sally and Benany Streter, int. Aug. 3, 1811.
Samuel Jr. and Elizabeth Davenson, int. Oct. 5, 1800.
Welcom and Anna M. Wilson, Sept. 22, 1822.*

ALLEXANDER (see Allaxander), Jennet and Henry Strongman, Oct. 27, 1757.*

ANDERSON, John of Dearfield [int. Deerfield], and Jenney [int. Jeny] McCraken, July 11, 1767.*
Thomas of Coldrain, and Mary Linsey, int. Nov. 10, 1750.
William and Elisabeth Queen, int. Sept. 23, 1763.

ANDRESS (see Andrews, Andros), Betsey of Hinsdale, Cheshier Co., N.H., and Isaac Briggs Jr., int. Sept. 20, 1816.

ANDREWS (see Andress, Andros), Polly [int. Polley] and Perez [int. Periss] Brown, Jan. 28 [1816].*
Stephan of Ware, and Bridget Southworth, int. Dec. 3, 1783.

ANDROS, (see Andress, Andrews) Abigal of Balchertown, and William Hunter, int. Sept. 28, 1801.

* Intention also recorded.

ARNOLD, Eliza [int. Elizabeth, dup. Elia, b. Belchertown], of Belchertown, and Hiram Ballou [int. Ballow], Nov. 30, [1843].*

Epharim of Belchertown, and Mary Crozier, int. Sept. 23, 1808.

Mary of Balchertown, and Agustius Chace, int. Oct. 24, 1802.

Polly and Pleney Hannum, int. June 9, 1808.

Samuel and Mrs. Chloe Jilson, Dec. 13, 1827.*

Saphrona [int. Sophronia], 20, d. Savannah, and Warner Pratt, Oct. 1, 1846.*

Savannah and Emeline Ballou, May 26, 1822.*

Savannah, widr., and Mary Newell, wid., May 4, 1848.*

Smith of Cumberland, R. I., and Susanna Hall, int. June 26, 1807.

ASHLEY, Calven and Matilda Mun, int. Oct. 14, 1797.

Lucy and Alden Parce, int. Sept. 17, 1792.

Will[ia]m and Nancy Pumroy, int. Apr. 2, 1786.

ATKINSON, John and Mary Woods, int. May 22, 1790.

Mary and Jedediah Jewett, int. Aug. 21, 1788.

Salley and Elijah Edson, int. Sept. 5, 1791.

AUSTIN, Charles, 21, s. Ebeneazer and Mary, and Maria E. Shaw, Aug. 1, 1848.*

Ebeneazer and Mrs. Bettiah Winslow, int. Apr. 6, 1846.

Eben[eze]r and Mary [int. Marry] Boynton, Nov. 28 [1824].*

Joel, 21, s. Ebeneazer and Mary, and Sarah M. Cowls [int. Cowles], May 27, 1847.*

AYER (see Ayres, Heirs), Patty and Elijah Carruth, int. Dec. 9, 1820.

AYRES (see Ayer, Heirs), Nancy [int. Ayers] and Jonas Bridge, Dec. 25 [1821].*

Ruth of Greenwich, and Josiah Pierce Jr., int. Apr. 8, 1811.

BABBET (see Babbott), Betsy [int. Betsey] and Hiram Abercrombie, Dec. 26, 1839.

BABBITT (see Babbet, Babbott).

BABBOTT (see Babbet), Susan E. [int. Babbitt], 52, b. Dana, d. Jonathan, and Simon Cook, May 2, 1844.*

BABEY, Nabby and Seth Bryent, int. Oct. 14, 1798.

* Intention also recorded.

BAILEY, Algenon S. and Marsha S. Davis, Nov. 28 [1839].*
Sarah C. and James Taylor, Dec. 18, 1829.*

BAKER, Ann and Jared T. Westcott, June 20, 1838, in Marcellus, Onondaga Co., N. Y.
Elisha and Ester Cuttler Latham, int. Sept. 18, 1803.
Eunice and William Shaw, int. Nov. 26, 1803.
John and Hannah Smith, int. Jan. 21, 1794.
Luice [Lewis] and Loise Walker, int. May 14, 1786.

BALDWIN, W[illia]m and Sarah Dunlap, int. Jan. 18, 1783.

BALL, Hoyt E., 27, of Amherst, b. Amherst, s. Abraham and Martha, and Mary Dodge, Oct. 5, 1847.
Josiah of Holden, and Almira Fales, Aug. 7, 1837.*

BALLOU (see Bellew), Emeline and Savannah Arnold, May 26, 1822.*
Emery and Maria Dunbar, int. June 14, 1837.
Hiram [int. Ballow] s. Stephen, and Elia [int. Elizabeth, dup. Eliza] Arnold, Nov. 30, 1843.*
Jane W. of Cumberland, R. I., and John B. Hall, int. Dec. 14, 1843.
Silas of Cumberland, R. I., and Sally Harlow, Mar. 22 [1821].*

BARBER (see Barbor), John and Zubee Warran, int. July 17, 1785.

BARBOR (see Barber), Hannah of Worcester, and Elot Gray, int. Feb. 7, 1761.
Margaret [int. Barbour] and John Lawson, Mar. 6, 1776.*
Robert and Sarah McFarland, May 16, 1751.*
Sarah and Matt[he]w Gray, Oct. 30, 1766.*

BARLOE (see Barlow), Deborah and Josiah McKee, int. May 14, 1786.
Mary. "May ye 7th [1787] then Personally apeared Mary Barloe of Pelham and Made Sollomn Oath that obed Hunt of Shutesbury Sollomnly Promised to Join with her in mariage Previous her entereng on Publication with him."
Polley [see Mary] and Obed Hunt, int. Feb. 12, 1786.

BARLOW (see Barloe), Isaac and Hannah Hacket, int. June 30, 1792.
Polly and Levi Tinkham, int. June 10, 1788.

* Intention also recorded.

BARLOW, Wyat [int. Wryot], widr., 58, of Belche[r]town, and Cleorinda Packard [int. Clarinda Packarrd], Nov. 25, 1847.*

BARNES (see Barns), Thomas of Greenwich, and Betsy Thurston, ——, 1836.

BARNS (see Barnes), Dwight and Louis Kentfield [female], int. Oct. 9, 1830.
Polly of Greenwich, and Eliphaz Eaton, int. July 2, 1797.

BARROWS, Willi[a]m and Philena C. Gaskill, int. Nov. 4, 1843.

BARRY (see Berrey, Berry), Lockard and Polly Childs, int. Sept. 29, 1800.
Polly and Gardner Sloan, int. Oct. 27, 1806.
William and Nancy McMillen, int. Mar. 18, 1798.
William 2d of New Salem, and Salley Ray, int. July 22, 1798.

BARTLET (see Bartlett), Alaxander Jr. and Susan Robinson, int. Nov. 13, 1841.
Alexander of Greenwich, and Lucy Jones, int. Mar. 1, 1814.
Benjaman and Rebeckah Hill, int. May 8, 1785.
Daniel and Cloe Rider, Aug. 20, 1828.
Ezube of Belshiretown, and Allexander Croser, int. June 4, 1780.
Lucy and William Butterfield, int. Dec. 4, 1841.
Luriah and Moses Williams, int. Oct. 7, 1814.
Susannah and Ebeneazer W. Robinson, int. Dec. 10, 1842.

BARTLETT (see Bartlet), Alexander and Deborah Robinson, wid., int. Nov. 15, 1838.
Chloe and John Torrence, int. Mar. 3, 1810.
Eliza of Endfield, and Jonathan Turner, int. Feb. —, 1825.
Rachel of Enfield, and Elias Shaw, July 20, 1827.

BARTON, Robert of Enfield, and Elinor [int. Elenor] Conkey, Dec. 25 [1817].*

BATCHELOR, Nathaniel K. and Lucretia Ward, Mar. 30, 1841.*

BATS, Laben Jr. of Bellingham, and Cloy Sampson, int. Sept. 9, 1804.

BEARS, Eloner and George Elot, Aug. 21, 1780.*

BELL, Abigial and William Abercrombie, int. Sept. 26, 1812.
James of Salem, N. Y., and Isabel Harkness, int. Apr. 10, 1791.
Sarah of Newport, R. I., and Thomas Johnston, int. Feb. 14, 1791.

* Intention also recorded.

BELLEW (see Ballou), Amariah and Anne Lotheridge, int.
Sept. 28, 1794.

BENIT (see Bennet), Eliza and Luke Willington, int. Mar. 10,
1811.

BENNET (see Benit), Sam[ue]ll and Eleies Michel, "Both of
Roadtown So Cd," int. Feb. 3, 1753.

BERREY (see Barry, Berry), Agness and Ebnezer Gray, int.
May 4, 1776.

BERRY (see Barry, Berrey), Elisabeth and John Allaxander [int.
Allex[an]d[e]r], Feb. 29, 1780.*
James and Margaret Smith, int. Oct. 27, 1768.
John of New Salem, and Mary Haskell [int. Haskel], Sept. 21,
1780.*
John and Betsy Millen, int. May 6, 1809.
John and Dorcas Thompson, int. Apr. 15, 1812.
Margaret [int. Berrey] and James Gillmore, Oct. 21, 1767.* [The
surname interlined in a modern hand.]
Will[ia]m and Naomi Petteson [int. Peteson], Jan. 27, 1780.*

BICKNELL, Alden, 21, of Foxboro, s. Joseph, and Esther
Harkness, Dec. 24, 1845.*

BIGELOW, Benson of Westminster, and Betsy Hamilton, int.
Apr. 8, 1833.

BILLING (see Billings), David of Amherst, and Hannah Hyde,
int. June 28, 1788.

BILLINGS (see Billing), Charles of Cazenovie [int. Casenovia,
Madison Co.], N. Y., and Sarah Heydon, Feb. 5, 1817.*

BISHOP, Phineas [int. Phinehas] and Rebecah [int. Rebeca]
Jenks, Apr. 7, 1833.*

BLACK, John of Murrayfield, and Jennet Blair, Dec. 25,
1766.*

BLACKEMORE (see Blackmore), Amos of Greenwich, and
Margret Gray, int. Mar. 7, 1802.

BLACKMORE (see Blackemore), Hiram of Belchertown, and
Emeline Chase, int. Feb. 10, 1849.

BLAIR, Elisabeth and George Gillmore, Oct. 17, 1765.*
* Intention also recorded.

BLAIR, Isebel [int. Isebal] and John McColluch, Nov. 8, 1768.*
James of Belchertown, and Mary Dick, Sept. 26, 1780.
Jennet and John Black, Dec. 25, 1766.*
John of Murreyfield, and Elisabeth Halbert, June 14, 1770.*
Parses and John Hench, int. Dec. 15, 1788.
Robert and Margret McKlyain, int. Mar. 18, 1749.
Sarah and Nathaniel Gray, Dec. 27, 1770.*
William and Silence Leach, int. Mar. 9, 1776.

BLAISDELL, L. George of Springfield, and Angelime Cook,
June 22, 1847.

BLISS, Mary of Ware Village, and Chester Gaskell, int. Mar. 3,
1844.

BLODGET, Cyrus of Brimfield, and Hannah Dewey, int. Mar.
25, 1822.

BOLSTER, Amy, wid. [dup. omits wid.; int. Miss], d. Dennis
Cook, and Varnum Jillson, Apr. 4, 1844.*

BOLTWOOD, John of Amherst, and Harmoney Briggs, int. Mar.
29, 1782.
John of Amharst, and Sarah Hayze, int. Oct. 21, 1784.
Kezeiah of Amherst, and Abia Southworth, int. Oct. 20, 1794.

BORDEN, Lydia and Theverick Weeks, int. Feb. 4, 1807.

BOSSWORTH (see Bosworth), Rufus and Mary Brown, wid.,
int. May 5, 1822.

BOSWORTH (see Bossworth), William and Lucey Thorp, int.
Nov. 7, 1802.

BOTHWELL, Lucretia and Dwight Marsh, July 4, 1839.*

BOYC, Sam[ue]ll of Blanford, and Ann Dick, int. June 2, 1782.

BOYDEN, Adaline and Dwight Marsh, int. Nov. 4, 1831.
Clarissa F. and Munroe Eaton, Mar. 14, 1838.*
Erastus P. and Mary R. Dunbar, int. Nov. 13, 1843.
Sanford and Mary N. Clark, int. Nov. 2, 1842.

BOYINGTON (see Boynton), Silas 3d and Eliza Gould, int.
Mar. 12, 1839.
Sylvia C., Mrs., and Edmond Thompson, int. Oct. 28, 1842.
William C. and Mersylva C. Davis, Sept. 9, 1840.*

* Intention also recorded.

BOYNTON (see Boyington), Emery and Mary Ann Augusta
    Wheeler, int. July 19, 1834.
Hannah and Stephen Hunter, June 15, 1836.*
Lucy and John M. King, Dec. 23 [1827].*
Mary [int. Marry] and Eben[eze]r Austin, Nov. 28 [1824].*
Mary, Mrs., and Henry Walker, Apr. 12 [1830].*
Mary and Peter Southwick, int. Apr. 9, 1836.
Sally and Moses Davis [int. Jr.], May 23, 1819.*

BRADSHAW, Elizabeth of Amherst, and Elihu Hollan[d], int.
    Mar. 19, 1789.

BRAILEY (see Braley, Braly), John and Almira Jillson, int.
    July 6, 1825.

BRAKENRIDGE, Francis of Palmer, and Margret Cowan, int.
    Mar. 29, 1755.

BRALEY (see Brailey, Braly), Collins and Mrs. Polly Kimball,
    int. Nov. 13 [18]49.

BRALY (see Brailey, Braley), Collins and Lurana Jilson, int.
    Sept. 27, 1813.

BRIDGE, Easter of Sutsbeary, and W[illia]m Harkness, int.
    Aug. 31, 1783.
Jonas of New Salem, and Nancy Ayres [int. Ayers], Dec. 25
    [1821].*
Melicent of Shutsbery, and Joshua Conkey, int. Mar. 14, 1782.
Ruth of Shutsbery [int. Shutsberry], and Jonas Conky, May 26,
    1778.*

BRIGGS, Asaph L., b. Shutesbury, s. Josiah L. of Shutesbury,
    and Lilly Eaton, Aug. 30, 1825.
Harmoney and John Boltwood, int. Mar. 29, 1782.
Harmony and Tho[ma]s Dale, int. Mar. 4, 1783.
Isaac Jr. and Betsey Andress, int. Sept. 20, 1816.

BRIGHAM, Barna and Anne Hinds, int. Mar. 11, 1805.
William and Harriot [int. Harriet] Horr, July 27 [1839].*

BRITEN, Samuel and Bashaba Haskens, int. Nov. 17, 1799.

BROOKS, Abigel of Heddley, and John Clark, int. July 13,
    1776.
John of Haddley, and Margaret Clark, Dec. 18, 1777.*

* Intention also recorded.

BROOKS, Thomas and Marthew Knapp, int. Sept. 5, 1791.

BROWN, Abel of Belchertown, and Hannah Ward, Dec. 17, 1829.*

Alsey and Giles Rider, int. Mar. 25, 1815;

Charles T. of Belchertown, and Mary Houston, int. Nov. 22, 1843.

Diana of Belchertown, and Samuel J. Lincoln, int. Jan. 29, 1814.

Easther of Belchertown, and Daniel Dodge, int. Mar. 27, 1812.

Elvira [int. Elmira] of Amherst, and Frederick [int. Fredirick] E. Dickinson, Aug. 15, 1833.*

Ezra and Polly Lincoln, int. Jan. 3, 1810.

Gennet [int. Genett] of Enfield, and Clarisa [int. Clarissa H.] Wheeler, Apr. 18, 1830.*

Harriot and Lyman Orcutt, int. Oct. 11, 1830.

Louisa and Waterman A. Fisher, May 4 [1836].*

Margret J. and Francis A. Talmage, int. Oct. 5, 1840.

Marrak [Mariah ?] of Conway, and Sumner O. Polley, int. Oct. 1, 1847.

Mary, wid., and Rufus Bossworth, int. May 5, 1822.

Matt[he]w of Merryfield, and Elisabeth Dick, Sept. 19, 1776.*

Perez [int. Periss] of Belchertown, and Polly [int. Polley] Andrews, Jan. 28 [1816].*

Sally and Asa Eveleth, both of Belchertown, Apr. 1, 1817.

Will[ia]m of Blandford [int. Blandfoard], and Agness King, Dec. 1, 1757.*

William of Ware [int. Vt.], and Ann K. Packard, Sept. 9 [1830].*

BRUCE, Harriet [int. N.] and Jason Luce, May 30, 1836.*

James of Greenwich, and Sally Wright, int. July 17, 1800.

BRYANT (see Bryent), Mary A. and Abiel Rankin, Dec. 26, 1822.*

Oliver of Enfield, and Rhoda A. Packard, int. Oct. 8, 1829.

BRYENT (see Bryant), Olive and William Hunter Conkey, int. Oct. 29, 1804.

Seth and Nabby Babey, int. Oct. 14, 1798.

BUCK, John of Wotherington [int. Worthington], and Elisabeth Selfridge, Feb. 4, 1773.*

BUCKLAND, George W. of Springfield [int. Hamsdon [sic] Co.], and Lydia Wood, Dec. 6, 1826.*

* Intention also recorded.

BUCKMUN, Samuel [int. Samuell] of Amherst, and Coziah [int. Cuziah] Wood, Mar. 6, 1780.*

BUFFUM, Angeline A., 18, d. Thomas and Betsy, and Joseph G. Ward, Mar. 2, 1847.*
Ruth and William Jenkes, int. Mar. 17, 1827.

BUGBEE, Henry S. of Ludlow, and Maryann Draper, int. May 20, 1844.

BUNCE, Ellis W. and Melinda Sanders,———[rec. during year preceding Apr. 2, 1827 ; int. Jan. 7, 1826].*

BUTLER, Mary [int. Buttler] and John Sloan, Dec. 3, 1761.*
Samuel H. and Rebecca Fisk, int. Sept. 10, 1844.

BUTTERFIELD, Sophronia of Belchertown, and William B. Kimball, int. Aug. 2, 1834.
William of Hadley, and Lucy Bartlet, int. Dec. 4, 1841.

CABOTT, Sebastain Collumbus, Rev., and Electa Osburnne, int. Sept. 9, 1809.

CAHOON, Dolley and Joseph Whipple, int. Feb. 23, 1806.
Hannah of Greenwich, and Calister Gray, int. June 27, 1802.
Mary of New Salem, and John Falton, int. Oct. 21, 1805.

CALESTER (see McCallister), Eloner and John Halbert, Dec. 27, 1764.*
Mary of Holden, and Patrick McMullen, int. Apr. 14, 1749.

CAMBEL (see Cambell), James and Maryann [int. Mary Ann] Dick, June 7, 1770.*

CAMBELL (see Cambel), William [int. Cambel] of Murrayfield [int. Murriefield], and Mary Young, Nov. 18, 1766.*

CARPENTER, Jason of Hardwick, and Sarah Gray, May 27, 1821.*

CARRUTH (see Keruth), Elijah of Barre, and Patty Ayer, int. Dec. 9, 1820.
Samuel Jr. of Barry, and Susannah Thomson, int. Mar. 23, 1806.

CASTLE, Lucinda and Samuel Abercrombie, int. Dec. 12, 1802.

CHACE (see Chase), Agustius and Mary Arnold, int. Oct. 24, 1802.

* Intention also recorded.

CHACE, Judah and Andrew Johnston, int. Nov. 11, 1804.

CHADWICK, Judiath [int. Judath] E. and Patrick Millen, Nov. 28, 1819.*

CHAPIN, Alanson and Almira Harrington, Nov. 21 [1819].*
Alanson, Lt., and Amy Westcott, Mar. 28 [1825].*
Calvin and Amy Wedge, int. Oct. 30, 1840.
Chester of Heath, and Pamela Gray, int. Oct. 1, 1814.
Eli W. and Martha Peirce, int. Nov. 4, 1831.
Esther W. and Cumming [int. Cummings] Fish, Mar. 29 [1825].*
Luther Jr. of Enfield, and Hannah Conkey, int. Nov. 12, 1831.
Luther, widr., 70, b. Chickopee, and Charlotte [int. Charlottee] Eaton, wid., Oct. 21, 1847.*
Polly and Lewis [int. Lewis B.] Fish, Oct. 13, 1828.*
Rachel and Cheney [int. Chene] Abbot, Nov. 29, 1827.*
Rhoda of Heath, and Naham Wedge, int. Mar. 10, 1812.

CHAPMAN, Daniel of Belchertown, and Nancy Smith, int. Apr. 4, 1809.
George W. [int. Chatman] of Maryland, and Abigail J. Whipple, Nov. 3 [1836].*

CHASE (see Chace), Emeline and Hiram Blackmore, int. Feb. 10, 1849.
Robert S. and Olive Jones, Dec. 4, 1832.*

CHILDS, Lovica of Enfield, and Chester Dodge, int. Mar. 7, 1824.
Polly and Lockard Barry, int. Sept. 29, 1800.

CHOTE, Will[ia]m Jr. and Mary Conkey, int. Oct. 25, 1786.

CLAPP, Abigail of Walpole, Norfolk Co., and Lt. Oliver Smith Jr., int. Sept. 6, 1817.
Lucius of Northampton, and Dorothy King, Sept. 14, 1824.*

CLAREY, David of Levereet, and Rhoda Hayward, int. Jan. 20, 1792.

CLARK (see Cleark), Adam and Jean Stewart, int. Sept. 3, 1773.
Clarrisa and Aaron Cook, int. Aug. 21, 1843.
Elisabeth and Jonathan Sprague, June 17, 1766.*
James of Colrain, and Mary Clark, Feb. 19, 1765.*
John of Blanfoard [int. Blanford], and Ann Meklem, Feb. 2, 1762.*

* Intention also recorded.

CLARK, John and Abigel Brooks, int. July 13, 1776.
John of Buckland, and Susannah Clark, int. Dec. 3, 1801.
Katuran and John Thompson Jr., int. Aug. 21, 1788.
Lucy and Stephen Graves, int. June 22 [1800].
Lydia and Mosess [int. Moses] Fulton, Nov. 18, 1777.*
Margaret and John Brooks, Dec. 18, 1777.*
Martha and Thomas Morrieson [int. Murrieson], Feb. 11, 1762.*
Martha and Job Packard, int. May 23, 1805.
Mary and James Clark, Feb. 19, 1765.*
Mary, Mrs., and Abijah Fales, Feb. 28, 1828.*
Mary, Mrs., and Abijah Fales, Oct. 15, 1840.*
Mary N. and Sanford Boyden, int. Nov. 2, 1842.
Matthew and Hannah Stevens, int. Sept. 14, 1771.
Polly and Uzial Taylor, int. Nov. 28, 1802.
Prudence [int. Cleark] and John Thompson, Dec. 13, 1757.*
Robert and Mary Patrick, Mar. 2, 1762.*
Samuel Jr. [int. Clerk] and Susan [int. Susanna] Gray, Nov. 27,
    1815.*
Susannah and John Clark, int. Dec. 3, 1801.
William of Colrain, and Mary Petteson, Nov. 22, 1764.*

CLEARK (see Clark), Jean and Andrew Smith, May 18, 1748.*
John and Sarah Gray, int. Dec. 5, 1746.

CLEAVELAND (see Cleavlin, Cleveland, Clevland), Simeon
    and Arthusa T. Daverson, both of Ware, ——, 1836.

CLEAVLIN (see Cleaveland, Cleveland, Clevland), Polley and
    Alvan Hill, int. June 24, 1814.

CLEVELAND (see Cleaveland, Cleavlin, Clevland), Battsey and
    David Griffen, int. Feb. 8, 1807.

CLEVLAND (see Cleaveland, Cleavlin, Cleveland), Battsey and
    Georg Smith, int. May 2, 1803.

CLOUGH (see Cluff), Ester of Balchertown, and David Gray,
    int. Nov. 25, 1805.
Joseph of S. Hadley, and Lucy Humphrey, May 24, 1832.*
Rhene and Nathen Thayer, int. Jan. 5, 1805.

CLUFF (see Clough), Jonathan of Belcherton [int. Belchire-
    town], and Elisabeth Croset, Nov. 25, 1773.*

COCHRAN, Agness and Thomas Torrance [int. Torrans], Oct.
    9, 1766.*

* Intention also recorded.

COCHRAN, Robert of Benningtown, and Mary Gillmore, June 18, 1767.*

COLE (see Cowls), John of New Salem, and Sarah Thompson, int. Jan. 19, 1795.

COLTON, Sarah of Springfield, and David Goodale, int. Nov. 19, 1819.

COMINS (see Cummings), Cooledge of Sunderland, and Sarah J. Hall, int. Dec. 10, [18]49.
Rhoda of Shutsbery, and Daniel Reniff, int. Oct. 3, 1814.

COMSTOCK, Anna and Learned [int. Lerned] Draper, Dec. 6, 1821.*

CONE, Elisabeth of Grotton, and Robert Pebels, int. Jan. 30, 1761.

CONKEY (see Conky), Alexander Jr. and Lucy McColough, int. Jan. 2, 1808.
Allexander and Eloner McConnel, int. June 18, 1791.
Andrus of Shutesbury, and Martha Slarah [?], int. Nov. 24, 1787.
Anne and James Stevenson, int. Nov. 2, 1806.
Austin W. [dup. Conky] and Charlotte Wallis, Apr. 29, 1830.*
David 2d and Eunice Tompson, int. May 25, 1797.
David Jr. and Pattey Washburn, int. May 31, 1801.
Elinor [int. Elenor] and Robert Barton, Dec. 25 [1817].*
Elisha and Susanah Thomson, int. Oct. 28, 1782.
Elizabeth and Eli Gray, int. Oct. 24, 1807.
Esther M. and Stillman Thurston, Apr. 14, 1842.*
Eunes and Sam[ue]ll Williey, int. Feb. 17, 1783.
Ezekiel and Elizebeth Thompson, int. Dec. 24, 1784.
Hannah and Isriel Conkey, int. Mar. 31, 1799.
Hannah and Luther Chapin Jr., int. Nov. 12, 1831.
Isaac A. and Vesta Hinds, int. Aug. 13, 1807.
Isriel and Hannah Conkey, int. Mar. 31, 1799.
James and Battey Cowan, int. Jan. 9, 1803.
Jemima and Antoney Cuttler, int. Sept. 6, 1789.
Jennet and William Dunlap, int. Mar. 11, 1788.
Juel and Molley Thompson, int. Jan. 2, 1796.
John, Maj., and Polley Dolan, int. Sept. 8, 1805.
John 2d and Sila Cowan, int. Apr. 30, 1813.
John Esq. and Joanna Dickinson, int. May 10, 1817.
Joshua and Melicent Bridge, int. Mar. 14, 1782.

* Intention also recorded.

CONKEY, Margret and Robert Gitte, int. Jan. 29, 1797.
Martha and Job Smith, int. Nov. 12, 1831.
Mary and Will[ia]m Chote Jr., int. Oct. 25, 1786.
Mary and Warren Conkey, int. May 18, 1806.
Mehetable and Andrew Sloan, Jan. 20 [1818].*
Merthew and Micaih Prate, int. Aug. 14, 1781.
Polly and James Crosett, int. Dec. 1, 1812.
Prudence and Rozel Knowlton, int. Aug. 12, 1809.
Rebekkah and Pattrick Peebles, int. Sept. 11, 1813.
Sarah and Ruben Holland, int. Nov. 15, 1782.
Sarah and James Forbs, int. Mar. 7, 1791.
Sarah and Robert King, int. Nov. 10, 1794.
Sarah and Daniel Thompson, int. Nov. 15, 1801.
Tho[ma]s and Elizabeth Paluske [?], int. May 21, 1784.
Warren and Mary Conkey, int. May 18, 1806.
Will[ia]m [int. Jr.] and Mary Maklam, Mar. 30, 1786.*
William Hunter and Olive Bryent, int. Oct. 29, 1804.

CONKY (see Conkey), Allex[an]d[e]r and Sarah Maklem [int. Meklem], Jan. 7, 1748.*
Allexand[e]r Jr. and Mary Pebels, June 11, 1776.*
Asa [int. Ese] and Margaret Hamilton, Feb. 2, 1775.*
David and Sarah Hunter, Apr. 29, 1773.*
Hannah and John M[c]Creelless [int. McCreelles], Oct. 21, 1760.*
Isaac and Rebekah Makem [int. Maklem], Dec. 5, 1780.*
Isebel [int. Isebal] and Robert Hamilton, May 6, 1768.*
James and Isabel [int. Iseball] Maklem, Apr. 16, 1747.*
John Jr. and Margaret Abercrombie, June 4, 1772.*
Jonas and Ruth Bridge, May 26, 1778.*
Joshua and Dinah Dick, Apr. 13, 1762.*
Luria[?] and Miner Gold, int. Aug. 30, 1833.
Margaret and John Young, Feb. 22, 1759.*
Margaret and Robert Hamilton, Oct. 1, 1767.*
Margary and James Abercrombie, Nov. 15, 1780.*
Mary and Andrew Abercrombie [int. Ebercrombie], Nov. 22, 1773.*
Sarah and John Peblels, int. May 2, 1752.
Will[ia]m and Rebekah Hamilton, Nov. 17, 1755.*

COOK, Aaron of Hadley, and Clarrisa Clark, int. Aug. 21, 1843.
Ammon and Harriet [int. Herriat] Whitemore, Apr. 7 [1825].*
Amy Ama and George L. Shaw, int. May 11, 1841.
Angelime, d. Lewis and Nancy, and L. George Blaisdell, June 22, 1847.

* Intention also recorded.

Cook, Emeline and Lucius E. Wilder, ———— [rec. during year preceding Apr. 13, 1839; int. July 20, 1838].*
Eseek 2d and Elmira Ward, int. Dec. 7, 1844.
Eseek, widr., and Lucena Cook, Oct. 31, 1847.*
Hannah and Harvy [int. Hervey] Spear, Mar. 26, 1823.*
Hannah and Giles Rider, int. Mar. 27, 1830.
James and Martha Moodey, int. Mar. 1, 1810.
Lavinia and Sumner Griffin, Aug. 27, 1837.*
Levi and Anna Harden, int. Nov. 2, 1806.
Levi and Anne Montgomery, int. Nov. 23, 1806.
Lewis and Nancy Fales, Mar. 1, 1821.*
Louisia and John B. Ward, int. Apr. 17, 1837.
Lovina [int. Lavina Cooke], 21, d. Zibe and Sally, and Albert L. Draper, July 4, 1848.*
Lucena and Eseek Cook, widr., Oct. 31, 1847.*
Lyman V. B. and Elsa Donning, int. Sept. 29, 1848.
Maria A. and Manley Jillson, int. Sept. 2, 1837.
Moody of Amherst, and Olive F. Jilson, int. Nov. 4, 1837.
Nancy F., d. Lewis and Nancy, and Samuel L. [dup. and int. N.] Miller, Nov. 31 [dup. 30], 1843.*
Nathaniel [int. Nathanil] and Bethiah Ward, Nov. 23, 1834.*
Oney and Emily Draper, int. June 1, 1828.
Polly and Samuel Kimboll, int. Jan. 12, 1811.
Silas and Sina Rawson, int. Mar. 9, 1816.
Silas, "lame," s. Silas dec'd, and Mrs. Daphna Mack, Dec. 21, 1843.*
Simon and Louisa Pierce, ———— [rec. during year preceding Apr. 2, 1827; int. Apr. 27, 1826].*
Simon, 44, b. Cumberland, R. I., s. Eseek, and Susan E. Babbott [int. Babbitt], May 2, 1844.*
Susan Jane, b. Baltimore, Md., d. Fenner and Susan dec'd, and Ralph K. Dodge, Dec. 27, 1848.*
Whipple and Asenath Grout, Apr. 2 [1817].*
Zebina and Mary Gray, Jan. 15, 1818.*

COOLEY (see Coolley, Cooly), Cheney and Relief Aldrich, int. Jan. 20, 1822.
John of Prescott, and Mrs. Maryann Horr, int. Apr. 1, 1848.
Lucy and Cullen Warner, Oct. 10, 1819.*

COOLLEY (see Cooley, Cooly), Moses of Petersham, and Sarah Sloan, June 16, 1774.*

COOLY (see Cooley, Coolley), Barnes of Petersham, and Eloner Sloan, int. Aug. 12, 1777.

* Intention also recorded.

COWAN (see Cowen, Cowin), Battey and James Conkey, int. Jan. 9, 1803.
Elisabeth [int. Elisebath] and David Thomas, Apr. 24, 1750.*
Eunice, wid., and Dea. Joseph Hamilton, int. Oct. 24, 1812.
Jam[e]s and Margret Hunter, Jan. 4, 1757.*
Jam[e]s Jr. and Elisabeth Hunter, Dec. 22, 1757.*
James and Lovina Millen, int. Sept. 3, 1814.
John and Abigail Page, int. Nov. 29, 1834.
Margret and Francis Brakenridge, int. Mar. 29, 1755.
Mary and James Tompson, July 24, 1766.*
Mary and Nelson Horr, int. Mar. 10, 1832.
Preston and Lorana S. Sloan, int. Sept. 18, 1848.
Sarah and Robert M[c]Colloch, Feb. 8, 1750.*
Sarah [int. Saram] and Samuel Wilson [int. Sam[ue]ll Willson], Nov. 24, 1761.*
Sila and John Conkey 2d, int. Apr. 30, 1813.
William and Eunice Dunbar, int. Mar. 13 [1787].

COWEN (see Cowan, Cowin), James and Mary Dunbar, int. Sept. 8, 1781.
Silvia [int. Cowan] and Joseph Hamilton, May 3, 1818.*

COWDAN (see Cowden, Cowdin), Sam[ue]ll of Worcester, and Margret Gillmore, Dec. 11, 1755.*

COWDEN (see Cowdan, Cowdin), Elisabeth and Samuel Rush, July 28, 1774.*
Jennet and Allexander McColluch [int. McColluh], Oct. 10, 1771.*
William and Jean Maklem, int. Apr. 2, 1774.

COWDIN (see Cowdan, Cowden), James and Rebakah [int. Rebekah] Hamilton, Jan. 9, 1778.*
Martha and Thomas M[c]Mullen, Jan. 29, 1778.*
Mary [int. Cowden] and James White, July 4, 1776.*
William [int. Cowden] and Sarah Crawford, Dec. 3, 1778.*

COWIN (see Cowan, Cowen), Sila [int. Silence] and Isaac Packard, Nov. 10, 1840.*

COWLS (see Cole), Sarah M. [int. Cowles], 18, b. Amherst, d.
——— [and] Roxana, and Joel Austin, May 27, 1847.*

CRAWFORD, Hannah and Eliot Gray 2d, int. Feb. 11, 1787.
John Jr. and Sussannah [int. Shusannah] Kelso, Feb. 8, 1753.*
L[e]vi, and Marthew Gray, int. Nov. 20, 1796.

* Intention also recorded.

CRAWFORD, Sarah and William Cowdin [int. Cowden], Dec. 3, 1778.*
Susannah and Daniel Car Gray, int. Jan. 19, 1795.

CROSER (see Crosier, Crozier), Allexander and Ezube Bartlet, int. June 4, 1780.

CROSET (see Crosett, Crossett, Crozet), Elisabeth and Jonathan Cluff, Nov. 25, 1773.*
Jacob and Eloner English, Dec. 3, 1772.*
James and Sarah ———, int. June 13, 1778.
Jinnet and Joseph Hinds, int. July 22, 1793.
Margaret and Joseph Thompson, June 30, 1774.*
Martha and Samuel Finten, Dec. 9, 1773.*
Mary and George Tompson, Dec. 5, 1765.*
Mary and William Ree, May 19, 1774.*
Robert and Nancey [int. Nancy] Hood, Dec. 8, 1782.*
William and Jenney Thomas, Dec. 10, 1778.*

CROSETT (see Croset, Crossett, Crozet), Isa and Robert Stutson, int. Feb. 19, 1795.
James and Polly Conkey, int. Dec. 1, 1812.
Rebekah and Epheriam Wheeler, int. Nov. 11, 1798.
William of Hebron, N. Y., and Margret Gray, int. Sept. 30, 1792.

CROSIER (see Croser, Crozier), Caroline, 23, d. Arthur, and Wiley Aldrich, Feb. 19, 1846.*
Moses [int. Crozier] and Lucinda Danforth, Oct. 8, 1821.*

CROSSETT (see Croset, Crosett, Crozet), Catherine A. of Prescott, and Chancelor L. Wheeler, [int.] Jan. 10, 1848.
Isreal and Martha Hamilton, int. Oct. 30, 1788.
Lavina of Prescott, and Dr. Irael H. Taylor, int. Dec. 10, 1842.

CROSSMAN, Tisdall [int. Tisdle] of Shutesbury, and Joanna Thurber, Dec. 22, 1825.*

CROZET (see Croset, Crosett, Crossett), Lidia and Thomas Gray, int. Oct. 6, 1785.
Sarah and Matthew Gray 3d, int. July 16, 1786.
Unice and John Maclam, int. May 8, 1785.

CROZIER (see Croser, Crosier), Arther and Submit Hall, int. Oct. 25, 1819.
Mary and Epharim Arnold, int. Sept. 23, 1808.

* Intention also recorded.

CUDWORTH, Salley of Barkley, and John Eaton Jr., int. June 23, 1794.

CUMMINGS (see Comins), Eliza A. of Lever[e]t, and William Hanks 2d, int. Aug. 11, 1841.

CUNNINGHAM, Mary [int. Cuningham] of Brookfield, and John Pebels [int. Pebles], Aug. 17, 1759.*

CURRIER, Samuel of Belchertown, and Malinda Danforth, Apr. 12 [1818].*

CUTLER (see Cuttler), Robert and Mrs. Esther Garnsey, Dec. 23, 1773.*

CUTTER, Hannah and Timothey Leach, int. Dec. 12, 1802.

CUTTLER (see Cutler), Antoney and Jemima Conkey, int. Sept. 6, 1789.

DALE, Tho[ma]s of Suffield, and Harmony Briggs, int. Mar. 4, 1783.

DANFORTH, Lucinda of Belchertown, and Moses Crosier [int. Crozier], Oct. 8, 1821.*
Malinda and Samuel Currier, Apr. 12 [1818].*

DARLING, Batsey of Amherst, and Thomas Sampson, int. Oct. 27, 1805.
Jemima and William Abercrombie, int. Jan. 1, 1804.
Orrin [int. Orin] E., 27, of Chickopee [int. Chickopie], s. Moses and Eunice, and Esther C. Wedge, June 13, 1848.*

DAVENSON (see Daverson, Davieson, Davison, Davission), Elizabeth and Samuel Allen Jr., int. Oct. 5, 1800.

DAVERSON (see Davenson, Davieson, Davison, Davission), Arthusa T. and Simeon Cleaveland, both of Ware, ——, 1836.

DAVIES (see Davis), Thankfull and Jacob Hinds, "Both of Quabin So Called," int. Aug. 23, 1749.

DAVIESON (see Davenson, Daverson, Davison, Davission), John and Sarah Stevens, int. Nov. 22, 1760.

DAVIS (see Davies), Marsha S. and Algenon S. Bailey, Nov. 28 [1839].*
Mersylva C. and William C. Boyington, Sept. 9, 1840.*

* Intention also recorded.

DAVIS, Moses [int. Jr.] of Milford, and Sally Boynton, May 23, 1819.*

Sarah Ann and William C. Jenck, int. Oct. 22, 1846.

DAVISON (see Davenson, Daverson, Davieson, Davission), Patty and Titus Randwell, int. Oct. 12, 1797.

Polly and Samuel Peso, int. Oct. 5, 1800.

Polly and John Ward Jr., int. Jan. 11, 1807.

DAVISSION (see Davenson, Daverson, Davieson, Davison), Lucy and Benjamin Randall, int. Apr. 18, 1812.

DEAN, James O., Rev., and Hannah Green, int. Apr. 13, 1839.

DEMMON, Martha and Dexter Rhodes, Mar. 2, 1829.*

DENIO, Frederick of Greenfield, and Lucy Wood, int. Nov. 29, 1773.

DEWEY, Hannah and Cyrus Blodget, int. Mar. 25, 1822.

DEXTER, David Jr. of Amherst, and Cynthia Rankin, int. Sept. 6, 1830.

DICK, Ann and Sam[ue]ll Boyc, int. June 2, 1782.

Catrin and Matt[he]w Gray, Sept. 25, 1777.*

Dinah and Robert Petteson, int. Apr. 4, 1761.

Dinah and Joshua Conky, Apr. 13, 1762.*

Elisabeth and Matt[he]w Brown, Sept. 19, 1776.*

Eunice [int. Eunis] and Sam[ue]ll Sloan, Nov. 30, 1779.*

Jean and David Heirs, May 13, 1777.*

John and Jean McColloch, Sept. 25, 1746.*

Ketrin and Isaac Hunter, Oct. 27, 1763.*

Margaret and James Dunlap, June 20, 1771.*

Mary and Daniel Gray, Oct. 23, 1760.*

Mary and James Blair, Sept. 26, 1780.

Maryann [int. Mary Ann] and James Cambel, June 7, 1770.*

Sarah and Hamillton McCallister [int. Hamilton McCalister], Oct. 15, 1767.*

Thomas and Mary McMullen, Apr. 27, 1780.*

DICKENSON (see Dickinson), Obed and Experience Smith, int. Aug. 14. 1804.

Pagay and Dea. Samuel Hide, int. Oct. 29, 1797.

DICKINSON (see Dickenson), Frederick [int. Fredirick] E. and Elvira [int. Elmira] Brown, Aug. 15. 1833.*

* Intention also recorded.

DICKINSON, Joanna of Amherst, and John Conkey Esq., int. May
    10, 1817.
Levy of Amherst, and Margrett Peebles, int. Sept. 6, 1782.

DILL, Nancy of Orleans, and Lewis Dodge, int. Mar. 15, 1819.

DILLON, Sidney of Troy, N. Y., and Hannak [Hannah?]
    Smith, int. July 11, 1841.

DOANE, Elkanah of Dana, and Adah Horr, int. Apr. 8, 1843.

DODGE, Ann Maria and James G. Whipple, Apr. 2, 1837.*
Chester and Lovica Childs, int. Mar. 7, 1824.
Cyrus B. and Sarah A. Spears, int. Jan. 10, 1844.
Daniel and Easther Brown, int. Mar. 27, 1812.
Isaac of Cha[r]lton, and Nancy McDonnal, int. Oct. 6, 1784.
Lewis and Nancy Dill, int. Mar. 15, 1819.
Mary, 19, d. John C. and Lavica, and Hoyt E. Ball, Oct. 5, 1847.
Nancy P., d. Daniel and Esther, and Josiah N. Holden, Dec. 27,
    1848.*
Ralph K., s. Daniel and Esther, and Susan Jane Cook, Dec. 27,
    1848.*
Sarah Ann, 20, d. Elison, and Samuel H. Packard, Oct. 23, 1844.*

DOLAN, Polley of New Salem, and Maj. John Conkey, int.
    Sept. 8, 1805.

DONNING, Elsa of Enfield, and Lyman V. B. Cook, int. Sept. 29,
    1848.

DORETY, Lucretia of Hardwick, and Nathen Peso, int. Mar. 3,
    1805.

DOWIN, Esther of Greenwich, and Thomas Packard, int. June 1,
    1811.

DRAPER, Albert L., 22, of Enfield, s. Lyman and Sally, and
    Lovina Cook [int. Lavina Cooke], July 4, 1848.*
Caroline E. [dup. same, int. Cordelia] d. Leornord, and Horrace
    N. Kendall [int. Horace N. Kendell], Apr. 29, 1844.*
Emily and Oney Cook, int. June 1, 1828.
Jena of Shutesbury, and Jonathan Griffin, int. Jan. 16, 1818.
Learned [int. Lerned] and Anna Comstock, Dec. 6, 1821.*
Lewis L. and Margret Henry, int. June 17, 1827.
Lucy and David Ide, int. Oct. 1, 1808.
Lyman and Sally Newell, June 8 [1819].*

* Intention also recorded.

DRAPER, Mariah and Levi B. Hall, int. June 9, 1827.

Maryann and Henry S. Bugbee, int. May 20, 1844.

Sarah Ann, 24, d. Lyman, and Samuel Flynn Jr., Feb. 25, 1845.*

Seth of Balchertown, and Poly Haden, int. May 11, 1800.

DUDLEY, Harriet E., 19, b. Douglas, d. Samuel and Chloe, of Douglas [int. Douglass], and Calvin D. Eaton, widr., Oct. 13, 1840.*

DUNBAR (see Dunbarr), Betsy P. of Belchertown, and Hiram Rankin, int. Mar. 2, 1843.

Eunice and William Cowan, int. Mar. 13 [1787].

Eunice of Belchertown, Hampshir Co., and Philip Lovel, Nov. 30, 1824, in Belchertown.

Maria of Belchertown, and Emery Ballou, int. June 14, 1837.

Mary of Winchester, and James Cowen, int. Sept. 8, 1781.

Mary R. of Belchertown, and Erastus P. Boyden, int. Nov. 13, 1843.

Nehemiah and Mary Hunter, int. May 12, 1788.

Seth of Carsinova, N. Y., and Anna McCollah, int. Nov. 16, 1800.

DUNBARR (see Dunbar), Eunice and Joseph Latham, int. July 24, 1784.

DUNLAP, Agness and Sam[ue]l Wilson [int. Sam[ue]ll Willson], Dec. 9, 1767.*

James and Margaret Dick, June 20, 1771.*

James and Nane Selfridg. int. Dec. 29, 1781.

John and Mary Oliver, int. Mar. 1, 1807.

Sarah and W[illia]m Baldwin, int. Jan. 18, 1783.

William and Jennet Conkey, int. Mar. 11, 1788.

DUNN, Anna and Benjamin Wheeler, int. Sept. 2, 1815.

DUNSETT, Cato of Stanford, and Zube Prat, int. Mar. 5, 1786.

EATON, Calvin D., 25, s. Marson and Charlottee, and Julia H. Kingman, Apr. 6, 1840.*

Calvin D., widr., 25, s. Marson and Charlotte, and Harriet E. Dudley, Oct. 13, 1840.*

Charlotte, wid., [int. Charlottee, Mrs.], 71, and Luther Chapin, widr., Oct. 21, 1847.*

Eliphaz and Polly Barns, int. July 2, 1797.

John Jr. and Salley Cudworth, int. June 23, 1794.

* Intention also recorded.

EATON, Lilly, d. Marson and Charlottee, and Asaph L. Briggs, Aug. 30, 1825.
Mary and David Abercrombie, Jan. 18, 1816.*
Munroe and Clarissa F. Boyden, Mar. 14, 1838.*
Orinda H., wid., and Asa Shumway, Jan. 3, 1838.*
Patience and John Strong, int. May 31, 1795.

EDSON, Abizer [int. Abiezer] and Rehoda [int. Rhoda] Peterson, Dec. 3, 1772.*
Anne and Benjaman Hanks, int. Nov. 10, 1781.
Betey and James Harkness, Sept. 15, 1784.
Cuziah and John Harkness, int. Sept. 1, 1781.
Elijah and Salley Atkinson, int. Sept. 5, 1791.
Polly and James Hunter, int. Apr. 4, 1808.

ELMER, William H. of Northampton, and Mary Randall, int. Apr. 4, 1840.

ELOT, George and Eloner Bears, Aug. 21, 1780.*

ENGLISH, Eloner of Greenwich, and Jacob Croset, Dec. 3, 1772.*

ENGRAM (see Ingraham, Ingram, Ingrem), Abigal and Peeter King, int. Apr. 25, 1783.

ENOCH, Benjamin and Martha Felton, int. May 8, 1846.

ERWIN, Eliza, Mrs., and Isaac Prouty Jr., int. Jan. 2, 1841.

EVELETH, Asa and Sally Brown, both of Belchertown, Apr. 1, 1817.

FAILES (see Fales), Alender of Holden, and Joel Johnson, int. Jan. 23, 1808.

FAIRFIELD, Allen, 22, of Northampton, b. Belchertown, s. Joel of Belchertown, and Caroline A. Hall, Feb. 25, 1845.*

FALES (see Failes), Abijah and Mrs. Mary Clark, Feb. 28, 1828.*
Abijah and Mrs. Mary Clark, Oct. 15, 1840.*
Almira and Josiah Ball, Aug. 7, 1837.*
Eunice and James Shaw, July 4 [1816].*
Nancy and Lewis Cook, Mar. 1, 1821.*

FALLEN, Nathen and Mary Hind, int. Sept. 7, 1800.

FALTON (see Felton), John and Mary Cahoon, int. Oct. 21, 1805.

* Intention also recorded.

FAY (see Faye), Benjamin, 25, of New Braintree, and Jane H. Presho, June 1, 1846.*

Jam[es] of Hardwick, and Sarah Horr, Apr. 2, 1843.*

FAYE (see Fay), Barnabas of Belshiertown, and Cloa Packard, int. Dec. 9, 1782.

FELTON (see Falton), Martha and Benjamin Enoch, int. May 8, 1846.

FERGESON (see Ferguson), James and Ester Thornton, Dec. 4, 1746.

FERGUSON (see Fergeson), Ann and John Sloan, Jan. 10, 1765.*

Jennet and Moses Ransom, Oct. 24, 1776.*

Susanna and James Hunter, Dec. 11, 1766.*

Thornton of Springfield, Madison Co., N. Y., and Lavonia Peck, June 6, 1831.*

William and Jennet Hood, Dec. 20, 1770.*

FESSENDEN, Lydia W. of "Guilford, V. T.," and Samuel W. Russell, May 1, 1844.*

FIELD, Jonathen of Amherst, and Elizabeth Johnston, int. June 23, 1794.

Robert and Sarah Abercrombie, Apr. 5, 1832.*

Seth of Loveriet, and Margrey Lotherige, int. Dec. 15, 1805.

FINTEN, Samuel of Greenwich, and Martha Croset, Dec. 9, 1773.*

FISH, Cumming [int. Cummings] of Shutesbury, and Esther W. Chapin, Mar. 29 [1825].*

Lewis [int. B.] of Shutesbury, and Polly Chapin, Oct. 13, 1828.*

Mary L., 17, d. Lewis B. and Polly, and David [int. N.] Hamilton, May 5, 1847.*

FISHER, Thomas and Venis Simons, int. Oct. 27, 1805.

Thomas and Abigal Robins, int. Oct. 8, 1813.

Waterman A. of Killingly, Conn. [int. "Killingsly, C. T."], and Louisa Brown, May 4 [1836].*

FISK, Rebecca of Sturbridge, and Samuel H. Butler, int. Sept. 10, 1844.

FLYNN, Samuel Jr., 22, of Springfield, b. Dover, N. H., s. Samuel of Dover, N. H., and Sarah Ann Draper, Feb. 25, 1845.*

* Intention also recorded.

FOARD (see Forde), Bass and Rosannah Gray, int. June 30, 1780.

FOLLET, Abraham of Cumberland, and Roxeyleney Michel, int. Dec. 7, 1805.

FORBS, James of Shoreham, Vt., and Sarah Conkey, int. Mar. 7, 1791.

FORDE (see Foard), Lyda of Abingtown, Plymoth Co., and Eliab Pakard, int. Oct. 15, 1803.

FOSTER, Edward Jr. and Vise Shirtlief, int. Apr. 12, 1789.
Seth and Hannah Shays, int. Feb. 5, 1793.

FREEMAN, Salley of Greenwich, and Jonathan McMillen, int. Mar. 8, 1785.

FREKER, Philip of Hardwick, and Elisabeth Ransom, Sept. 6, 1776.*

FROST, John of Springfield, and Deborah Herres, int. Apr. 19, 1754.

FULLER, Bethani and Live [Levi?] Wood, int. Oct. 19, 1786.
Heman of S. Hadley, and Harriet A. Hamilton, int. June 7, 1845.
Mercy and George Hecket, int. Oct. 6, 1785.
Waterman of Ludlow, and Sally Abercrombie, Apr. 20, 1824.*

FULTON, Mosess [int. Moses] of Colrain, and Lydia Clark, Nov. 18, 1777.*

GAMWELL, Hannah and Samuel Kimball Jr., both of Belchertown, Sept. 27, 1831.

GARDNER (see Guardner), Thomas of Enfield, and Mary M. Lother, int. Nov. 2, 1833.

GARNSEY, Esther, Mrs., of Amherst, and Robert Cutler, Dec. 23, 1773.*

GASKELL (see Gaskill), Chester and Mary Bliss, int. Mar. 3, 1844.
Phebe [int. Gaskill], Mrs., and Ozias Thurber, Aug. 30, 1825.*

GASKILL (see Gaskell), Joanna C. and George N. Wood, int. Sept. 10, 1834.

* Intention also recorded.

GASKILL, Lucy D. and John Taylor Jr., Nov. 17 [1836].*
Philena C. and Willi[a]m Barrows, int. Nov. 4, 1843.

GATES (see Gats), Levi Jr. of Wendell, and Anna Houston,
int. June 29, 1823.
Levi, widr., and Sally Horton, wid., July 2, 1849.*
Margaret and George S. Wyllie, int. Sept. 2, 1843.

GATS (see Gates), Ebenezer and Salley Washburn, int. Nov. 30,
1797.

GAY, Sarah of Walpole, and Oliver Smith, int. Nov. 8, 1808.

GAYLORD, Lucinda of Amherst, and Chandler Manley, int.
Aug. 10, 1831.
William of Amherst, and Mrs. Lucinda Thayer, int. Jan. 9, 1830.

GIBBS, Isreal H. and Brookey [int. Broocky] W. Whipple, Mar.
17 [1825].*

GILLMORE, Agnos and Rob[er]t Synet, int. May 9, 1752.
George of New Cambridge, and Elisabeth Blair, Oct. 17, 1765.*
Isebel and William Henry [int. Henrey], Jan. 15, 1760.*
James and Margaret Berry [int. Berrey], Oct. 21, 1767.*
          [Berry interlined in a modern hand.]
James of Conway, and Jean M[c]Colluch, Dec. 18, 1776.*
Margret and Sam[ue]ll Cowdan, Dec. 11, 1755.*
Mary and Robert Cochran, June 18, 1767.*
Rob[er]t of Roadtown, and Dolley Gray, int. Nov. 8, 1754.
Robert and Jean Gray, June 2, 1763.*

GITTE (see Gittee), Robert of Hebron, N. Y., and Margret
Conkey, int. Jan. 29, 1797.

GITTEE (see Gitte), John of Black Creek, and Sarah Gray,
Feb. 13, 1781.*

GLEASON (see Gleson), Oliver of Holden [int. Worcester Co.],
and Mrs. Anna Allen, Nov. 26, 1826.*

GLESON (see Gleason), Maria of Brimfield, and James Thurston, int. Nov. 1, 1827.

GOLD, Miner and Luria [?] Conky, int. Aug. 30, 1833.

GOODALE, David of Amherst, and Sarah Colton, int. Nov. 19,
1819.

* Intention also recorded.

GOODALE, George T., 22, of Conway, s. Thomas and w. of Amherst, and Lucy A. Rowland, May 28, 1844.*

GOODENOUGH, William H. [int. Goodenow], 28, of Greenwich, b. Greenwich, s. William and Abagail, and Susan [int. Susannah] Thurston, Nov. 24, 1846.*

GOULD, Aaron [int. Goul] and Lydia Gray, May 29, 1781.*
Eliza of Enfield, and Silas Boyington 3d, int. Mar. 12, 1839.
Emeline and Zechariah Weston, Dec. 16, 1833.*
Haffield and Betsy Phelps, int. May 6, 1809.
Jane L., 27, b. Newport, R. I., d. James and Sarah, and Augustus Hamilton, Apr. 12, 1848.*
Sarah, Mrs., and Elijah Randall, int. Dec. 5, 1840.

GRAVES, Elihu "late of Leverett," and Sarah Hinds, int. July 9, 1808.
Stephen of Deerfield, and Lucy Clark, int. June 22 [1800].

GRAY, Aaron [int. Aron] and Isebal [int. Isebel] Lucore, Feb. 22, 1759.*
Aaron and Ruth Powers, int. Oct. 23, 1796.
Andrew and Sally Harkness, int. Dec. 1, 1805.
Anne and William Hartness, July 28, 1748.*
Battsey and Oliver Hamilton, int. Nov. 15, 1801.
Calister and Hannah Cahoon, int. June 27, 1802.
Callister and Phebee Tolymon, int. May 13, 1799.
Chester and Lydia Shaw, May 8, 1817.*
Daniel and Elesabeth Lawman, int. Mar. 28, 1752.
Daniel and Mary Dick, Oct. 23, 1760.*
Daniel Car and Susannah Crawford, int. Jan. 19, 1795.
David and Ester Clough, int. Nov. 25, 1805.
Dolley and Rob[er]t Gillmore, int. Nov. 8, 1754.
Easter [int. Ester] and James Hood, Apr. 2, 1747.*
Ebenezer and Sarah Johnston, Feb. 12, 1767.*
Ebenezer Jr. and Anne Peebles, int. Nov. 23 [1800].
Ebenezer of Madison, N. Y., and Mrs. Sarah Thompson, Jan. 23, 1828.*
Ebnezer and Agness Berrey, int. May 4, 1776.
Eli and Elizabeth Conkey, int. Oct. 24, 1807.
Elihu and Martha Wilson, int. Aug. 20, 1791.
Eliot 2d and Hannah Crawford, int. Feb. 11, 1787.
Elisabeth and Joseph Rinken, Apr. 21, 1748.*
Elisabeth and Rob[e]rt Young, Dec. 20, 1764.*

* Intention also recorded.

GRAY, Eliza and William Haydon, both of Belchertown, Aug. 25, 1830.
Elot and Hannah Barbor, int. Feb. 7, 1761.
Estar and Asaph Lyon, int. June 10, 1781.
Hannah and James Thompson 2d, int. Mar. 4, 1788.
Horace and Louisa M. Jillson, int. Aug. 30, 1834.
Isaac and Mary Meklem, Sept. 10, 1754.*
Isabel [int. Isebal] and William Harkness Jr., June 11, 1778.*
Isabel and Jacob Shaw, int. Oct. 4, 1795.
Jacob and Jean Smith, Sept. 26, 1780.*
Jean and Robert Gillmore, June 2, 1763.*
Jenney and Pattrick Peebles, int. July 19, 1801.
Jeremiah and Margret Gray, int. Aug. 22, 1790.
Joel and Marthe Linsey, int. Oct. 15, 1786.
John Jr. [int. omits Jr.] and Martha Savige, Apr. 17, 1755.*
John and Susannah Hunter, int. Mar. 25, 1792.
John 2d and Battsey Rinken, int. Sept. 24, 1797.
John, Lt., and Patty Smith, int. Aug. 29, 1814.
John, Lt., and Amanda Hubbard, int. Mar. 16, 1823.
Jonathan and Margret Patrick, int. July 19, 1754.
Jonathan and Elisabeth Willey, Mar. 8, 1774.*
Justus and Lucey Sekiel [Sekins?], int. Feb. 12, 1792.
Kelso of Worcester, and Phebe Gray, int. Apr. 14, 1764.
Lamond [int. Lawman] and Isabel Hamilton, May 26, 1778.*
Levi and Abigal Robbens, int. Sept. 13, 1798.
Lorania and William W. Oliver, Oct. 4, 1826.*
Lydia and Robert Oliver, Sept. 13, 1759.*
Lydia and Aaron Gould [int. Goul], May 29, 1781.*
Margaret and John Henricks [int. Henriks], Oct. 27, 1768.*
Margret and Jeremiah Gray, int. Aug. 22, 1790.
Margret and William Crosett, int. Sept. 30, 1792.
Margret and Amos Blackemore, int. Mar. 7, 1802.
Martha and James Tafts [int. Teft], Feb. 26, 1761.*
Marthew and L[e]vi Crawford, int. Nov. 20, 1796.
Mary and Robert McKee, Aug. 21, 1746.*
Mary and Zebina Cook, Jan. 15, 1818.*
Maryan and James Linsey, int. Jan. 30, 1789.
Matt[he]w and Sarah Barbor, Oct. 30, 1766.*
Matt[he]w and Catrin Dick, Sept. 25, 1777.*
Matthew 3d and Sarah Crozet, int. July 16, 1786.
Matthew, Dea., and Jemima McCreeles, int. Feb. 2, 1788.
Moses and Marcy Whitehom, int. July 8, 1793.
Nancy and James Harkness, Apr. 7, 1757.*

* Intention also recorded.

GRAY, Nancy and Stuard James Parks, int. Apr. 29, 1798.
Naomi and Francis Adams, June 10 [1817].*
Nathaniel and Sarah Blair, Dec. 27, 1770.*
Nathenial and Phelina Macomber, int. Dec. 1, 1805.
Pamela and Chester Chapin, int. Oct. 1, 1814.
Patrick and Abigail Sloan, int. June 29 [1782].
Patrick Jr. and Sally Peirce, int. Mar. 24, 1810.
Pattrick and Lowes Hunter, int. Aug. 9, 1795.
Pattrick and Battsey Moor, int. Aug. 11, 1799.
Phebe and Kelso Gray, int. Apr. 14, 1764.
Phebe and Bildad Sarl, int. Nov. 23 [1794].
Polly and David Haskel, int. Feb. 15, 1794.
Polly and Salvenus Wood, int. Jan. 1, 1797.
Polly and Barnabas [int. Barnabus] Sears Jr., May 21 [1818].*
Rosannah and Foard Bass, int. June 30, 1780.
Roxana and Gardner Sloan, int. Apr. 14, 1812.
Sarah and John Cleark, int. Dec. 5, 1746.
Sarah and Abraham Nut, Sept. 13, 1759.*
Sarah and John Gittee, Feb. 13, 1781.*
Sarah and Jason Carpenter, May 27, 1821.*
Sarah H. and Erastus C. Thompson, int. Aug. 31, 1830.
Susan [int. Susanna] and Samuel Clark [int. Clerk] Jr., Nov. 27, 1815.*
Thomas and Lidia Crozet, int. Oct. 6, 1785.
Whitcomb and Maria Sibley, both of Belchertown, Apr. 21, 1830.

GREEN, Elisabeth of Westron, and James McCartney, int. Sept. 19, 1772.
Hannah of Leyden, and Rev. James O. Dean, int. Apr. 13, 1839.
Mary and James Petteson, Dec. 11, 1777.*

GRIFFEN (see Griffin), David and Battsey Cleveland, int. Feb. 8, 1807.

GRIFFIN (see Griffen), Hannah and Charles Randell, Aug. 13, 1827.*
Jonathan and Jena Draper, int. Jan. 16, 1818.
Sumner and Lavinia Cook, Aug. 27, 1837.*

GROUT, Annis and Samuel Robbins, Nov. 7, 1837.*
Asenath and Whipple Cook, Apr. 2 [1817].*
Austin and Susan A. Hall, int. Mar. 30, 1829.
Martin and Clarissa Johnson, int. Sept. 6, 1816.
Orra and Melinda Randall, int. Nov. 20, 1830.

* Intention also recorded.

GROUT, Rufus and Clarisa [int. Clarissa] A. Hall, Jan. 27, 1825.*
Rufus and Nancy Reniff, Jan. 24, 1841.*

GUARDNER (see Gardner), Benjamin and Nancy Rider, both of Enfield, Sept. 29, 1828.

GUERNSEY (see Garnsey).

GUN, Almira of Enfield, and Ira Hanks, int. Mar. 1, 1830.

HACKET (see Hecket, Heket), Gideon and Lydia Peeso, int. Feb. 7, 1796.
Hannah and Isaac Barlow, int. June 30, 1792.
Lidia and Daniel Harkness, int. Oct. 6, 1785.
Ruth and Ichabode Hayward, int. Apr. 15, 1790.

HADEN (see Hayden, Haydon, Heydon), Poly and Seth Draper, int. May 11, 1800.
Richard and Ellis Hyde, int. Aug. 25, 1783.

HALBERT, Elisabeth and John Blair, June 14, 1770.*
James and J[e]nnet Hunter, Nov. 23, 1760.*
John of Chesterfield, and Eloner Calester, Dec. 27, 1764.*
Mary and Timothy Rice, July 25, 1769.*

HALL, Amelia M., d. Lemuel, and William C. Rankin, Dec. 31, 1843.*
Caroline A., 17, d. Levi B., and Allen Fairfield, Feb. 25, 1845.*
Clarisa [int. Clarissa] A. and Rufus Grout, Jan. 27, 1825.*
John B. and Jane W. Ballou, int. Dec. 14, 1843.
Levi B. and Mariah Draper, int. June 9, 1827.
Levi B. and Mrs. Susan E. Parker, int. Apr. 26, 1849.
Mary and Silas C. Newell, int. Mar. 30, 1833.
Sarah J. and Cooledge Comins, int. Dec. 10, [18]49.
Submit of Amherst, and Arther Crozier, int. Oct. 25, 1819.
Susan A. and Austin Grout, int. Mar. 30, 1829.
Susanna and Smith Arnold, int. June 26, 1807.
Vienna and Ansel A. Rankin, int. Dec. 17, 1832.

HALLEY, Phibe of Amherst, and Micah Prett Jr., —— [1778].

HAMELTON (see Hamilton), Janet and Nathaniel Tagert, Jan. 16, 1753.*

HAMILTON (see Hamelton), Anna and John Lewis, May 31, 1825.*

* Intention also recorded.

HAMILTON, Anne and Pattrick Peebles, int. Jan. 3, 1802.

Augustus, 27, s. Joseph and Sylvia, and Jane L. Gould, Apr. 12, 1848.*

Betsy and Benson Bigelow, int. Apr. 8, 1833.

David [int. N.], 21, b. Shutesbury, s. David and Hannah of Shutsbury, and Mary L. Fish, May 5, 1847.*

Eli of Greenfield, and Avis Southward, int. Oct. 21 [1787].

Elizabith and David Peebles, int. Nov. 6, 1803.

Ephraim [int. Ephriam] of Blanford, and Margaret Hamilton, July 7, 1768.*

Frank and Charles Kid, Nov. 30, 1773.*

Harriet A. and Heman Fuller, int. June 7, 1845.

Isabel and Lamond [int. Lawman] Gray, May 26, 1778.*

Isaac and Rachel Hoar, int. Feb. 2, 1811.

Jam[e]s and Sarah Lucore, Jan. 19, 1758.*

James of Colrain, and Phebe Henderson, Feb. 14, 1764.*

Joel and Abigail Hoar, int. Feb. 23, 1811.

John [int. Jr.] and Agness Sloan, Dec. 27, 1759.*

John Jr. and Mary Thomas, int. May 21, 1786.

Joseph and Ann [int. Anne] Oliver, Nov. 11, 1773.*

Joseph, Dea., and Eunice Cowan, wid., int. Oct. 24, 1812.

Joseph and Silvia Cowen [int. Cowan], May 3, 1818.*

Margaret and Ephraim [int. Ephriam] Hamilton, July 7, 1768.*

Margaret and Asa [int. Ese] Conky, Feb. 2, 1775.*

Martha and Henery McCollock, int. Jan. 6, 1787.

Martha of Shutsbury, and Isreal Crossett, int. Oct. 30, 1788.

Oliver and Battsey Gray, int. Nov. 15, 1801.

Rebekah and Will[ia]m Conky, Nov. 17, 1755.*

Rebakah of Shutsberry, [int. Rebekah of Shutsbry] and James Cowdin, Jan. 9, 1778.*

Robert of "Rutland District," and Margaret Conky, Oct. 1, 1767.*

Robert and Isebel [int. Isebal] Conky, May 6, 1768.*

Rob[er]t Jr. and Elisabeth Kid, Apr. 19, 1757.*

Thomas Jr. and Jennet McColloch, Dec. 9, 1762.*

HANKS, Benjaman of Belchiertown, and Anne Edson, int. Nov. 10, 1781.

Ira and Almira Gun, int. Mar. 1, 1830.

James 2d and Sophrona Oldes [int. Olds], May 4, 1842.*

Sam[ue]l C. of Enfield, and Arminda Randall, int. Nov. 6, 1848.

William of Enfield [int. of Belchertown], and Nancy Randall [int. Rendell], Oct. 29, 1833.*

* Intention also recorded.

HANKS, William 2d and Eliza A. Cummings, int. Aug. 11, 1841.

HANNUM, Grove Wright and Amelia Brown Newell, Apr. 4 [1820].*
Henry and Mitty Abell, int. Apr. 9, 1820.
Moses and Mary Maria Vatakin, int. Mar. 4, 1848.
Pleney of Belchertown, and Polly Arnold, int. June 9, 1808.

HARDEN, Anna and Levi Cook, int. Nov. 2, 1806.

HARKNES (see Harkness, Hartness), Daniel and Battsey Holland, int. Aug. 23, 1801.

HARKNESS (see Harknes, Hartness), Abigail, Mrs., and Esq. John Rankin, int. Nov. 12, 1832.
Anne and George Macomber, int. Aug. 30, 1801.
Chloe and Josiah Smith, int. Jan. 29, 1814.
Daniel and Lidia Hacket, int. Oct. 6, 1785.
Esther, 20, d. John, and Alden Bicknell, Dec. 24, 1845.*
Isabel and James Bell, int. Apr. 10, 1791.
James and Nancy Gray, Apr. 7, 1757.*
James and Betey Edson, int. Sept. 15, 1784.
James of Salem, N. Y., and Polley Rhoads, int. Dec. 29, 1798.
John and Cuziah Edson, int. Sept. 1, 1781.
John 2d and Rachel McNall, int. Oct. 28, 1781.
John Jr. and Esther Wilson, int. Dec. 8, 1810.
John and Amy Wilson, int. Mar. 6, 1837.
Jonathen and Elizebeth Thompson, int. July 31, 1789.
Lovicy and Oliver Smith, int. Jan. 29, 1814.
Nancy and Nathaniel Samson [int. Sampson], Sept. 21, 1780.*
Nancy and James Hood, int. Aug. 21, 1813.
Polly and Joseph Rinken, int. Nov. 17, 1805.
Sally and Andrew Gray, int. Dec. 1, 1805.
Sumner and Mrs. Mary A. Perkins, int. Jan. 17, 1845.
Vesta and Daniel Wilson, int. Dec. 8, 1810.
William Jr. and Isabel [int. Isebal] Gray, June 11, 1778.*
W[illia]m and Easter Bridge, int. Aug. 31, 1783. ----.
William and Abigail Turner, Dec. 12 [1816].*

HARLOW, Sally and Silas Ballou, Mar. 22 [1821].*
Thomas and Salley King, int. Mar. 11, 1792.

HARPER, Elisabeth of Lancaster [int. Lancester], and David Thomas, Nov. 18, 1755.*

* Intention also recorded.

HARRINGTON (see Herrington), Almira and Alanson Chapin, Nov. 21 [1819].*

HARRIS (see Herres).

HARTNESS (see Harknes, Harkness), William and Anne Gray, July 28, 1748.*

HARTWELL, Phinehas P. of Westminster, and Abigail D. Polly, int. May 28, 1846.

HASE (see Hayze, Heas), Jeremiah and Levince White, int. June 10, 1791.

HASKEL (see Haskell), David and Polly Gray, int. Feb. 15, 1794.

HASKELL (see Haskel), Eli of Belchertown, and Betsy Tower, int. Feb. 16, 1808.
Mary [int. Haskel] and John Berry, Sept. 21, 1780.*
Polly of Belchertown, and Isaac Tower Jr., int. Feb. 17, 1809.

HASKENS, Bashaba of New Salem, and Samuel Briten, int. Nov. 17, 1799.

HATHAWAY (see Hathay, Hatheway, Hathway), Mary and Daniel There, int. July 12, 1777.

HATHAY (see Hathaway, Hatheway, Hathway), Sam[ue]ll of Midelberry [int. Middelberry], and Sarah Stevens, Aug. 24, 1780.*

HATHEWAY (see Hathaway, Hathay, Hathway), Battsey and William Conkey Pratt, int. Nov. 11, 1804.

HATHWAY (see Hathaway, Hathay, Hatheway), Dexter [int. Hathaway] and Sally Hooker, Dec. 30, 1819.*

HAWARD (see Hayward, also Howard), Elihu and Tryol Hayward, int. Apr. 19, 1789.
Mary and Jonathan Ingraham, int. July 11, 1788.

HAWKS, James A. and Ruth Peaso, int. Oct. 22, 1842.

HAWLEY, Martha of Amherst, and Harmon P. Hoar, int. Aug. 18, 1832.

HAYDEN (see Haden, Haydon, Heydon), Fanny and Johnthan [int. Johnathan] Wood, Mar. 3, 1842.*

* Intention also recorded.

HAYDON (see Haden, Hayden, Heydon), William and Eliza Gray, both of Belchertown, Aug. 25, 1830.

HAYES (see Hase, Hayze, Heas).

HAYWARD (see Haward), Ichabode and Ruth Hacket, int. Apr. 15, 1790.
Polly and John Thayer 3d, int. Mar. 16, 1807.
Rhoda and David Clarey, int. Jan. 20, 1792.
Tryol of Milford, and Elihu Haward, int. Apr. 19, 1789.

HAYZE (see Hase, Heas), Sarah and John Boltwood, int. Oct. 21, 1784.

HEAS (see Hase, Hayze), Elisabeth of Belchiretown, and Eligah McFarland, int. Sept. 9, 1770.

HECKET (see Hacket, Heket), George and Mercy Fuller, int. Oct. 6. 1785.

HEIRS (see Ayer, Ayres), David of Colrain, and Jean Dick, May 13, 1777.*

HEKET (see Hacket, Hecket), Presila and Allexander Torrance, Mar. 2, 1781.*

HEMENWAY, Harding and Mary Henry, int. May 11, 1836.

HENCH, John and Parses Blair, int. Dec. 15, 1788.

HENDERSON, Mary and Starling King, int. Sept. 3, 1769.
Phebe and James Hamilton, Feb. 14, 1764.*

HENREY (see Henry), Joseph [int. Henery] of Colrain, and Margaret M[c]Colluch, Nov. 29, 1774.*

HENRICKS, John [int. Henriks] of Shelborn, and Margaret Gray, Oct. 27, 1768.*

HENRY (see Henrey), Margret of Shutesbury, and Lewis L. Draper, int. June 17, 1827.
Mary of Priscott, and Harding Hemenway, int. May 11, 1836.
William [int. Henrey] of Coldrain, and Isebel Gillmore, Jan. 15, 1760.*

HERRES, Deborah of Roadtown, and John Frost, int. Apr. 19, 1754.

* Intention also recorded.

HERRINGTON (see Harrington), Fathfull and Nathaniel Wheeler, int. June 25, 1808.

HERROON, Oliver of Cambrige, and Molley McCollock, int. Jan. 1, 1787.

HEYDON (see Haden, Hayden, Haydon), Phebe and Cyrus Kingman, Mar. 27 [1817].*
Sarah and Charles Billings, Feb. 5, 1817.*
Thomas Jr. [int. omits Jr. and adds Lt.] and Chloe Wallis, Nov. 27 [1823].*

HIDE (see Hyde), Samuel and Hannah Meklem, Dec. 19, 1765.*
Samuel, Dea., and Pagay Dickenson, int. Oct. 29, 1797.

HILL, Alvan of Shutsbery, and Polley Cleavlin, int. June 24, 1814.
Oliver of Shutesbury, and Susan M. Thurston, int. Apr. 17, 1843.
Rebeckah and Benjaman Bartlet, int. May 8, 1785.
Sampson and Prudence Rugg, int. Aug. 17, 1764.

HIND (see Hinds), Mary and Nathen Fallen, int. Sept. 7, 1800.

HINDS (see Hind), Anne and Barna Brigham, int. Mar. 11, 1805.
Jacob and Thankfull Davies, "Both of Quabin So Called," int. Aug. 23, 1749.
Joseph of "Jorman flats," N. Y., and Jinnet Croset, int. July 22, 1793.
Nehemiah of Greenwich, and Anne Pebels, Dec. 1, 1774.*
Sarah and Elihu Graves, int. July 9, 1808.
Vesta and Isaac A. Conkey, int. Aug. 13, 1807.

HINTEN, William and Mary Moss, int. Aug. 18, 1749.

HOAR (see Horr), Abigail and Joel Hamilton, int. Feb. 23, 1811.
George Washington of Prescott, and Mary Thompson, int. Mar. 8, 1834.
Harmon P. and Martha Hawley, int. Aug. 18, 1832.
Rachel and Isaac Hamilton, int. Feb. 2, 1811.

HODGEKINS (see Hodgkin), Joseph Jr. and Roxsa Wedge, int. Aug. 12, 1821.

HODGKIN (see Hodgekins), Clarissa and Absalom Lord, Apr. 24 [1816].*

HOLCOMB, Berijah of Hadley, and Sarah Peeso, int. Jan. 10, 1796.

* Intention also recorded.

HOLDEN, Josiah N. of Prescott, and Nancy P. Dodge, Dec. 27, 1848.*

HOLAN, Hanah and Levi Smith, int. July 1, 1781.

HOLLAN, Elihu and Elizebeth Bradshaw, int. Mar. 19, 1789.

HOLLAND, Ana and Dr. James Wood, Sept. 25, 1784.
Battsey and Daniel Harknes, int. Aug. 23, 1801.
Mary and Jonathan Kellogg, int. Mar. 22, 1783.
Oliver and Martha Rinken, June 1, 1775.*
Ruben and Sarah Conkey, int. Nov. 15, 1782.
Sarah and Jonathan Hood, Oct. 3, 1774.*

HOOD, James and Easter [int. Ester] Gray, Apr. 2, 1747.*
James and Nancy Harkness, int. Aug. 21, 1813.
Jennet and William Ferguson, Dec. 20, 1770.*
Jonathan and Sarah Holland, Oct. 3, 1774.*
Nancey [int. Nancy] and Robert Croset, Dec. 8, 1782.*

HOOKER, Esther and John Hunt, Feb. 15 [1816].*
Sally and Dexter Hathway [int. Hathaway], Dec. 30, 1819.*

HORR (see Hoar), Adah and Elkanah Doane, int. Apr. 8, 1843.
Harriot [int. Harriet] and William Brigham, July 27 [1839].*
Maryann, Mrs., and John Cooley, int. Apr. 1, 1848.
Mercia and Isaac Thompson, int. Apr. 14, 1822.
Nelson of Enfield, and Mary Cowan, int. Mar. 10, 1832.
Nelson [int. Wilson] widr., b. Prescott, s. John, and Caroline
    Rhodes, Dec. 19, 1849.*
Sarah and Jam[es] Fay, Apr. 2, 1843.*

HORTON, Sally, wid., and Levi Gates, widr., July 2, 1849.*

HOUSTEN (see Houston, Huston), David of Londonderry, and
    Mary Pebels [int. Pebbels], Apr. 26, 1757.*

HOUSTON (see Housten, Huston), Anna and Levi Gates Jr.,
    int. June 29, 1823.
David and Sarah Pebbles, int. Jan. 26, 1785.
John, Rev. [int. Husten], of Bedford, and Mrs. Ann Peebles,
    Nov. 17, 1757.*
John O. and Lucy Taylor, June 17 [1819].*
Mary and Charles T. Brown, int. Nov. 22, 1843.
Sarah and Capt. John Taylor, July 1, 1827.*

HOWARD (see also Haward), Davis of Boston, and Martha
    Southworth, Mar. 15 [1825].*

* Intention also recorded.

HOWARD, Joseph and Olive Lanord, int. May 20, 1805.
Rebekah and Marvel Leach, int. Oct. 14, 1798.

HUBBARD, Amanda of Leverett, and Lt. John Gray, int. Mar.
16, 1823.

HULET, Joseph of Belshireton, and Jean Johnston, int. Apr.
27, 1776.

HUMPHREY (see Humphry), Lucy and Joseph Clough, May
24, 1832.*

HUMPHRY (see Humphrey), Sarah P. [int. Humphrey] and
Rev. Benjamin C. Phelps, ———— [rec. during the year preceding Apr. 13, 1839; int. May 31, 1838].*

HUNT, Caroline Augusta of Northampton, and Dr. Daniel
Thompson, int. June 2, 1827.
John of Belchertown, and Esther Hooker, Feb. 15 [1816].*
Obed of Shutsbury, and Polley Barloe [see Barloe, Mary], int.
Feb. 12, 1786.
Obed of Shutesbury, and Lucy Whitney, int. Apr. 28, 1787.
William of Shutesbery, and Polly Orzen [?], int. Sept. 22, 1793.

HUNTER, Anne and John Rinken Jr., int. Oct. 17, 1802.
Elisabeth and Jam[e]s Cowan Jr., Dec. 22, 1757.*
Isaac and Ketrin Dick, Oct. 27, 1763.*
Isaac Cowan of Greenwich, and Allice Wilson, int. Feb. 16,
1795.
James and Susanna Ferguson, Dec. 11, 1766.*
James of Ware, and Polly Edson, int. Apr. 4, 1808.
J[e]nnet and James Halbert, Nov. 23, 1760.*
Lowes of Greenwich, and Pattrick Gray, int. Aug. 9, 1795.
Lucy and Horice Vinton, Oct. 20 [1824].*
Margret and Jam[e]s Cowan, Jan. 4, 1757.*
Mary of Greenwich, and Nehemiah Dunbar, int. May 12, 1788.
Sarah and David Conky, Apr. 29, 1773.*
Sarah and James Rinken, int. Aug. 21, 1788.*
Stephen of Hadley, and Hannah Boynton, June 15, 1836.*
Susannah and John Gray, int. Mar. 25, 1792.
William and Abigal Andros, int. Sept. 28, 1801.

HUSTON (see Housten, Houston), David and Martha Prat,
int. Jan. 10, 1792.

HUTER, Mary and Allex[an]d[e]r Line, int. Aug. 3, 1751.
* Intention also recorded.

HYDE (see Hide), Andrew and Mary Morton, int. Jan. 18, 1793.
Chester of Bethleham, N. Y., and Catharine Pacckard [int. Katherine Packard], Dec. 6, [1821].*
Ellis and Richard Haden, int. Aug. 25, 1783.
Eunice and Rufus Millen, int. June 6, 1807.
Hannah and David Billing, int. June 28, 1788.
Isabel and Joseph Pack, int. Aug. 11, 1799.
James and Martha Thompson, int. Feb. 11, 1787.
Polly and John Lindsy [int. L.] Millen, July 4 [1816].*
Samuel and Rachel Peebles, int. Nov. 10, 1792.

IDE, David of Amherst, and Lucy Draper, int. Oct. 1, 1808.

INGRAHAM (see Engran, Ingram, Ingrem), Gideon of Amherst, and Polly King, int. Apr. 17, 1796.
Jonathan and Mary Haward, int. July 11, 1788.

INGRAM (see Engram, Ingraham, Ingrem), Aron H. of Amherst, and Martha Ward, int. Aug. 21, 1841.

INGREM (see Engram, Ingraham, Ingram), Timothy and Percila Richman, Sept. 6, 1776.*

JENCK (see Jenkes, Jenks), William C. and Sarah Ann Davis, int. Oct. 22, 1846.

JENKES (see Jenck, Jenks), William of Cumberland, R. I., and Ruth Buffum, int. Mar. 17, 1827.

JENKS (see Jenck, Jenkes), Rebecah [int. Rebeca] and Phineas [int. Phinehas] Bishop, Apr. 7, 1833.*

JEPSON, Betsy M. of Ashfield, and John T. Thurston, int. Apr. 4, 1842.
Forris of Belchertown, and Emily Thurston, int. Mar. 16, 1838.

JEWETT, Jedediah of Killinglee, Conn., and Mary Atkinson, int. Aug. 21, 1788.

JILLSON (see Jilson), Almira and John Brailey, int. July 6, 1825.
Louisa M. and Horace Gray, int. Aug. 30, 1834.
Lucy and Lemuel C. Wedge, int. Dec. 15, 1842.
Manley and Maria A. Cook, int. Sept. 2, 1837.
Marinda and Daniel Purinton, int. Mar. 28, 1824.
Varnum and Amy Bolster, wid. [dup. omits wid.; int. Miss], Apr. 4, 1844.*

* Intention also recorded.

JILSON (see Jillson), Chloe, Mrs., and Samuel Arnold, Dec. 13, 1827.*
Lurana and Collins Braly, int. Sept. 27, 1813.
Olive F. and Moody Cook, int. Nov. 4, 1837.

JOANS (see Jones), James of Shoutesbery, and Sarah Leach, int. Jan. 5, 1793.

JOHNSON, Anna and Noble Keep, int. Mar. 1, 1809.
Clarissa of Amherst, and Martin Grout, int. Sept. 6, 1816.
George A. and Jane Johnston, Mar. 7, 1841.*
Joel and Alender Failes, int. Jan. 23, 1808.

JOHNSTON (see Jonston), Agness and Benjamen [int. Benjamin] Kid, Feb. 7, 1771.*
Andrew and Judah Chace, int. Nov. 11, 1804.
Earl and Nancy Oliver, both of Amherst, Nov. 21, 1821.
Elizabeth and Jonathen Field, int. June 23, 1794.
Hugh Moore and Levina Powers, int. Feb. 5, 1793.
Jane and George A. Johnson, Mar. 7, 1841.*
Jean and Joseph Hulet, int. Apr. 27, 1776.
John and Jean Jonston, May 15, 1777.*
Sarah and Ebenezer Gray, Feb. 12, 1767.*
Thomas and Sarah Bell, int. Feb. 14, 1791.
Thomas and Sarah Walker, int. July 30, 1792.
William and Margaret Meklem, Aug. 2, 1770.*

JONES (see Joans), Lucy and Alexander Bartlet, int. Mar. 1, 1814.
Olive and Robert S. Chase, Dec. 4, 1832.*
Patty and Ira Millen, Sept. 23 [1817].*

JONSTON (see Johnston) Jean [int. Johnston] and John Johnston, May 15, 1777.*

JORDAN (see Jurden).

JOSLIN (see Joslyn), Nabby, wid., and Daniel Woods, int. Mar. 17, 1815.

JOSLYN (see Joslin), John M. of Utica, N. Y., and Nancy Packard, int. Sept. 11, 1828.

JURDEN, John T. of Greenwich, and Mary Thurston, int. Jan. 8, 1830.

KEEP, Almedia and Andrew Thompson, int. Mar. 15, 1810.
* Intention also recorded.

KEEP, Noble of Jeffery, Chashire Co., N. H., and Anna Johnson, int. Mar. 1, 1809.

KEET, Jemima of Leverick, and Joseph Renken, int. June 10 [1788].

KEITH (see Keth).

KELLOGG, Jonathan of Amherst, and Mary Holland, int. Mar. 22, 1783.
Olive M. of Amherst, and Gilbert Southwick, int. Sept. 29, [18]49.

KELSO, Sussannah [int. Shusannah] and John Crawford Jr., Feb. 8, 1753.*

KENDALL, Horrace N. [int. Horace N. Kendell] of Ludlow, and Caroline E. Draper [dup. same, int. Cordelia] Apr. 29, 1844.*

KENTFIELD, Louis [female] of Ware, and Dwight Barns, int. Oct. 9, 1830.

KERUTH (see Carruth), Samuel of Barry, and Martha Thompson, int. Sept. 16, 1786.

KETH, John M. [int. Keith] of Uxbridge, and Mary Ann Whipple, Sept. 16, 1833.*

KID, Benjmen [int. Benjamin] of Chesterfield, and Agness Johnston, Feb. 7, 1771.*
Charles of Chesterfield, and Frank Hamilton, Nov. 30, 1773.*
Elisabeth and Rob[er]t Hamilton Jr., Apr. 19, 1757.*

KIMBALL (see Kimboll), Polly, Mrs., and Collins Braley, int. Nov. 13, [18]49.
Samuel Jr. and Hannah Gamwell, both of Belchertown, Sept. 27, 1831.
William B. and Sophronia Butterfield, int. Aug. 2, 1834.

KIMBOLL (see Kimball), Samuel of Shutesburry, and Polly Cook, int. Jan. 12, 1811.

KING, Agness and Will[ia]m Brown, Dec. 1, 1757.*
Albigame [int. Abbigane] Dr., and Rebekah Smith, Mar. 26, 1825.*
Damaries of Tanton, and Abisha Sampson, int. Sept. 7, 1794.
Dorothy and Lucius Clapp, Sept. 14, 1824.*

* Intention also recorded.

KING, Eloner and William M[c]Creeliss, int. Oct. 7, 1758.
James and Elisabeth McColluch, Sept. 9, 1779.*
John M. of Enfield, and Lucy Boynton, Dec. 23 [1827].*
Margarett and Edmund Mirick, int. Aug. 15, 1819.
Margret and Will[ia]m Petteson, May 18, 1749.*
Nancy and John Lotherige, int. Aug. 19, 1804.
Peeter and Abigal Engram, int. Apr. 25, 1783.
Polly and Gideon Ingraham, int. Apr. 17, 1796.
Polly and Robert Lotheridge, int. Aug. 31, 1800.
Robert and Sarah Conkey, int. Nov. 10, 1794.
Salley of New Salem, and Thomas Harlow, int. Mar. 11, 1792.
Starling of Chesterfield, and Mary Henderson, int. Sept. 3, 1769.

KINGMAN, Cyrus and Phebe Heydon, Mar. 27 [1817].*
Francis, s. Cyrus and Phebe, and Sophia J. Tomson, Mar. 9,
    1848.*
Harvy, Capt., and Sally Robsion, int. Mar. 7, 1812.
Julia H., 18, d. Martin and Phebe, and Calvin D. Eaton, Apr. 6,
    1840.*
Mary H. and Nathaniel Pratt, May 10, 1827.*
Sally, d. Henry, and Moses L. Ward, Apr. 3, 1845.*

KNAPP, Marthew and Thomas Brooks, int. Sept. 5, 1791.

KNIGHT, Philander S. and Mary Ward, June 11, 1837.*

KNOWLTON (see Nolten), Rozel of Belchertown, and Prudence
    Conkey, int. Aug. 12, 1809.

LANE, Elijah of Enfield, and Margret Thurston, int. May 23,
    1829.

LANORD, Olive of New Salem, and Joseph Howard, int. May 20,
    1805.

LARRABEE, wid. [of] Phinius, and Amos Tylor, int. Dec. 5, 1807.

LASON (see Lawson). William of Greenfield, and Polly Mount-
    gomerey, int. Nov. 2, 1793.

LATHAM, Bashshaba and Daniel Russell Jr., int. May 31, 1795.
Esther Cuttler and Elisha Baker, int. Sept. 18, 1803.
Joseph and Eunice Dunbarr, int. July 24, 1784.
Mendall and Mary A. Winslow, int. May 11, 1834. (Winslow
    Latham, father of Mendall, minor, forbade the giving of a
    certificate, May 25, 1834.)

* Intention also recorded.

LATHAM, Sally and Seth Ludden, int. May 1, 1796.

LAWMAN, Elesabeth of Licester, and Daniel Gray, int. Mar. 28, 1752.

LAWSON (see Lason), John of Shelburn, and Margaret Barbor, [int. Barbour], Mar. 6, 1776.*

LAZELL, Isaac of Wardsborough, Vt., and Lucy Wilson, int. Mar. 12, 1808.

LEACH, Bethiah and Daniel Rankin, int. Apr. 1, 1783.
Hannah of New Salem, and Ebenezer Lyskem, int. May 25, 1800.
Hannah and James Sloan, int. Apr 29, 1804.
Jonathan and Anne [int. Anna] Williams, May 26, 1784.*
Jonathen and Lydia Amerson Pettengal, int. Apr. 3, 1796.
Marvel and Rebekah Howard, int. Oct. 14, 1798.
Nabby and Robeson Shepard, int. Jan. 25, 1801.
Sarah and James Joans, int. Jan. 5, 1793.
Silence and William Blair, int. Mar. 9, 1776.
Silence and Robert Pirkens, int. Sept. 2, 1776.
Timothey and Hannah Cutter, int. Dec. 12, 1802.

LEONARD (see Lanord).

LEWIS, James and Rachel Abercrombie, int. Mar. 5, 1814.
John of Westminster, and Anna Hamilton, May 31, 1825.*
Sally and Arba Albe [int. Albee], Dec. 24 [1817].*
William of Northfield, and Sally Sears, int. Oct. 26, 1803.

LINCOLN, Hannah J. and Chandler Manley, int. Dec. 8, 1827.
Luther and Lucy Whitemore, Mar. 7, 1826.*
Marshal T. and Lucinda Myrick [int. Mirick], May 5, 1827.*
Polly and Ezra Brown, int. Jan. 3, 1810.
Samuel J. and Diana Brown, int. Jan. 29, 1814.

LINE, Allex[an]d[e]r of Haddem, and Mary Huter, int. Aug. 3, 1751.

LINDSEY (see Linsey, Linzie), John and Mary Thompson [int. Tompson], Dec. 17, 1761.*

LINSEY (see Lindsey, Linzie), Agness and John Walless, Oct. 13, 1761.*
Georg and Anne McMillen, int. Nov. 17, 1791.
James and Maryan Gray, int. Jan. 30, 1789.

* Intention also recorded.

LINSEY, Jean of New Salem, and William McMillen, int. Sept. 30, 1792.
Jennet and Charles Stewart, int. Apr. 24, 1759.
Marthe of New Salem, and Joel Gray, int. Oct, 15, 1786.
Mary and Thomas Anderson, int. Nov. 10, 1750.
Nancy and Jeremiah McMillen, int. Oct. 3, 1791.
William and Jean Murdah, int. Oct. 21, 1749.
William and Susannah McMillen, int. Aug. 23, 1789.

LINZIE (see Lindsey, Linsey), Stacy [male] and Haley Wilder, int. July 24, 1816.

LORD, Absalom of Athol, and Clarissa Hodgkin, Apr. 24 [1816].*

LOTHER, Mary M. and Thomas Gardner, int. Nov. 2, 1833.

LOTHERIDGE (see Lotherige, Rothridge), Anne and Amariah Bellew, int. Sept. 28, 1794.

LOTHERIGE (see Lotheridge, Rothridge), John and Nancy King, int. Aug. 19, 1804.
Margrey and Seth Field, int. Dec. 15, 1805.
Robert and Polly King, int. Aug. 31, 1800.

LOVEL (see Lovell), Philip and Eunice Dunbar, Nov. 30, 1824, in Belchertown.

LOVELL (see Lovel), Lovina [int. Lavinia] S., 21, of Amherst [int. of Belchertown], b. Belchertown, s. Phillip and ———— of Belchertown, and Emerson Abercrombie, Oct. 23, 1848.*

LUCE, Jason of Canton, Conn. [int. of "Collins Ville, C. T."], and Harriet [int. N.] Bruce, May 30, 1836.*

LUCORE, Isebal [int. Isebel] and Aaron [int. Aron] Gray, Feb. 22, 1759.*
Sarah and Jam[e]s Hamilton, Jan. 19, 1758.*

LUDDEN, Seth of Hadley, and Sally Latham, int. May 1, 1796.

LYON, Asaph and Hannah Wood, int. Sept. 9, 1775.
Asaph of Shutsbery, and Estar Gray, int. June 10, 1781.

LYSKEM, Ebenezer and Hannah Leach, int. May 25, 1800.

MacCALLISTER, etc. (see McCallister, etc.).

MACK, Daphna, Mrs., and Silas Cook, Dec. 21 [1843].*

* Intention also recorded.

MACK, John F. and Mrs. Sophia Packard, int. Apr. 23, 1842.

MACLAM (see Maklam, Maklem, McKliam, McKlyain, Meklem), John of Blanford, and Unice Crozet, int. May 8, 1785.

MACOMBER, George and Anne Harkness, int. Aug. 30, 1801.
Phelina of Shutesbery, and Nathenial Gray, int. Dec. 1, 1805.
Polly and William Oliver, int. Oct. 12, 1800.

MAKLAM (see Maclam, Maklem, McKliam, McKlyain, Meklem), Mary and Will[ia]m Conkey [int. Jr.], Mar. 30, 1786.*

MAKLEM (see Maclam, Maklam, McKliam, McKlyain, Meklem), Isabel [int. Iseball] and James Conky, Apr. 16, 1747.*
Jean and William Cowden, int. Apr. 2, 1774.
John and Rachel Works, int. Feb. 7, 1767.
John and Martha Thomas, Jan. 9, 1772.*
Rebekah (Makem) [int. Maklem] and Isaac Conky, Dec. 5, 1780.*
Sarah [int. Meklem] and Allex[an]d[e]r Conky, Jan. 7, 1748.*

MANLEY, Chandler of Northampton, and Hannah J. Lincoln, int. Dec. 8, 1827.
Chandler and Lucinda Gaylord, int. Aug. 10, 1831.

MARCH, Edwin A. of Northfield, and Betsy F. Presho, int. Feb. 17, 1849.

MARKS, Hannah and Ephriam Whiler, "both of Quaben [int. Quabin] So Called," Nov. 10, 1746.*

MARSH, Dwight of Hatfield, and Adaline Boyden, int. Nov. 4, 1831.
Dwight of Hadley, and Lucretia Bothwell, July 4, 1839.*
Edwin A., 22, of Northfield, b. Northfield, s. Isaac and Lucretia, and Betsey F. Presho, Mar. 7, 1849.

McCALLEY, Tho[ma]s and Katrine M[c]Donel, int. Apr. 27, 1754.

McCALLISTER (see Calester), Hamillton [int. Hamilton Mc-Calister], of White Creek, and Sarah Dick, Oct. 15, 1767.*

McCARTNEY, James and Elisabeth Green, int. Sept. 19, 1772.

McCLELAND, Mary and James Wallas, Apr. 8, 1756.*

McCOLLAH (see McColloch, McCollock, McColluch, McColluh, McColoch, McColough), Anna and Seth Dunbar, int. Nov. 16, 1800.

* Intention also recorded.

McCollah, Martha and Ens. Isaac Abercrombie, int. Dec. 5, 1789.

McCOLLOCH (see McCollah, McCollock, McColluch, McColluh, McColoch, McColough), Allex[an]d[e]r and Sarah Pebbels [int. Pebels], Feb. 10, 1755.*
Jean [int. McColluch] and John Dick, Sept. 25, 1746.*
Jennet and Thomas Hamilton Jr., Dec. 9, 1762.*
John and Molley Thompson, int. Mar. 31 [1788].
Rob[er]t and Margret Smith, Nov. 13, 1746.*
Robert and Sarah Cowan, Feb. 8, 1750.*

McCOLLOCK (see McCollah, McColloch, McColluch, McColluh, McColoch, McColough), Henery and Martha Hamilton, int. Jan. 6, 1787.
Molley and Oliver Herroon, int. Jan. 1, 1787.

McCOLLUCH (see McCollah, McColloch, McCollock, McColluh, McColoch, McColough), Alexander [int. McColluh of New Cambridge] and Jennet Cowden, Oct. 10, 1771.*
Elisabeth and James King, Sept. 9, 1779.*
Jean and James Gillmore, Dec. 18, 1776.*
John of New Cambridge, and Isebel [int. Isebal] Blair, Nov. 8, 1768.*
Margaret and Joseph Henrey [int. Henery], Nov. 29, 1774.*

McCOLLUH (see McCollah, McColloch, McCollock, McColluch, McColoch, McColough), Sarah 3d [int. McColluch] and James Caldwell M[c]Mullen, Nov. 29, 1774.*

McCOLOCH (see McCollah, McColloch, McCollock, McColluch, McColluh, McColough), Margr[e]t [int. McColloch] and Jam[e]s Smith, Oct. 27, 1748.*

McCOLOUGH (see McCollah, McColloch, McCollock, McColluch, McColluh, McColoch), Lucy of Colrain, and Alexander Conkey Jr., int. Jan. 2, 1808.

McCONNEL, Eloner and Allexander Conkey, int. June 18, 1791.
Jean and William Mills, Apr. 6, 1780.*

McCRAKEN, Jenney [int. Jeny] and John Anderson, July 11, 1767.*
Joseph of Worcester, and Sarah Torner, Feb. 12, 1760.*

* Intention also recorded.

McCREELES (see McCreeliss, McCreelless), Jemima of Coldrain, and Dea. Matthew Gray, int. Feb. 2, 1788.

McCREELISS (see McCreeles, McCreelless), William 2d of Cold Rain, and Eloner King, int. Oct. 7, 1758.

McCREELLESS (see McCreeles, McCreeliss), John [int. McCreelles] of Coldrain and Hannah Conky, Oct. 21, 1760.*

McDONEL (see McDonnal), Katrine of Heddley, and Tho[ma]s M[c]Calley, int. Apr. 27, 1754.

McDONNAL (see McDonel), Nancy and Isaac Dodge, int. Oct. 6, 1784.

McFALL, Jennet and Hugh Smith, int. Dec. 17, 1783.
William and Judith Purkins, wid., int. Jan. 11, 1809.

McFARLAND, Eligah and Elisabeth Heas, int. Sept. 9, 1770.
Sarah and Robert Barbor, May 16, 1751.*

McKEE, John and Lucy Ramsdel, int. Apr. 22, 1775.
Josiah and Deborah Barloe, int. May 14, 1786.
Robert and Mary Gray, Aug. 21, 1746.*

McKLIAM (see Maclam, Maklam, Maklem, McKlyain, Meklem), Elizabeth and John Stevenson, int. Sept. 13, 1801.

McKLYAIN (see Maclam, Maklam, Maklem, McKliam, Meklem), Margret of Worcester, and Robert Blair, int. Mar. 18, 1749.

McMASTER, Catrin [int. Catren] of Palmer, and William Selfridge, Mar. 17, 1757.*

McMILLEN (see Millen), Anne and Georg Linsey, int. Nov. 17, 1791.
Jeremiah and Nancy Linsey, int. Oct. 3, 1791.
Jonathan and Salley Freeman, int. Mar. 8, 1785.
Nancy and William Barry, int. Mar. 18, 1798.
Susannah and William Linsey, int. Aug. 23, 1789.
William and Jean Linsey, int. Sept. 30, 1792.

McMULLEN (see McMullin), James Caldwell and Sarah M[c]Colluh 3d [int. McColluch], Nov. 29, 1774.*
Mary and Thomas Dick, Apr. 27, 1780.*
Patrick and Mary Calester, int. Apr. 14, 1749.
Thomas and Martha Cowdin, Jan. 29, 1778.*

* Intention also recorded.

McMULLIN (see McMullen), W[illia]m and Hanah Smith, int.
Nov. 3, 1781.

McNALL, Rachel of Union, and John Harkness 2d, int. Oct.
28, 1781.

McNUTT (see Nut), Allex[an]d[e]r and Elisabeth Meklem, Apr.
14, 1749.*

MEKLEM (see Maclam, Maklam, Maklem, McKliam, McKlyain),
Ann and John Clark, Feb. 2, 1762.*
Elisabeth and Allex[an]d[e]r M[c]Nutt, Apr. 14, 1749.*
Hannah and Samuel Hide, Dec. 19, 1765.*
Jean and Thomas Thompson, Sept. 11, 1777.*
Margaret and William Johnston, Aug. 2, 1770.*
Mary and Isaac Gray, Sept. 10, 1754.*
Rob[er]t and Rebekah ———, int. Sept. 7, 1751.

MELLIN, Anna and Isaac Powers, int. June 19, 1807.

MICHEL, Eleies and Sam[ue]ll Bennet, "Both of Roadtown
So Cd," int. Feb. 3, 1753.
Roxeyleney and Abraham Follet, int. Dec. 7, 1805.

MILLEN (see McMillen, also Miller), Betsy and John Berry,
int. May 6, 1809.
David and Hannah Patch, int. Sept. 16, 1808.
David and Patty Rankin, int. Mar. 20, 1813.
David and Laura Wetherby [int. Witherby], May 15 [1817].*
Hannah and John M. Thompson, int. Apr. 27, 1812.
Ira of Temple, N. H., and Patty Jones, Sept. 23 [1817].*
John Lindsy [int. L.] and Polly Hyde, July 4 [1816].*
Levi and Polly Sears, int. July 27, 1809.
Lovina and James Cowan, int. Sept. 3, 1814.
Lucius of Marcellus, N. Y., and Abigail Mills, Jan. 29, 1820.
Patrick and Livena Sadler, int. Nov. 4, 1809.
Patrick and Judiath [int. Judath] E. Chadwick, Nov. 28,
1819.*
Polly and James Peebles, int. Sept. 18, 1803.
Rufus and Eunice Hyde, int. June 6, 1807.
Samuel and Jinney Sloan, int. Dec. 18, 1801.
Susannah and Charles Staples, May 27 [1817].*
William Jr. and Sally Snow, int. Sept. 12 [1809].
William "Cenior" and Hannah Thompson, wid., int. Dec. 31,
1814.

* Intention also recorded.

MILLER (see also Millen), Job S. of Southampton, and Marilla Thurston, int. Feb. 23, 1847.

Samuel L. [dup. and int. N.] of S. Hadley, and Nancy F. Cook, Nov. 31 [dup. 30], 1843.*

MILLS, Abigail and Lucius Millen, Jan. 29, 1820.

William and Jean M[c]Connel, Apr. 6, 1780.*

MIRICK (see Myrick), Chloe and William Newell, int. Oct. 6, 1827.

Edmund and Margarett King, int. Aug. 15, 1819.

MONTGOMERY (see Mountgomerey), Anne and Hanery Strobridge, int. Oct. 5, 1799.

Anne and Levi Cook, int. Nov. 23, 1806.

Mary and Irra Wood, both of Enfield, Hampshire Co., June 20, 1839.

MOODEY (see Moody), Martha of Amherst, and James Cook, int. Mar. 1, 1810.

MOODY (see Moodey), Mary of Amherst, and Paul Thuston, int. Aug. 31, 1806.

MOOR, Abeih of Unen, and James Taylor, int. May 7, 1763.

Battsey of Chaster, and Pattrick Gray, int. Aug. 11, 1799.

MORRIESON, Thomas [int. Murrieson] of Londonderry, and Martha Clark, Feb. 11, 1762.*

MORTON, Mary of Amherst, and Andrew Hyde, int. Jan 18, 1793.

Seth of Hatfield, and Mary Sloan, Mar. 15, 1770.*

MOSS, Mary "of Quaben So Called," and William Hinten, int. Aug. 18, 1749.

MOUNTGOMEREY (see Montgomery), Polly and William Lason, int. Nov. 2, 1793.

MUN, Matilda and Calven Ashley, int. Oct. 14, 1797.

MURDAH, Jean of Londonderry, and William Linsey, int. Oct. 21, 1749.

MYRICK (see Mirick), Lucinda [int. Mirick] and Marshal T. Lincoln, May 5, 1827.*

* Intention also recorded.

NEWCOMB, Poley and David Winters, int. July 22, 1798.

NEWEL (see Newell), Benjamin and Charlottee Newel, int. July 1, 1814.
Charlottee and Benjamin Newel, int. July 1, 1814.

NEWELL (see Newel), Amelia Brown and Grove Wright Hannum, Apr. 4 [1820].*
David and Huldah Reniff, int. Mar. 10, 1835.
Mary, wid., and Savannah Arnold, widr. [int. omits widr.], May 4, 1848.*
Reuben and Serena Packard, Oct. 28 [1817].*
Sally and Lyman Draper, June 8 [1819].*
Silas C. and Mary Hall, int. Mar. 30, 1833.
William and Chloe Mirick, int. Oct. 6, 1827.
William of Amherst, and Mrs. Harriet M. Wescott, Apr. 24, 1844.*

NOLTEN (see Knowlton), Margrey [int. Margary] and Reuben Rothridge [int. Lothridge], Nov. 8, 1770.*

NORTH, Benjamin of Northampton, and Dorcas Thompson, int. May 10, 1845.

NOWLEY, Rufus and Olive Prat, int. July 6, 1811.

NUT (see McNutt), Abraham [int. Nutt] of Pequige, and Sarah Gray, Sept. 13, 1759.*

OLDES, Sophrona [int. Olds] of Greenwich, and James Hanks 2d, May 4, 1842.*

OLIVER, Ann [int. Anne] and Joseph Hamilton, Nov. 11, 1773.*
Eunice [int. H.] and Daniel Stratton, May 1, 1828.*
Mary and John Dunlap, int. Mar. 1, 1807.
Mary Given and Pattrick Phillips, int. Jan. 29, 1804.
Nancy and Earl Johnston, both of Amherst, Nov. 21, 1821.
Robert of Pequige, and Lydia Gray, Sept. 13, 1759.*
William and Polly Macomber, int. Oct. 12, 1800.
William W. and Lorania Gray, Oct. 4, 1826.*

ORCUTT, Lyman of Monson, and Harriot Brown, int. Oct. 11, 1830.
Samuel of Wendal, and Mary Wood, wid., int. Aug. 27, 1808.

ORZEN [?], Polly and William Hunt, int. Sept. 22, 1793.

* Intention also recorded.

OSBORN (see Osburnne), Elem and Almira Wellman, both of Enfield, Apr. —, 1818.

OSBURNNE (see Osborn), Electa of Belchertown, and Rev. Sebastain Collumbus Cabott, int. Sept. 9, 1809.

OTIS, Betsey and James Smith, int. Jan. 6, 1816.

OWEN, Hannah [int. Owens] and Jacob Ramsdell, "Both of Quabin [int. Quaben] So Called," Jan. 23, 1747.*

PACCKARD (see Packard, Pakard), Catharine [int. Katherine Packard] and Chester Hyde, Dec. 6 [1821].*

PACK (see Peck), Joseph of Amherst, and Isabel Hyde, int. Aug. 11, 1799.

PACKARD (see Pacckard, Pakard), Ambrose and Elizabeth B. Smith, int. Mar. 17, 1822.
Ann K. and William Brown, Sept. 9 [1831].*
Barzillia of Belchertown, and Olive Rider, int. Nov. 14, 1807.
Cloa and Barnabas Faye, int. Dec. 9, 1782.
Cleorinda [int. Clarinda Packarrd], 42, d. Daniel and Nancy, and Wyat [int. Wryot] Barlow, widr. [int. omits widr.], Nov. 25, 1847.
David [int. Packord] of Enfield, and Azubah [int. Azuba] Whipple, Sept. 30 [1819].*
Eliza of Enfield, and Joel Packard, int. Dec. 29, 1838.
Isaac of Enfield, and Sila [int. Silence] Cowin, Nov. 10, 1840.*
Jene and Freeman Peppr [?] Jr., int. Aug. 17 [? or 27 or 12], 1833.
Job and Martha Clark, int. May 23, 1805.
Joel and Eliza Packard, int. Dec. 29, 1838.
Justin and Sophia Wood, Dec. 26, 1822.*
Maryann and Abial Robinson, int. Apr. 29, 1827.
Nancy and Zebina Rankin, int. Mar. 17, 1815.
Nancy and John M. Joslyn, int. Sept. 11, 1828.
Philena and Horatio N. Randall, int. Apr. 6, 1843.
Rhoda A. and Oliver Bryant, int. Oct. 8, 1829.
Sally, Mrs., of N. Bridgewater, and John Rankin Esq., int. Jan. 26, 1830.
Samuel H., 25, of Enfield, s. Abram of Enfield, and Sarah Ann Dodge, Oct. 23, 1844.*
Serena and Reuben Newell, Oct. 28 [1817].*
Sophia, Mrs., and John F. Mack, int. Apr. 23, 1842.
Thomas and Esther Dowin, int. June 1, 1811.

* Intention also recorded.

PAGE, Abigail of Prescott, and John Cowan, int. Nov. 29, 1834.

PAKARD (see Pacckard, Packard), Eliab and Lyda Forde, int. Oct. 15, 1803.

PALUSKE [?], Elizabeth and Tho[ma]s Conkey, int. May 21, 1784.

PARCE, Alden of New Salem, and Lucy Ashley, int. Sept. 17, 1792.
Metilda of Shutesbery, and James Thompson Jr., int. Mar. 6, 1796.

PARKER, Susan E., Mrs., and Levi B. Hall, int. Apr. 26, 1849.

PARKS, Stuard James and Nancy Gray, int. Apr. 29, 1798.

PATCH, Hannah of Stow, and David Millen, int. Sept. 16, 1808.

PATRICK, Margret of Rutland, and Jonathan Gray, int. July 19, 1754.
Mary of Rutland, and Robert Clark, Mar. 2, 1762.*

PAUL, William of Greenwich, and Catrin Rice, int. Dec. 25, 1804.

PEASE, Marcus J. of Collinsvill, Conn. [int. "Collinsville, C. T."], and Sarah C. Aldrich, Sept. 6 [1836].*

PEASO (see Peeso, Peso), Ruth of Belchertown, and James A. Hawks, int. Oct. 22, 1842.

PEBBELS (see Pebbles, Pebels, Peblels, Peebles), Patrick and Margret Taylor, Mar. 8, 1757.*
Sarah [int. Pebels] and Allex[an]d[e]r M[c]Colloch, Feb. 10, 1755.*

PEBBLES (see Pebbels, Pebels, Peblels, Peebles), John and Anne Shaw, int. Mar. 17, 1770.
Sarah and David Houston, int. Jan. 26, 1785.

PEBELS (see Pebbels, Pebbles, Peblels, Peebles), Anne and Nehemiah Hinds, Dec. 1, 1774.*
James and Rachel Young, May 5, 1768.*
John [int. Pebles] and Mary Cunningham [int. Cuningham], Aug. 17, 1759.*
Mary [int. Pebbels] and David Housten, Apr. 26, 1757.*
Mary and Allexand[e]r Conky Jr., June 11, 1776.*
Robert and Elisabeth Cone, int. Jan. 30, 1761.

* Intention also recorded.

PEBLELS (see Pebbels, Pebbles, Pebels, Peebles), John and Sarah Conky, int. May 2, 1752.

PECK (see Pack), Jesse F. and Matilda Tingley, int. Nov. 19, 1819.

Lavonia and Thornton Ferguson, June 6, 1831.*

Simeon of Amherst, and Francis [int. Frances] Zuill, Oct. 17, 1776.*

Winchester of Amherst, and Lydia Pirkens, int. Feb. 13, 1789.

PEEBLES (see Pebbels, Pebbles, Pebels, Peblels), Ann, Mrs., and Rev. John Houston [int. Husten], Nov. 17, 1757.*

Anne and Ebenezer Gray Jr., int. Nov. 23 [1800].

David of Hamilton, N. Y., and Elizabith Hamilton, int. Nov. 6, 1803.,

Frank and Joseph Sears, int. Jan. 8, 1797.

James of Hamilton, N. Y., and Polly Millen, int. Sept. 18, 1803.

Margrett and Levy Dickinson, int. Sept. 6, 1782.

Pattrick and Jenney Gray, int. July 19, 1801.

Pattrick and Anne Hamilton, int. Jan. 3, 1802.

Pattrick of Maddison, N. Y., and Rebekkah Conkey, int. Sept. 11, 1813.

Rachel and Samuel Hyde, int. Nov. 10, 1792.

William Forbush of Salem, N. Y., and Elizabeth Religh, int. Apr. 10, 1791.

PEESO (see Peaso, Peso), Lydia and Gideon Hacket, int. Feb. 7, 1796.

Sally of Belchertown, and Joseph Randell, int. Jan. 3, 1819.

Sarah and Berijah Holcomb, int. Jan. 10, 1796.

PEIRCE (see Pierce), Martha of Prescott, and Eli W. Chapin, int. Nov. 4, 1831.

Sally of New Salem, and Patrick Gray Jr., int. Mar. 24, 1810.

PEPPR [?], Freeman Jr., of Ware, and Jene Packard, int. Aug. 17 [? or 27, or 12], 1833.

PERKINS (see Pirkens, Purkins), Mary A., Mrs., of Palmer, and Sumner Harkness, int. Jan. 17, 1845.

PERRY, Nathan C. of Belchertown, and Lois Tomson, int. Mar. 30, 1843.

PESO (see Peaso, Peeso), Nathen and Lucretia Dorety, int. Mar. 3, 1805.

* Intention also recorded.

PESO, Samuel and Polly Davison, int. Oct. 5, 1800.

PETERSON, Rehoda [int. Rhoda] and Abizer [int. Abiezer] Edson, Dec. 3, 1772.*

PETTENGAL (see Pettingel), Lydia Amerson of Belshertown, and Jonathen Leach, int. Apr. 3, 1796.

PETTESON, Adam of Shutsbery, and Jennet Rinken, July 7, 1778.*
James and Mary Green, Dec. 11, 1777.*
Mary and William Clark, Nov. 22, 1764.*
Naomi [int. Peteson] and Will[ia]m Berry, Jan. 27, 1780.*
Robert and Dinah Dick, int. Apr. 4, 1761.
Will[ia]m and Margret King, May 18, 1749.*

PETTINGEL (see Pettengal), Nathan of Belchertown, and Lurana Tower, int. Nov. 25, 1808.

PHELPS, Asahel of Northampton, and Polly Sears, int. Oct. 31, 1802.
Benjamin C., Rev. [int. omits Rev.], of Mystic, Conn., and Sarah P. Humphry [int. Humphrey], ——— [rec. during year preceding Apr. 13, 1839; int. May 31, 1838].*
Betsy of Holden, and Haffield Gould, int. May 6, 1809.

PHILLIPS, Pattrick of Boston, and Mary Given Oliver, int. Jan. 29, 1804.

PIERCE (see Peirce), Hezekiah H. and Elcey Works, int. July 19, 1839.
Josiah Jr. and Ruth Ayres int. Apr. 8, 1811.
Louisa of Amherst, and Simon Cook, ——— [rec. during year preceding Apr. 2, 1827; int. Apr. 27, 1826].*

PIRKENS (see Perkins, Purkins), Lydia and Winchester Peck, int. Feb. 13, 1789.
Robert of Rutland, and Silence Leach, int. Sept. 2, 1776.

POLLEY (see Polly), Sumner O. and Marrak [Mariah ?] Brown, int. Oct. 1, 1847.

POLLY (see Polley), Abigail D. and Phinehas P. Hartwell, int. May 28, 1846.

POMROY (see Pumroy), Luther of Amherst, and Sibeliah Tower, int. Jan. 4, 1812.

* Intention also recorded.

POWERS, Isaac of Madison, N. Y., and Anna Mellin, int. June 19, 1807.

Joanna and Moses Wilder, " Both of Roadtown So Called," int. Nov. 6, 1756.

Levina of Shutesbry, and Hugh Moore Johnston, int. Feb. 5, 1793.

Ruth of Shutesbery, and Aaron Gray, int. Oct. 23, 1796.

PRAT (see Prate, Pratt, Prett), Margaret and James Rankin, int. Nov. 1, 1811.

Martha and David Huston, int. Jan. 10, 1792.

Nathan and Abigail Whitten, int. July 30, 1779.

Olive and Rufus Nowley, int. July 6, 1811.

Zube and Cato Dunsett, int. Mar. 5, 1786.

PRATE (see Prat, Pratt, Prett), Micaih and Merthew Conkey, int. Aug. 14, 1781.

PRATT (see Prat, Prate, Prett), John and Adaline Aldrich, Jan. 5, 1826.*

Nathaniel of Belchertown, and Mary H. Kingman, May 10, 1827.*

Silvanes and Lidiah Southworth, int. Dec. 6, 1783.

Virgil, 30, b. Belchertown, s. Elihu and Abagail of Belche[r]-town, and Maryann [int. Mary Ann] Randall, Nov. 1, 1847.*

Warner, 22, b. Belchertown, s. Elisha Pratt of Belchertown, and Saphrona [int. Sophronia] Arnold, Oct. 1, 1846.*

William Conkey and Battsey Hatheway, int. Nov. 11, 1804.

PRESHO, Betsey [int. Betsy] F., 18, and Edwin A. Marsh [int. March], Mar. 7, 1849.*

Jane H., 22, d. Zadoc, and Benjamin Fay, June 1, 1846.*

PRETT (see Prat, Prate, Pratt), Micah Jr. and Phibe Halley, int. —— [1778].

PROUTY, Isaac Jr. of Shutesbury, and Mrs. Eliza Erwin, int. Jan. 2, 1841.

PUMROY (see Pomroy), Nancy and Will[ia]m Ashley, int. Apr. 2, 1786.

PURINTON, Daniel of Munson, and Marinda Jillson, int. Mar. 28, 1824.

* Intention also recorded.

PURKINS (see Perkins, Pirkens), Judith, wid., and William McFall, int. Jan. 11, 1809.

PUTNUM, Hannah of New Salem, and Abiel B. Smith, int. Apr. 24, 1825.

QUEEN, Elisabeth and William Anderson, int. Sept. 23, 1763.

RAMSDALE (see Ramsdel, Ramsdell), Abner and Susannah Sekiel, int. Oct. 24, 1783.

RAMSDEL (see Ramsdale, Ramsdell), Lucy of Greenwich, and John McKee, int. Apr. 22, 1775.

RAMSDELL (see Ramsdale, Ramsdel), Jacob and Hannah 'Owen [int. Owens], "Both of Quabin [int. Quaben] So Called," Jan. 23, 1747.*

RANDALL (see Randel, Randell), Arminda and Sam[ue]l C. Hanks, int. Nov. 6, 1848.
Benjamin of Belchertown, and Lucy Davission, int. Apr. 18, 1812.
Elijah and Mrs. Sarah Gould, int. Dec. 5, 1840.
Fidelia S. and Henry Strong 2d, Nov. 22, 1848.*
Horatio N. of Belchertown, and Philena Packard, int. Apr. 6, 1843.
Mary and William H. Elmer, int. Apr. 4, 1840.
Maryann [int. Mary Ann], 24, d. Ephran and Hannah, and Virgil Pratt, Nov. 1, 1847.*
Melinda and Ora Grout, int. Nov. 20, 1830.
Nancy [int. Rendell] and William Hanks, Oct. 29, 1833.*
Warren and Asenath P. Aldrich, int. Mar. 11, 1840.

RANDEL (see Randall, Randell), Arba [int. Randell] of Belchertown, and Esther N. Smith, Apr. 19 [1821].*

RANDELL (see Randall, Randel), Charles and Hannah Griffin, Aug. 13, 1827.*
Joseph and Sally Peeso, int. Jan. 3, 1819.

RANDWELL, Titus of Greenwich, and Patty Davison, int. Oct. 12, 1797.

RANKIN (see Renken, Rinken), Abiel and Mary A. Bryant, Dec. 26, 1822.*
Ansel A. and Vienna Hall, int. Dec. 17, 1832.
Cynthia and David Dexter Jr., int. Sept. 6, 1830.

* Intention also recorded.

RANKIN, Daniel and Bethiah Leach, int. Apr. 1, 1783.
Hiram and Betsy P. Dunbar, int. Mar. 2, 1843.
James and Margaret Prat, int. Nov. 1, 1811.
John Esq. and Mrs. Sally Packard, int. Jan. 26, 1830.
John Esq. and Mrs. Abigail Harkness, int. Nov. 12, 1832.
Margaret, Mrs., and Asahel Aldrich, Nov. 17, 1825.*
Patty and David Millen, int. Mar. 20, 1813.
Silas and Sally Robbins, int. Dec. 9, 1813.
William C. of Westfield, s. James dec'd, and Amelia M. Hall,
    Dec. 31, 1843.*
Zebina and Nancy Packard, int. Mar. 17, 1815.

RANSOM, Elisabeth and Philip Freker, Sept. 6, 1776.*
Moses and Jennet Ferguson, Oct. 24, 1776.*

RAWSON, Sina of Cumberland, Providence Co., R. I., and Silas
    Cook, int. Mar. 9, 1816.

RAY, Salley and William Barry 2d, int. July 22, 1798.

REE, William of Greenwich, and Mary Croset, May 19, 1774.*

RELIGH, Elizabeth and William Forbush Peebles, int. Apr. 10,
    1791.

RENIFF, Daniel and Rhoda Comins, int. Oct. 3, 1814.
Huldah and David Newell, int. Mar. 10, 1835.
Nancy and Rufus Grout, Jan. 24, 1841.*

RENKEN (see Rankin, Rinken), Joseph and Jemima Keet,
    int. June 10 [1788].

RHOADS (see Rhodes), Polley and James Harkness, int. Dec.
    29, 1798.

RHODES (see Rhoads), Caroline, d. Joel and Nelson [int. Wil-
    son] Horr, widr., Dec. 19, 1849.*
Dexter and Martha Demmon, Mar. 2, 1829.*
Joel [int. Rodes] and Lucy Allen, Oct. 2, 1828.*
Relief, 16, d. Joel and Lucy, and John Rider, Dec. 17, 1846.*

RICE, Catrin and William Paul, int. Dec. 25, 1804.
Timothy of Chesterfield, and Mary Halbert, July 25, 1769.*

RICHARDSON, Henry [int. Lt.] and Saloma Snow, June 20,
    1816.*

RICHMAN, Percila and Timothy Ingrem, Sept. 6, 1776.*

* Intention also recorded.

RIDER, Cloe of Enfield, and Daniel Bartlet, Aug. 20, 1828.
Giles of Belchertown, and Alsey Brown, int. Mar. 25, 1815.
Giles and Lucy Wood, Apr. 16, 1822.*
Giles and Hannah Cook, int. Mar. 27, 1830.
John and Rebekah [int. Rebecca] Wood, Nov. 10, 1819.*
John, 24, s. John and Rebecca, and Relief Rhodes, Dec. 17, 1846.*
Lucy and Ichabod Wood Jr., int. May 25, 1816.
Nancy and Benjamin Guardner, both of Enfield, Sept. 29, 1828.
Olive and Barzillia Packard, int. Nov. 14, 1807.

RIGHT (see Wright), Gaius and Lucy Shalden, int. Oct. 10, 1799.

RINKEN (see Rankin, Renken), Battsey and John Gray Sd [?], int. Sept. 24, 1797.
James and Sarah Hunter, int. July 18, 1788 [dup. int. Aug. 21, 1788].
Jennet and Adam Petteson, July 7, 1778.*
John and Mary Torrance, Oct. 6, 1774.*
John Jr. and Anne Hunter, int. Oct. 17, 1802.
Joseph and Elisabeth Gray, Apr. 21, 1748.*
Joseph and Polly Harkness, int. Nov. 17, 1805.
Martha and Oliver Holland, June 1, 1775.*
Matthew and Martha Torrance [int. Torranc], June 26, 1777.*

ROBBENS (see Robbins, Robins), Abigal of Balchertown, and Levi Gray, int. Sept. 13, 1798.

ROBBINS (see Robbens, Robins), Sally of Belchertown, and Silas Rankin, int. Dec. 9, 1813.
Samuel of Montague, and Annis Grout, Nov. 7, 1837.*

ROBESON (see Robsion), Joseph of Greenwich, and Sarah Wilson, int. Sept. 22, 1793.

ROBINS (see Robbens, Robbins), Abigal of Shutsbery, and Thomas Fisher, int. Oct. 8, 1813.
Daniel [int. Robbins] of Boston, and Harriot [int. Herriot] Wilson, May 21 [1818].*

ROBINSON, Abial and Maryann Packard, int. Apr. 29, 1827.
Deborah, wid., of Hardwich, and Alexander Bartlett, int. Nov. 15, 1838.
Ebeneazer W. of Hardwick, and Susannah Bartlet, int. Dec. 10, 1842.

* Intention also recorded.

ROBINSON, Prudence and Joseph Shaw, int. Aug. 20, 1791.
Smith of Greenwich, and Ama Sears, int. Nov. 12, 1820.
Susan of Hardwick, and Alaxander Bartlet Jr., int. Nov. 13, 1841.

ROBSION (see Robeson), Sally and Capt. Harvy Kingman, int. Mar. 7, 1812.

ROGERS, Mary of Ware, and Paul Thuston, int. Jan. 8, 1790.

ROTHRIDGE (see Lotheridge, Lotherige), Reuben [int. Loth-ridge] and Margrey [int. Margary] Nolten, Nov. 8, 1770.*

ROWLAND, Lucy A., 20, d. Lyman and w., and George T. Goodale, May 28, 1844.*

RUGG, Prudence of Greenwich, and Sampson Hill, int. Aug. 17, 1764.

RUGGLES, Adin [int. Aiden] and Cynthia [int. Cyntha] Snow, Apr. 25 [1816].*

RUSH, Samuel and Elisabeth Cowden, July 28, 1774.*

RUSSELL, Daniel Jr. of Hadley, and Bashshaba Latham, int. May 31, 1795.
Samuel W. and Lydia W. Fessenden, May 1, 1844.*

SADLER, Livena of Ashfield, and Patrick Millen, int. Nov. 4, 1809.

SAMPSON (see Samson), Abisha and Damaries King, int. Sept. 7, 1794.
Cloy and Laben Bats Jr., int. Sept. 9, 1804.
Thomas and Batsey Darling, int. Oct. 27, 1805.

SAMSON (see Sampson), Nathaniel [int. Sampson] and Nancy Harkness, Sept. 21, 1780.*

SANDERS, Melinda and Ellis W. Bunce, ——— [rec. during year preceding Apr. 2, 1827 ; int. Jan. 7, 1826].*

SARL, Bildad of South Hampton, and Phebe Gray, int. Nov. 23, 1794.

SAVIGE, Martha and John Gray Jr. [int. omits Jr.], Apr. 17, 1755.*
Thankfull of Rutland, and Isaac Stivenson [int. Stevinson], Nov. 15, 1764.*

SCOT, Elisabeth of Leicester, and David Sloan, June 2, 1774.*

* Intention also recorded.

SEAGRAVES, Horatio of Uxbridge, and Berthia [int. Bethiah] Ward, May 9, 1834.*

SEARS, Ama and Smith Robinson, int. Nov. 12, 1820.
Barnabas [int. Barnabus] Jr. and Polly Gray, May 21 [1818].*
Jonathan F. and Polley Town, int. Aug. 16, 1813.
Joseph and Frank Peebles, int. Jan. 8, 1797.
Polly and Asahel Phelps, int. Oct. 31, 1802.
Polly and Levi Millen, int. July 27, 1809.
Sally and William Lewis, int. Oct. 26, 1803.

SEKIEL, Lucey [Sekins?] of Deerfield, and Justus Gray, int. Feb. 12, 1792.
Susannah and Abner Ramsdale, int. Oct. 24, 1783.

SELFRIDG (see Selfridge), Nane and James Dunlap, int. Dec. 29, 1781.

SELFRIDGE (see Selfridg), Elisabeth and John Buck, Feb. 4, 1773.*
Oliver and Ester Smith, Dec. 28, 1756.*
Will[ia]m and Catrin [int. Catren] M[c]Master, Mar. 17, 1757.*

SHALDEN (see Sheldon), Lucy of Ludlow, and Gaius Right, int. Oct. 10, 1799.

SHAW, Anne of S. Brimfield, and John Pebbles, int. Mar. 17, 1770.
Elias of Balshartown, and Mary Thuston, int. Mar. 24, 1799.
Elias of Belchertown, and Rachel Bartlett, July 20, 1827.
George L. of Enfield, and Amy Ama Cook, int. May 11, 1841.
Jacob of Shutesbery, and Isabel Gray, int. Oct. 4, 1795.
James of Granby, and Eunice Fales, July 4 [1816].*
Joseph of Canterbery, Conn., and Prudence Robinson, int. Aug. 20, 1791.
Lois of Greenwich, and Thomas Vaughn Jr., int. May 29, 1813.
Lydia of New Salem, and Chester Gray, May 8, 1817.*
Maria E., 18, d. Steward and Mary, and Charles Austin, Aug. 1, 1848.*
William of Balchertown, and Eunice Baker, int. Nov. 26, 1803.

SHAYS, Hannah and Seth Foster, int. Feb. 5, 1793.

SHELDON (see Shalden), Legrand C., 24, of Southampton, s. Wareham and Rebecca of Southampton, and Ataline Wedge, Sept. 10, 1846.*

* Intention also recorded.

SHEPARD, Robeson of Hamilton, N. Y., and Nabby Leach, int. Jan. 25, 1801.

SHIRTLIEF (see Shirtlieff), Vise and Edward Foster Jr., int. Apr. 12, 1789. '

SHIRTLIEFF (see Shirtlief), Iroa and Anne Taylor, int. June 23, 1794.

SHUMWAY, Asa of Palmer, and Orinda H. [int. omits H.] Eaton, wid., Jan. 3, 1838.*

SIBLEY, Maria and Whitcomb Gray, both of Belchertown, Apr. 21, 1830.
Polly B., Mrs., and Nathan Washburn, Feb. 16, 1828.*

SIMONS, Venis of Shutesbery, and Thomas Fisher, int. Oct. 27, 1805.

SLARAH [?], Martha and Andrus Conkey, int. Nov. 24, 1787.

SLOAN, Abigail of New Salem, and Patrick Gray, int. June 29 [1782].
Agness and John Hamilton [int. Jr.], Dec. 27, 1759.*
Andrew of Watterford [int. Waterford], N. Y., and Mehetable Conkey, Jan. 20 [1818].*
David and Elisabeth Scot, June 2, 1774.*
Elisabith and John White, int. Apr. 21, 1783.
Eloner and Barnes Cooly, int. Aug. 12, 1777.
Gardner and Polly Barry, int. Oct. 27, 1806.
Gardner and Roxana Gray, int. Apr. 14, 1812.
James and Hannah Leach, int. Apr. 29, 1804.
Jinney and Samuel Mullen, int. Dec. 18, 1801.
John of Selam [Salem], and Mary Butler [int. Buttler], Dec. 3, 1761.*
John and Ann Ferguson, Jan. 10, 1765.*
Lorana S. of Prescott, and Preston Cowan, int. Sept. 18, 1848.
Martha and Samuel Stevenson, int. Mar. 31, 1787.
Mary and Seth Morton, Mar. 15, 1770.*
Sam[ue]ll and Eunice [int. Eunis] Dick, Nov. 30, 1779.*
Sarah and Moses Coolley, June 16, 1774.*

SMITH, Abiel B. and Hannah Putnum, int. Apr. 24, 1825.
Andrew of Holden, and Jean Cleark, May 18, 1748.*
Elisabeth of Worcester, and John Young, int. Feb. 2, 1760.
Elizabeth B. of Needham, and Ambrose Packard, int. Mar. 17, 1822.

* Intention also recorded.

SMITH, Ester and Oliver Selfridge, Dec. 28, 1756.*

Esther N. and Arba Randel [int. Randell], Apr. 19 [1821].*

Experiance of Whatley, and Obed Dickenson, int. Aug. 14, 1804.

Georg and Battsey Clevland, int. May 2, 1803.

Hanah of Holden, and W[illia]m McMullin, int. Nov. 3, 1781.

Hannah of Hardwick, and John Baker, int. Jan. 21, 1794.

Hannak [Hannah?] and Sidney Dillon, int. July 11, 1841.

Hugh and Jennet McFall, int. Dec. 17, 1783.

Jam[e]s of Kingstown, and Margr[e]t M[c]Coloch [int. Margret McColloch], Oct. 27, 1748.*

James and Betsey Otis, int. Jan. 6, 1816.

Jean of Holden, and Jacob Gray, Sept. 26, 1780.*

Job and Mahetable Abercrombie, int. Nov. 11, 1804.

Job and Martha Conkey, int. Nov. 12, 1831.

Josiah of Boston, and Chloe Harkness, int. Jan. 29, 1814.

Levi of Amhast, and Hanah Holan, int. July 1, 1781.

Margaret of "Rutland Destrick," and James Berry, int. Oct. 27, 1768.

Margret of Kingstown [int. "So Called"], and Rob[er]t M[c]Colloch, Nov. 13, 1746.*

Mecy [int. Mecie] and Tho[ma]s [int. Tomas] Thompson, Aug. 31, 1780.*

Nancy and Daniel Chapman, int. Apr. 4, 1809.

Oliver and Sarah Gay, int. Nov. 8, 1808.

Oliver of Boston, and Lovicy Harkness, int. Jan. 29, 1814.

Oliver Jr., Lt., and Abigail Clapp, int. Sept. 6, 1817.

Patty of Rutland, and Lt. John Gray, int. Aug. 29, 1814.

Rebekah and Dr. Albigame [int. Abbigane] King, Mar. 26, 1825.*

Sally C. and Jared T. Wescott, Dec. 29 [1829].*

William and Rebeca Albercrombie, int. Nov. 6, 1803.

SNOW, Cynthia [int. Cyntha] and Adin [int. Aiden] Ruggles, Apr. 25 [1816].*

Sally of Greenwich, and William Millen Jr., int. Sept. 12 [1809].

Saloma and [int. Lt.] Henry Richardson, June 20, 1816.*

SOUTHWARD, Avis and Eli Hamilton, int. Oct. 21 [1787].

SOUTHWICK, Gilbert and Olive M. Kellogg, int. Sept. 29, [18]49.

Hepsibah and Charles N. Woods, int. Dec. 27, 1834.

* Intention also recorded.

SOUTHWICK, Peter and Mary Boynton, int. Apr. 9, 1836.

SOUTHWORTH, Abia and Kezeiah Boltwood, int. Oct. 20, 1794.
Bridget and Stephan Andrews, int. Dec. 3, 1783.
Lidiah and Silvanes Pratt, int. Dec. 6, 1783.
Martha and Davis Howard, Mar. 15 [1825].*

SPEAR (see Spears), Harvy [int. Hervey] of Shutesbury, and Hannah Cook, Mar. 26, 1823.* [Prob. m., but rec. among int. Int. Mar. 9.]

SPEARS (see Spear), Sarah A. of Belchertown, and Cyrus B. Dodge, int. Jan. 10, 1844.

SPRAGUE, Jonathan of Ashfield, and Elisabeth Clark, June 17, 1766.*

STANFORD, Sarah and Edward Adams, int. Dec. 12, 1777.

STAPLES, Charles and Susannah Millen, May 27 [1817].*

STEARNS, Jasper and Patty Wyman, int. Oct. 10, 1807.

STEVENS, Hannah of Sutesbery, and Matthew Clark, int. Sept. 14, 1771.
Sarah and John Davieson, int. Nov. 22, 1760.
Sarah and Sam[ue]ll Hathay, Aug. 24, 1780.*

STEVENSON (see Stivenson), James of Greenwich, and Anne Conkey, int. Nov. 2, 1806.
John of Greenwich, and Elizabeth McKliam, int. Sept. 13, 1801.
Samuel and Martha Sloan, int. Mar. 31, 1787.

STEWART, Charles of Coldrain, and Jennet Linsey, int. Apr. 24, 1759.
Jean of Braintree, and Adam Clark, int. Sept. 3, 1773.

STIVENSON (see Stevenson), Isaac [int. Stevinson] and Thankfull Savige, Nov. 15, 1764.*

STRATTON, Daniel of Athol, and Eunice [int. H.] Oliver, May 1, 1828.*

STRETER, Benany of Cumberland, and Sally Allen, int. Aug. 3, 1811.

STROBRIDGE, Hanery of Northfield, and Anne Montgomery, int. Oct. 5, 1799.
* Intention also recorded.

STRONG, Henry 2d [int. of Northampton], and Fidelia' S. Randall, Nov. 22, 1848.*

John of Northampton, and Patience Eaton, int. May 31, 1795.

STRONGMAN, Henry of Greenfield, and Jennet Allexander, Oct. 27, 1757.*

STUTSON, Robert of Greenwich, and Isa Crosett, int. Feb. 19, 1795.

SUMNER, Clark of Hardwick, and Louisa Turner, int. Jan. 12, 1846.

SYNET, Rob[er]t of Bladfoard, and Agnos Gillmore, int. May 9, 1752.

TAFTS, James [int. Teft] of Worcester, and Martha Gray, Feb. 26, 1761.*

TAGERT, Nathaniel of Blanfoard, and Janet Hamelton, Jan. 16, 1753.*

TALMAGE, Francis A. of Ludow, and Margret J. Brown, int Oct. 5, 1840.

TAYLOR, Anne and Iroa Shirtlieff, int. June 23, 1794.

Irael H., Dr., and Lavina Crossett, int. Dec. 10, 1842.

James and Abeih Moor, int. May 7, 1763.

James and Sarah C. Bailey, Dec. 18, 1829.*

John and Marthew Thompson, int. Mar. 31, 1799.

John, Capt., of Rowe [int. Franklin Co.], and Sarah Houston, July 1, 1827.*

John Jr. and Lucy D. [int. omits D.] Gaskill, Nov. 17 [1836].*

Lucy and John O. Houston, June 17 [1819].*

Margret and Patrick Pebbels, Mar. 8, 1757.*

Uzial of S. Hadley, and Polly Clark, int. Nov. 28, 1802.

THAYER (see There), Gideon S. of Belchertown, and Eunice A. Wheeler, int. Mar. 20, 1835.

John 3d of Belchertown, and Polly Hayward, int. Mar. 16, 1807.

Lucinda, Mrs., and William Gaylord, int. Jan. 9, 1830.

Nathen of Boston, and Rhene Clough, int. Jan. 5, 1805.

Susannah of Belchertown, and James Thurston, int. Mar. 3, 1817.

THERE (see Thayer), Daniel of Chesterfield, and Mary Hathaway, int. July 12, 1777.

* Intention also recorded.

THOMAS, David and Elisebeth [int. Elisabeth] Cowan, Apr. 24, 1750.*
David and Elisabeth Harper, Nov. 18, 1755.*
Jenney of Worcester, and William Croset, Dec. 10, 1778.*
Martha and John Maklem, Jan. 9, 1772.*
Mary and John Hamilton Jr., int. May 21, 1786.
Susanna of Worcester, and James Torner, Apr. 1, 1760.*

THOMPSON (see Thomson, Tompson, Tomson), Andrew and Almedia Keep, int. Mar. 15, 1810.
Daniel and Sarah Conkey, int. Nov. 15, 1801.
Daniel, Dr., and Caroline Augusta Hunt, int. June 2, 1827.
Dorcas and John Berry, int. Apr. 15, 1812.
Dorcas and Benjamin North, int. May 10, 1845.
Edmond and Mrs. Sylvia C. Boyington, int. Oct. 28, 1842.
Elizebeth and Ezekiel Conkey, int. Dec. 24, 1784.
Elizebeth and Jonathen Harkness, int. July 31, 1789.
Erastus C. and Sarah H. Gray, int. Aug. 31, 1830.
Hannah and Pliney Wilson, int. Oct. 8, 1808.
Hannah, wid., and William Millen "Cenior," int. Dec. 31, 1814.
Isaac and Mercia Horr, int. Apr. 14, 1822.
James 2d and Hannah Gray, int. Mar. 4, 1788.
James Jr. and Metilda Parce, int. Mar. 6, 1796.
John and Prudence Clark [int. Cleark], Dec. 13, 1757.*
John Jr. and Katuran Clark, int. Aug. 21, 1788.
John M. and Hannah Millen, int. Apr. 27, 1812.
Joseph and Margaret Croset, June 30, 1774.*
Martha and Samuel Keruth, int. Sept. 16, 1786.
Martha and James Hyde, int. Feb. 11, 1787.
Marthew and Squire Abbet, int. Oct. 19, 1795.
Marthew and John Taylor, int. Mar. 31, 1799.
Mary [int. Tompson] and John Lindsey, Dec. 17, 1761.*
Mary and George Washington Hoar, int. Mar. 8, 1834.
Molley and John McColloch, int. Mar. 31 [1788].
Molley and Joel Conkey, int. Jan. 2, 1796.
Peleg P. and Pamilia White, int. Mar. 19, 1833.
Perm....a, wid., 35, b. Ashfield, d. Sylvenus —— and Martha of Chesterfield, and Cheney Abbott, widr., Aug. 30, 1846.*
Sarah and John Cole, int. Jan. 19, 1795.
Sarah, Mrs., and Ebenezer Gray, Jan. 23, 1828.*
Thomas and Jean Meklem, Sept. 11, 1777.*
Tho[ma]s [int. Tomas] and Mecy [int. Mecie] Smith, Aug. 31, 1780.*

* Intention also recorded.

THOMSON (see Thompson, Tompson, Tomson), Susanah and
 Elisha Conkey, int. Oct. 28, 1782.
Susannah and Samuel Carruth Jr., int. Mar. 23, 1806.

THORNTON, Ester and James Fergeson, Dec. 4, 1746.

THORP, Lucey and William Bosworth, int. Nov. 7, 1802.

THURBER, Joanna and Tisdall [int. Tisdle] Crossman, Dec. 22,
 1825.*
Ozias and Mrs. Phebe Gaskell [int. Miss Phebe Gaskill], Aug. 30,
 1825.*
William M. and Harriet L. Williams, int. Dec. 4, 1847.
William W. and Pamelia [int. Permelia] Wheeler, May 2,
 1822.*

THURSTING (see Thurston, Thusten, Thuston), Mary, wid.,
 and Reuben Westcott, int. June 13, 1839.

THURSTON (see Thursting, Thusten, Thuston), Betsy and
 Thomas Barnes, ———, 1836.
Emily and Forris Jepson, int. Mar. 16, 1838.
James and Susannah Thayer, int. Mar. 3, 1817.
James and Maria Gleson, int. Nov. 1, 1827.
John T. and Betsy M. Jepson, int. Apr. 4, 1842.
Margret and Elijah Lane, int. May 23, 1829.
Marilla and Job S. Miller, int. Feb. 23, 1847.
Mary and John T. Jurden, int. Jan. 8, 1830.
Stillman and Esther M. Conkey, Apr. 14, 1842.*
Susan [int. Susannah], 28, d. Paul and Mary, and William H.
 Goodenough [int. Goodenow], Nov. 24, 1846.*
Susan M. and Oliver Hill, int. Apr. 17, 1843.
Thomas and Lydia Westcott, int. May 4, 1837.

THUSTEN (see Thursting, Thurston, Thuston), Elizabeth and
 Caleb Tilson, int. Mar. 18, 1803.

THUSTON (see Thursting, Thurston, Thusten), Mary and Elias
 Shaw, int. Mar. 24, 1799.
Mary and Robert Abecrombie, int. Oct. 7, 1799.
Paul and Mary Rogers, int. Jan. 8, 1790.
Paul and Mary Moody, int. Aug. 31, 1806.

TILSON, Caleb of Greenwich, and Elizabeth Thusten, int. Mar.
 18, 1803.

* Intention also recorded.

TINGLEY, Matilda of Attleborough, and Jesse F. Peck, int. Nov. 19, 1819.

TINKHAM, Levi and Polly Barlow, int. June 10, 1788.

TOLMAN, John C. and Sarah Jane Whipple, Oct. 4, 1837.*

TOLYMON, Phebee and Callister Gray, int. May 13, 1799.

TOMPSON (see Thompson, Thomson, Tomson), Eunice and David Conkey 2d, int. May 25, 1797.
George and Mary Croset, Dec. 5, 1765.*
James and Mary Cowan, July 24, 1766.*

TOMSON (see Thompson, Thomson, Tompson), Lois and Nathan C. Perry, int. Mar. 30, 1843.
Sophia J., b. Palmer, d. Asa and Ruth, and Francis Kingman, Mar. 9, 1848.*

TORNER, James and Susanna Thomas, Apr. 1, 1760.*
Sarah and Joseph M[c]Craken, Feb. 12, 1760.*

TORRANCE (see Torrence), Allexander and Presila Heket, Mar. 2, 1781.*
Martha [int. Torranc] and Matthew Rinken, June 26, 1777.*
Mary of Belchiretown, and John Rinken, Oct. 6, 1774.*
Thomas [int. Torrans] of Braintree, and Agness Cochran, Oct. 9, 1766.*

TORRENCE (see Torrance), John of Belchertown, and Chloe Bartlett, int. Mar. 3, 1810.

TOWER, Betsy and Eli Haskell, int. Feb. 16, 1808.
Isaac Jr. and Polly Haskell, int. Feb. 17, 1809.
Lurana and Nathan Pettingel, int. Nov. 25, 1808.
Sibeliah and Luther Pomroy, int. Jan. 4, 1812.

TOWN, Polley of Greenwich, and Jonathan F. Sears, int. Aug. 16, 1813.

TURNER, Abigail and William Harkness, Dec. 12 [1816].*
Caroline and John Willace, int. May 21, 1847.
Jonathan and Eliza Bartlett, int. Feb. —, 1825.
Jonathan, widr. [int. omits widr.], 55, s. Ellis and Thankful, and Persis Allen, Jan. 29, 1846.*
Louisa and Clark Sumner, int. Jan. 12, 1846.
Zylphia and Nahum Wallis, Nov. 6, 1823.*

* Intention also recorded.

TYLOR, Amos of Hinsdale, and wid. [of] Phinius Larrabee, int. Dec. 5, 1807.

VATAKIN, Mary Maria of Amherst, and Moses Hannum, int. Mar. 4, 1848.

VAUGHAN (see Vaughn), Sally and John Wheeler, int. July 23, 1807.

VAUGHN (see Vaughan), Thomas Jr. and Lois Shaw, int. May 29, 1813.

VINTON, Horice of Monson, and Lucy Hunter, Oct. 20 [1824].*

WALKER, Henry of Upton, and Mrs. Mary Boynton, Apr. 12 [1830].*
Loise of Hardwick, and Luice [Lewis] Baker, int. May 14, 1786.
Sarah of Adams, and Thomas Johnston, int. July 30, 1792.

WALLAS (see Walless, Wallis), Jam[e]s of Ruttland, and Mary M[c]Cleland, Apr. 8, 1756.*

WALLESS (see Wallas, Wallis), John of Colrain [int. Coldrain], and Agness Linsey, Oct. 13, 1761.*

WALLIS (see Wallas, Walless), Charlotte and Austin W. Conky [dup. and int. Conkey], Apr. 29, 1830.*
Chloe and Thomas Heydon Jr. [int. omits Jr. and adds Lt.], Nov. 27 [1823].*
Nahum and Zylphia Turner, Nov. 6, 1823.*

WARD, Berthia [int. Bethiah] and Horatio Seagraves, May 9, 1834.*
Bethiah of Belchertown, and Nathaniel [int. Nathanil] Cook, Nov. 23, 1834.*
Elmira and Eseek Cook 2d, int. Dec. 7, 1844.
Hannah and Abel Brown, Dec. 17, 1829.*
John Jr. of Balchertown, and Polly Davison, int. Jan 11, 1807.
John B. of Ware Village, and Louisia Cook, int. Apr. 17, 1837.
Joseph G., 27, b. Canidy, s. Joseph and Greecash of Canidy, and Angeline A. Buffum, Mar. 2, 1847.*
Lucretia and Nathaniel K. Batchelor, Mar. 30, 1841.*
Martha and Aron H. Ingram, int. Aug. 21, 1841.
Mary and Philander S. Knight, June 11, 1837.
Moses L., s. Moses of Belchertown, and Sally Kingman, Apr. 3, 1845.*

* Intention also recorded.

WARNER, Cullen of New Marlborough, and Lucy Cooley, Oct. 10, 1819.*

WARRAN, Zubee and John Barber, int. July 17, 1785.

WASHBURN, Nathan [int. of Easton], and Mrs. Polly B. Sibley, Feb. 16, 1828.*
Pattey and David Conkey Jr., int. May 31, 1801.
Salley and Ebenezer Gats, int. Nov. 30, 1797.

WEBSTER, Cha[rle]s N., 24, s. Ezekiel and Matilda, and Sarah E. Webster, Mar. 28, 1849.*
Martha L., 21, d. Augustus and Amy, and Warren C. Wedge, Mar. 28, 1849.*
Sarah E., 24, d. Augustus and Amy, and Cha[rle]s N. Webster, Mar. 28, 1849.*

WEDGE, Amy and Calvin Chapin, int. Oct. 30, 1840.
Ataline, 23, d. Lemuel C. and Cintha, and Legrand C. Sheldon, Sept. 10, 1846.*
Esther C., 22, d. Lemuel C. and Cyntha, and Orrin [int. Orin] E. Darling, June 13, 1848.
Lamuel C. of Shutesbury [int. Shutesbary], and Cynthia Wescott [int. Cyntha Westcott], Nov. 11, 1821.*
Lemuel C. and Lucy Jillson, int. Dec. 15, 1842.
Naham and Rhoda Chapin, int. Mar. 10, 1812.
Roxsa and Joseph Hodgekins Jr., int. Aug. 12, 1821.
Warren C., 21, s. Lemuel and Cynthia, and Martha L. Webster, Mar. 28, 1849.*

WEEKS, Theverick of Petersham, and Lydia Borden, int. Feb. 4, 1807.

WELLINGTON (see Willington).

WELLMAN, Almira and Elem Osborn, both of Enfield, Apr. —, 1818.

WESCOTT (see Westcott), Cynthia [int. Cyntha Westcott] and Lamuel C. Wedge, Nov. 11, 1821.*
Harriet M., Mrs., d. William Wilson, and William Newell, Apr. 24, 1844.*

WESTCOTT (see Wescott), Amy and Lt. Alanson Chapin, Mar. 28 [1825].*
Jared T. and Sally C. Smith, Dec. 29 [1829].*

* Intention also recorded.

WESTCOTT, Jared T. and Ann Baker, June 20, 1838, in Marcellus, Onondaga Co., N. Y.
Lydia and Thomas Thurston, int. May 4, 1837.
Reuben and Mary Thursting, wid., int. June 13, 1839.
Walter and Harriet M. Willson, int. Nov. 18, 1833.

WESTON, Zechariah and Emeline Gould, Dec. 16, 1833.*

WETHERBY, Laura [int. Witherby] and David Millen, May 15 [1817].

WHEELER, Benjamin of New Marlborough, and Anna Dunn, int. Sept. 2, 1815.
Chancelor L. and Catherine A. Crossett, [int.] Jan. 10, 1848.
Clarisa [int. Clarissa H.] and Gennet [int. Genett] Brown, Apr. 18, 1830.*
Epheriam of Shutesbery, and Rebekah Crosett, int. Nov. 11, 1798.
Eunice A. and Gideon S. Thayer, int. Mar. 20, 1835.
John of Greenwich, and Sally Vaughan, int. July 23, 1807.
Mary Ann Augusta and Emery Boynton, int. July 19, 1834.
Nathaniel of Shutesbury, and Fathfull Herrington, int. June 25, 1808.
Pamelia [int. Permelia] and William W. Thurber, May 2, 1822.*

WHILER, Ephriam and Hannah Marks, "Both of Quaben [int. Quabin] So Called," Nov. 10, 1746.*

WHIPPLE, Abigail J. and George W. Chapman [int. Chatman], Nov. 3 [1836].*
Azubah [int. Azuba] and David Packard, Sept. 30 [1819].*
Brookey [int. Broocky] W. and Isreal H. Gibbs, Mar. 17 [1825].*
James G. and Ann Maria Dodge, Apr. 2, 1837.*
Joseph and Dolley Cahoon, int. Feb. 23, 1806.
Mary Ann and John M. Keth [int. Keith], Sept. 16, 1833.*
Sarah Jane and John C. Tolman, Oct. 4, 1837.*

WHITE, James and Mary Cowdin [int. Cowden], July 4, 1776.*
John of Belshiertown, and Elisabith Sloan, int. Apr. 21, 1783.
Levince and Jermiah Hase, int. June 10, 1791.
Pamilia and Peleg P. Thompson, int. Mar. 19, 1833.

WHITEHOM, Marcy of New Salem, and Moses Gray, int. July 8, 1793.

WHITEMORE, Harriet [int. Herriat] and Ammon Cook, Apr. 7 [1825].*

* Intention also recorded.

WHITEMORE, Lucy and Luther Lincoln, Mar. 7, 1826.*

WHITNEY, Lucy and Obed Hunt, int. Apr. 28, 1787.

WHITTEN, Abigail of Braintree, and Nathan Prat, int. July 30, 1779.

WILDER, Haley of Stirling, and Stacy Linzie [male], int. July 24, 1816.
Lucius E. of Philipston [int. Phillipston], and Emeline Cook, ——— [rec. during year preceding Apr. 13, 1839; int. July 20, 1838].*
Moses and Joanna Powers, " Both of Roadtown So Called," int. Nov. 6, 1756.

WILLACE, John and Caroline Turner, int. May 21, 1847.

WILLEY (see Williey, Wyllie), Elisabeth of Worcester, and Jonathan Gray, Mar. 8, 1774.*

WILLIAMS, Anne of Shutesbury [int. Anna of Shuttsbury], and Jonathan Leach, May 26, 1784.*
Harriet L. of Amherst, and William M. Thurber, int. Dec. 4, 1847.
Moses of Amherst, and Luriah Bartlet, int. Oct. 7, 1814.

WILLIEY (see Willey, Wyllie), Sam[ue]ll of Worcester, and Eunes Conkey, int. Feb. 17, 1783.

WILLINGTON, Luke of Sterling, and Eliza Benit, int. Mar. 10, 1811.

WILLIS (see Willace).

WILLSON (see Wilson), Harriet M. and Walter Westcott, int. Nov. 18, 1833.

WILSON (see Willson), Allice and Isaac Cowan Hunter, int. Feb. 16, 1795.
Amy of Belchertown, and John Harkness, int. Mar. 6, 1837.
Anna M. and Welcom Allen, Sept. 22, 1822.*
Asa Jr. [int. Willson] of Belchertown, and Rachel Aldrich, Aug. 27, 1828.*
Daniel of Belchertown, and Vesta Harkness, int. Dec. 8, 1810.
Esther of Belchertown, and John Harkness Jr., int. Dec. 8, 1810.
Harriot [int. Herriot] and Daniel Robins [int. Robbins], May 21 [1818].*
Lucy and Isaac Lazell, int. Mar. 12, 1808.

* Intention also recorded.

WILSON, Martha of Okham, and Elihu Gray, int. Aug. 20, 1791.

Pliney of Belchertown, and Hannah Thompson, int. Oct. 8, 1808.

Samuel [int. Samll Willson of Colran] of Colrain, and Sarah [int. Saram] Cowan, Nov. 24, 1761.*

Sam[ue]l [int. Samll Willson] of Colrain, and Agness Dunlap, Dec. 9, 1767.*

Sarah and Joseph Robeson, int. Sept. 22, 1793.

William Jr. and Margret Abercrombie, int. Sept. 25, 1803.

WINSLOW, Bettiah, Mrs., of Belchertown, and Ebeneazer Austin, int. Apr. 6, 1846.

Mary A. and Mendall Latham, int. May 11, 1834.

WINTERS, David and Poley Newcomb, int. July 22, 1798.

WOOD (see Woods), Coziah [int. Cuziah] and Samuel Buckmun, Mar. 6, 1780.*

George N. of New York City, and Joanna C. Gaskill, int. Sept. 10, 1834.

Hannah and Asaph Lyon, int. Sept. 9, 1775.

Ichabod Jr. of Enfield, and Lucy Rider, int. May 25, 1816.

Irra and Mary Montgomery, both of Enfield, Hampshire Co., June 20, 1839.

James, Dr., of Springfield, and Ana Hollond, int. Sept. 25, 1784.

Johnthan [int. Johnathan] and Fanny Hayden, Mar. 3, 1842.*

Live [Levi?] and Bethani Fuller, int. Oct. 19, 1786.

Lucy and Frederick Denio, int. Nov. 29, 1773.

Lucy of Enfield, Hampshire Co., and Giles Rider, Apr. 16, 1822.*

Lydia and George W. Buckland, Dec. 6, 1826.*

Mary, wid., and Samuel Orcutt, int. Aug. 27, 1808.

Rebekah [int. Rebecca] of Enfield, and John Rider, Nov. 10, 1819.*

Salvenus and Polly Gray, int. Jan. 1, 1797.

Sophia and Justin Packard, Dec. 26, 1822.*

WOODS (see Wood), Charles N. and Hepsibah Southwick, int· Dec. 27, 1834.

Daniel of New Braintree, and Nabby Joslin, wid., int. Mar. 17, 1815.

Mary of Shutes[b]ery, and John Atkinson, int. May 22, 1790.

WORKS, Elcey of Shutesbury, and Hezekiah H. Pierce, int. July 19, 1839.

* Intention also recorded.

WORKS, Rachel and John Maklem, int. Feb. 7, 1767.

WRIGHT (see Right), Sally and James Bruce, int. July 17, 1800.

WYLLIE (see Willey, Williey), George S. of Ware, and Margaret Gates, int. Sept. 2, 1843.

WYMAN, Patty of Wenchendon, and Jasper Stearns, int. Oct. 10, 1807.

YOUNG, John and Margaret Conky, Feb. 22, 1759.*
John and Elisabeth Smith, int. Feb. 2, 1760.
Mary and William Cambell [int. Cambel], Nov. 18, 1766.*
Rachel and James Pebels, May 5, 1768.*
Rob[er]t of Athull, and Elisabeth Gray, Dec. 20, 1764.*

ZUILL, Francis [int. Frances] and Simeon Peck, Oct. 17, 1776.*

UNIDENTIFIED.

———, Rebekah of "ye Union So Calld," and Rob[er]t Meklem, int. Sept. 7, 1751.
———, Sarah of Lovrik [Leverett ?], and James Croset, int. June 13, 1778.

* Intention also recorded.

PELHAM DEATHS.

PELHAM DEATHS.

To the year 1850.

ABBOTT, Rachel, w. Cheney, Nov. 30, 1839.

ABERCROMBIE, Fanny, d. David and Mary, Apr. 5, 1839.
Ira, s. Isaac and Marthew, Apr. 5, 1797.
James, Dec. 14, 1836.
Jemima, w. William, Feb. 13, 1808.
Lucindia, w. Samuel, July 27, 1807.
Margart, w. Robert (Ebercrombie), Nov. 2, 1765.
Robert, Dec. 19, 1834.
Sinday, d. Isaac and Marthew, July 11, 1800.
William, Mar. 28, 1822.
William H., s. Isaac and Martha, Oct. 20, 1811.

ALDRICH, Olive, w. Asahel, July 10, 1825.

ALLEN, Charles Medcalf, s. Jesse and Anna, Aug. 17, 1810.
Jesse, Feb. 27, 1818.
Nancy, d. Jesse and Anna, Apr. 12, 1816.
Phinehas, Mar. 25, 1833.
Susan A., b. Deerfield, d. David and Hannah, lung fever, Feb. 4,
    1846, a. 4m. 5d.

ALLEXANDER, Margaret, d. John and Jennet, Mar. [torn ;
    prob. 1772–6].
[torn], h. [torn], Nov. 2 [? 1765–6 ; torn].

ARNOLD, Rhoda, w. Samuel, May 6, 1826.
Samuel, Nov. 19, 1838.
Suzanna, w. Smith (Arnold), Oct. 28, 1807.
Welcome, Sept. 24, 1826.
———, inf. Smith and Suzanna, Oct. 28, 1807.

AUSTIN, Mary, m., d. Ebenezur Boynton and Mary, June 9,
    1845, a. 44.

BABBIT (see Babbott), Betsey, wid., b. Taunton, consumption,
    May 22, 1848, a. 80.

BABBIT, Jonathan, m., b. Freetown, R. I., fever, May 6, 1844, a.
76 [*sic*; rec. 1849].

BABBOTT (see Babbit), Jonathan, May 7, 1843.

BAILEY, Clarissa, w. Jedediah, Apr. 21, 1838.
Norman Westley, s. Sidney and Marsha, Jan. 9, 1842, a. 1.

BAKER, Isaac [h. Rebekah], Dec. 13, 1820.
John, s. Ezkial and Hannah, Nov. 1, 1800.
Jonathan, Oct. 27, 1821.
Rebekah, w. Isaac [dec'd], Dec. 23, 1820.
————, inf. John and Hannah, Feb. 23, 1821.

BALDWIN, Sarah, wid., Apr. 1, 1837.

BALLOU, Alonzo, s. Leonard, Mar. 9, 1820.
Bethany, d. Stephen, Oct. 18, 1817.
Edward, Mar. —, 1833.
Eliab, s. Stephen, Oct. 13, 1817.
John Braley, s. Learned and Pheebe, Dec. 21, 1823.
Susannah, d. Leonard, Sept. 26, 1817.
Theadore Sampson, s. Leonard and Pebe, Nov. 13, 1829.
Welcome, s. Stephen and Alice, June 22, 1817.

BARBER, Chaster, s. John and Azubah, Nov. 22, 1802.

BARNES, Martha A., b. Hardwick, d. Ansel and Deborah,
Nov. 6, 1848, a. 8.
Vila, w. Dwight (Barns), Apr. 2, 1830.

BARRY (see Berry), James, h. Jean, Sept. 4, 1783.

BARTLET (see Bartlett), Phebe, Nov. 25, 1843.

BARTLETT (see Bartlet), Lucy, w. Alexander, June 20, 1838.
Rebecca, w. Lemuel, Feb. 1, 1832. " Formerly from Shutesbury."
Samuel Baxter, s. Horace, Jan. 10, 1838.

BENTSON, Artemas, Apr. 28, 1841, a. 14.

BERRY, (see Barry), Betsey, w. John, Nov. 12, 1811.
Jean, w. James, Jan. 4, 1808.

BLAIR, Calvin Dunia, s. Samuel and Ruba, July 23, 1822.

BOYINGTON (see Boynton), Jeremiah, s. Olive, wid., July 12,
1839.
William C., Feb. 10, 1841.

BOYNTON (see Boyington), Alfa, Sept. 23, 1818.
Anna, d. Eben[eze]r and Mary, Oct. 5, 1811.
Asa, Feb. 22, 1828.
Ebenezar, s. Eben[eze]r and Mary, Dec. 8, 1808.
Ebenezer, June 22, 1822.
Emory, m., s. Ebenezur and Mary, consumption, Feb. 24, 1849,
    a. 40.
Silas, June 23, 1838.

BRAINARD, Joseph, s. Elijah and Parthina, Oct. 31, 1810.

BRIGGS, Francis Wayland, s. Isaac and Betsey, Sept. 23, 1826.

BRIGHAM, Bashua [dup. Basha] Hamilton, d. Barna and Anna
    [dup. Barney and Anne], Sept. 28, 1806.
Nehemiah [dup. Nehimiah] Hinds, s. Barna and Anna, Sept. 18,
    1811.
Tilly, s. Barna and Anna, Sept. 26, 1811.

BROWN, Lucy Ann, d. R. Brown Jr., Oct. 21, 1829.
Milton, s. Ezra Esq., Oct. 27, 1837.
William, Mar. 28, 1814.

BRUCE, Lendol, s. Abijah and Rizpah, killed by " the fall of a
    tree," May 30, 1806, in Dover, Vt.
———, inf. s. Abijah and Rizpah, Apr. 15, 1821.

BRYANT, Elizebath, wid. Seth, Feb. 20, 1823.
Nancy, d. Ichabod and w., Mar. 10, 1815.

BUFFOM (see Buffum), Joseph C., s. Thomas and Betsy, Nov.
    20, 1840.

BUFFUM (see Buffom), William Foster, s. Tho[ma]s, Mar. 30,
    1837.

BUMP, Isaac, s. Zenes and Bridgett, Nov. 26, 1810.

BUTTERWORTH, Welcome, May 7, 1831.

CARTER, Bethia J., b. New Salem, w. John, consumption, Aug.
    6, 1848, a. 21.

CENEDY, Betsey, Feb. 12, 1844.

CHAISE, Clarissa, w. Robert (Chase), Oct. 24, 1828.

CHAPEN (see Chapin), Battsey [dup. Chapens], d. Luther and
    Mary, Mar. 26, 1802.

CHAPEN, ———, ch. Alanson and Amy, Feb. 7, 1835.

CHAPIN (see Chapen), Almira, w. Ens. Alanson, Jan. 16, 1824.
Elizabeth, w. Elijah, Jan. 30, 1825.
Hirum Johnson, s. Alanson and Amy, Dec. 19, 1834.

CHASE (see Chaise).

CLARK, John, h. Sarah, Sept. 1, 1785, in 80th y.
Samuel, Apr. 6, 1831, a. 78.
Samuel Wild, s. Samuel and Susanna, Oct. 8, 1828.
Sarah, w. John [dec'd], Mar. 13, 1787, in 70th y.

CLEAVELAND (see Cleavland), George W., s. Aseph and Nancy,
    Aug. 20, 1840.

CLEAVLAND (see Cleaveland), Elvira, Feb. 8, 1838.

CLOUGH, Sybil, d. Benjamin, Apr. 14, 1808.

COMSTOCK (see Cumstock), Lorenzo B., Sept. 17, 1843.

CONKEY (see Conky), Betsey, d. Warren and Polly, July 14, 1831,
    a. 16.
David, Mar. 31, 1828.
Dolley, d. Elisha and Susanah, June 17, 1794.
Elleazar, s. Maj. John and Margaret, Feb. 7, 1808.
Elisha, Mar. 27, 1827.
Elisha 2d, Mar. 14, 1826.
Hannah, d. Thomas and Elizebeth, Aug. 25, 1795.
Isaac, h. Rebecah, Mar. 14, 1810.
James, s. Elisha and Susannah, Apr. 9, 1802.
John Esq., Apr. 15, 1824.
[Josh‡]ua, s. John and Margret, Apr. 12, 1790.
Lactie, d. Thomas and Elizabeth, Aug. 15, 1803.
Levi Washburn, s. David and Martha, Aug. 20, 1803.
Lezetta, d. Isaac and Vashti, Aug. 10, 1811.
Margret, w. Maj. John, Feb. 1, 1801.
Mary, w. Alexander, Apr. 1, 1820.
Mary, d. David and Patty, Oct. 11, 1843, a. 29.
Molly, w. John, Sept. 5, 1811.
Nehemiah, s. Alexander and Mary, Dec. 11, 1793.
Patty, w. David, fever, Oct. 1, 1848, a. 74.
Rebecah, w. Isaac, Jan. 30, 1796.
Robert, Nov. 28, 1826.
Sally, Feb. 28, 1823.

‡ Torn in original record ; supplied from town copy.

CONKEY, Sarah, d. Elisha and Susanah, Sept. 18, 1797.

CONKY (see Conkey), Martha, d. Will[ia]m [torn], Jan. 29, 1749.
Mary, w. [torn], Sept. 9, 1754.

COOK, Abner, s. Adams and Susanna, Sept. 12, 1806.
Adennis, Apr. 29, 1833.
Francis O. [dup. Olney], s. Olney and Emily, fracture of the head, Jan. 10, 1848 [dup. 1838], a. 8 y. 9 m.
Harriet M. [dup. Mariah], d. Olney and Emily [dup. Emely], inflamation in the head, Sept. 10, 1843, a. 1 y. 4 m.
Ira Gray, s. Zebina and Mary, Oct. 8, 1822.
Joanna, w. Silas, Feb. 6, 1815.
Louisa, w. Simon, Jan. 3, 1844, a. 37.
Lucy, d. Lewis and Nancy, June 30, 1829.
Mary, w. Zebina, Oct. 10, 1822.
Preston, s. Hannah, July 14, 1828.
Silas, Feb. 12, 1842, a. 88.
Silvestus, s. Simon and Louisa, Feb. 14, 1844.
Washington, s. Simon and Louisa, Jan. 2, 1841.

COOLEY, Benjamin Walker [dup. Waker], s. Obediah and Lucy, June 16, 1809.

COWAN, George, h. Sarah, Oct. 28, 1765.
George, Jan. 24, 1808.
Justice, s. James and Mary, Aug. 22, 1803.
Lucy, d. James and Mary, Aug. 4, 1803.
Lucy,.d. James and Margart, June 22, 1808.
Lyman, inf. s. William and Eunice, Jan. 30, 1809.
Margart, w. James, Apr. 23, 1808.
Mary, d. James and Mary, Aug. 2, 1803.

CRAWFORD, Anne, d. John and Susannah, Aug. 1, 1772.
Harvey, s. Levi and Patty, Sept. 18, 1810.
John, s. John and Susanna, Aug. 14, 1761.
John, h. Isabel dec'd, Sept. 17, 1761.
John, s. John and Susannah, Sept. 24, 1767.
Susanna, w. Dea. John, Nov. 5, 1808.

CROSET (see Crosett), [John‡] Savige, s. Archabald and Sarah, Apr. 3, 1770.

CROSETT (see Croset), Anna, d. Robert and Nancy, Feb. 16, 1795.

‡ Torn in original record; supplied from town copy.

CROSETT, Fanney, d. Isreal and Marthew, Aug. 8, 1796.
Nancy, w. Robert, Apr. 11, 1808.
Robert, h. Nancy, July 27, 1811.
Robert, s. Robert and Nancy, Nov. 6, 1811.
William, s. Robert and Nancy, Jan. 6, 1806.

CROSIER, Arthur, Dec. 1, 1843.

CUMSTOCK (see Comstock), Leonard D., s. William and Elmira,
    Sept. 13, 1843, a. 20 m.

CUNDEL (see Cundell), Fanny W., w. Capt. John, May 11, 1827.

CUNDELL (see Cundel), Abner, Capt., June 12, 1828.

CURTICE, Oliver, Mar. 17, 18[1]5.

DANFORTH, Benjamin, s. Samuel and Mehitable, Mar. 9, 1814.
Elijah, Oct. 28, 1814.
Richard Sears, s. Samuel and Mehitable, Aug. 4, 1818.

DANIELS, Lucy, w. Joseph, Apr. 5, 1830.
Ruth, d. Joseph and Lucy, Aug. 26, 1814.

DAVINSON, Patty, wid., Feb. 23, 1829.
Phineas, May 5, 1826.

DAVIS, Elizabeth, wid., Oct. 26, 1836.
Sally, [w.] Moses, consumption, Sept. 15, 1848, a. 50.

DICK, John, s. Tho[ma]s [torn], Sept. 17, 1749.
John, h. Jean, Apr. 24, 1781.
Lois, d. Tho[ma]s and [torn], [Jan.‡] 28, 1776.
[? Dick] Margaret [about 1777].
M[ary‡]an, d. [torn], Feb. 1, 1741.
[Pr]udence, d. [torn], Aug. 27, 1759.
Rob[er]t, s. Tho[ma]s [torn], Jan. 11, 1750.
[T]homas, h. Margare[t], Sept. 11, 1774.
[torn]hn, s. John and Is[torn], Feb. 10, 1758.

DICKINSON, Esther Maria, d. Henry and Esthe, Oct. 3, 1834.

DITSON, Josiah, Aug. 21, 1840.

DOANE (see Done).

DODGE, Axey, d. Nathaniel and w., Mar. 18, 1814.
Nathaniel, July 21, 1814.

        ‡ Torn in original record ; supplied from town copy.

Dodge, Ora, s. John C. and Lovcia, drowned, May 19, [18]48, a. 17.

DONE, Emeziah, Feb. 1, 1821.

DRAPER, Alonso Orne, s. Learned O. and Anna, July 31, 1830.
Lewis, Nov. 5, 1843.
Sally, w. Lyman, Mar. 2, 1827.

DUNLAP, Agness, w. James, Dec. 27, 1813.
James, s. James and Margaret, [Fe‡]b. 16, 1774.
James, Jan. 4, 1815.
W[illia]m, second son John and Mary, Sept. 28, 1822.
William, May 24, 1837.

DWELLEY (see Dwelly), Deborah, Nov. 1, 1822.

DWELLY (see Dwelley), Aaron, pauper, old age, ———.
[Rec. Jan. 23, 1850.]

EATON, Hannah, d. Marson and Charlotty, Oct. 15, 1811.
Julia H., w. Calvin D., June 20, 1840.
Madison, Oct. 19, 1836.
Rufus, Feb. 3, 1823.

EDSON, Seth, Feb. 17, 1818.

FAIRBANKS, Nancy, d. Stephen and Nancy, Dec. 28, 1815.

FALES, Caroline Augusta, d. Daniel and Elizabeth, Aug. 8, 1836.
Emeline, d. Daniel and Lucy, Feb. 22, 1820.
Francis Edwin, s. Daniel and Elizabeth, Sept. 25, 1829.
Joseph [h. Sarah], Feb. 9, 1818.
Sarah, w. Joseph [dec'd], June 25, 1818.
Silas, s. Lois, wid., Mar. 8, 1828.

FELTON, Augustus Wales, s. Nathan and Mary, Aug. 20, 1811.
Charles Shepherd, s. Nathan and Mary, Aug. 21, 1811.

FERGUSON, John [torn]. [Prob. rec. about 1777.]

FISH, Mary Angeline, d. Cummings and Esther, Dec. 12, 1834.

FRY, Bathsheba, d. Benjamin and Siene, Feb. 7, 1828.
Siene, w. Benjamin, Feb. 17, 1828.

GATES, Ann, [w.] Levi, consumption, Mar. 21, 1847, a. 48.

‡ Torn in original record ; supplied from town copy.

GILLMORE, [Da‡]vid, s. Will[ia]m and E[lsa], Feb. 25, 1749.
[E‡]lse, d. W[illia]m [torn], Oct. 24, 1753.
Else, w. William, [Jan.‡] 18, 1774.
[R‡]ob[er]t, s. Will[ia]m [torn], Aug. 16, 1745.
[R‡]ob[er]t, s. W[illia]m [torn], Apr. 18, 1756.

GOLD, Polly, w. Joseph, July 5, 1823.
———, inf. Miner, July 3, 1836.

GOOLD (see Gould), Judith, d. Haffield and Betsey, Sept. 4, 1811.

GOULD (see Goold), James, Sept. 14, 1833.

GRAHAM, Richard Crouch, Rev., h. Madam Molley, Feb. 26, 1771.

GRAY, Aaron, h. Ruth, Feb. 4, 1805.
Abigal, w. Pattrick, Sept. 1, 1795.
Agnes, w. Dea. Eben[e]z[er], Aug. 10, 1831, a. 78.
Amos, Feb. 6, 1823.
Anson, s. Calister and Phebe, Feb. 4, 1800.
Betsy, w. John, Dec. 24, 1840.
Clarisa, d. Eben[eze]r and Agnas, Apr. 7, 1812.
Daniel, Dn. [sic], h. Mary, Dec. 14, 1803.
Ebenezer, Dea., Jan. 18, 1834.
Elizabath, w. Jonathan, Oct. 11, 1808.
Ira, s. John and Battsey, Oct. 22, 1802.
Isabal, d. Jerimiah and Margaret, June 22, 1809.
Isabel, d. Moses and Marcy, July 2, 1801.
James, s. Eben[e]z[e]r and Agnas, Apr. 8, 1802.
Jean, w. William, Aug. 12, 1780.
Jerimiah, s. Jerimiah and Margaret, Sept. 4, 1803, in Greenwich.
Jonathen, h. Elizabeth, Jan. 11, 1801.
Joseph Wiley, s. Jonathen and Elizabeth, June 19, 1778.
Levi, s. Justice and Lucy, Feb. 3, 1799.
Lowes, w. Pattrick, Nov. 17, 1799.
Margaret, w. Jonathan, Dec. 8, [177‡]1.
Matthew, Dea., Mar. 24, 1803.
Molley, d. Jonathen and Elizabeth, June 4, 1788.
Moses, Dec. 16, 1819.
Olive, d. Dea. Matthew and Sarah, Jan. 6. 1775.
Pheebe, w. Calister, Jan. 18, 1802.
Salomy Right, d. Nathaniel and Philena, Aug. 28, 1811.

‡ Torn in original record ; supplied from town copy.

GRAY, Whiticmb, s. Capt. Moses and Mercy, Apr. 11, 1807.
[Wi‡]lliam, h. Jean, Jan. 17, 1759.
[Willi‡]am, s. Jonathan and Margar[torn], Mar. 14, 1759.
[Willi‡]am, [torn] Feb. 21, 1777.
William 2d, s. Jonathen and Margret, Jan. 17, 1771.
————, s. Eliot and Hannah, May 5, 1799.

GRIFFIN, Charles, s. Jonathan and Lydia, July 4, 1816.
Lydia, w. Jonathan, July 5, 1817.
Phebe, d. Jonathan, Apr. 12, 1811.
Vicy, d. Jonathan, Sept. 20, 1814.

GROUT, Clarrissa, w. Rufus, Aug. 31, 1834.
Elizabeth Walker, d. Austin, Mar. 27, 1838.
Huldah, w. Rufus, Feb. 4, 1840.
Joel, July 21, 1835.
Nancy Hall, d. Rufus, Dec. 12, 1834.

HADEN (see Heydon), Josiah, s. Thomas and Molley, Aug. 6, 1799.

HALL, Henry Clay, s. Levi B. and Merah, Sept. 29, 1833.

HAMILTON, Anna, w. Joseph, June 17, 1811.
Eunice, w. Dea. Joseph, Mar. 4, 1813.
Oliver, Sept. 13, 1829.
Rebekah, [w]id., May 25, 1759.
Vina Franklin, d. Oliver and Elizabeth, Aug. 25, 1829.
Willice, May 4, 1833.
[torn]mes, "formerly of Worcester" [torn].
[torn] d. Thomas and Jannet, Aug. 6, 1766.
[torn] s. Robert [torn]bel, Sept. 16, 1772.

HANKS, Ira, Nov. 29, 1836.
John Marshall, s. John and Esther, Jan. 3, 1830.

HANNAM (see Hannum), Nathenial Little, s. David and Elizabeth, Dec. 24, 1806.

HANNUM, (see Hannam), Henry C., s. G. W. and Amelia, inflamation of bowels, Apr. 6, 1845, a. 6 y. 10 m.
John Qincy Adams, s. Grove W. and Pamelia, Dec. 25, 1825.
Leonard Arnold, s. David and Elizabeth, Feb. 7, 1808.
Pliny Jr., s. Pliny and Polly, Sept. 11, 1817.
[torn]ny Jr., s. Pliny and Polly, Sept. 11, 1817.

‡ Torn in original record ; supplied from town copy.

HARDY, Elizabeth Nancy, Jan. 31, 1835.

HARKNESS (see Harkniss), Adeline, Sept. 26, 1836.
Ambrose, s. John, Feb. 24, 1840.
Amy, d. John and Esther, July 30, 1835.
David, Mar. 19, 1816.
Dexter Right, s. Daniel and Betsey, Nov. 6, 1811.
Edward, Feb. 17, 1839.
Esther, w. John, Nov. 5, 1836.
Grove, s. John and Esther, Feb. 13, 1817.
Isaac, s. John and Keziah, May 26, 1807.
John, June 4, 1821.
Lonzo Oliver, s. Daniel and Betsey, May 20, 1810.
Lyda, d. Daniel and Lyda, Mar. 15, 1800.
Lyda, w. Daniel, May 15, 1800.
Polly, wid., Sept. 11, 1829. [This entry has been crossed out.]
Sarah, w. David, July 19, 1825.
Susanna, d. David and w., Nov. 17, 1815.
William, h. Abigail, Dec. 18, 1831.

HARKNISS (see Harkness), James [torn]y (Harkness), Apr. 16, 1776.

HARLOW, Sarrah, w. Thomas, Jan. 21, 1812.
Thomas, Sept. 21, 1826.

HEYDON (see Haden), Chloe, w. Capt. Thomas, Nov. 4, 1833, a. 34.
Thomas, Sept. 21, 1827.
Thomas, Capt., Aug. 30, 1836.

HINDS, Lezetta, d. Dr. Neh[emia]h and Ann, Apr. 5, 1807.

HOAR, Elizabeth, wid. Calvin of Prescott, Jan. 3, 1838.

HODGKINS, Mary Carline, d. Joseph and Sally, Aug. 25, 1811.

HOOD, Esther, w. James, Feb. 4, 1811.
Jonathan, Jan. 7, 1827.
Sally, w. Jonathan, Apr. 26, 1819.
Sally Ann, d. James and Nancy, Feb. 19, 1823.

HOUSTIN (see Houston, Huston), John, s. Robert and Catharine, Feb 20, 1814.

HOUSTON (see Houstin, Huston), Martha, wid., Oct. 21, 1839.

HOWARD, Charles Carrol, Sept. 16, 1838.

HUBBARD, Lucresha, d. Elijah and Abi, Jan. 8, 1801.

HUNTER, Agnas, ———. [Recorded after Susanah, w. James.]
James, July 14, 1807.
John, s. James and Susannah, Aug. 29, 1803.
Susanah [dup. Susannah], w. James, Dec. 18, 1780.

HUSTON (see Houstin, Houston), David, h. Mary, Oct. 29, [torn ; 1765 ?].
Mary, w. David [dec'd], Mar. [torn], 1766.

HYDE, Charles Austin, s. James and Martha, Aug. 27 [1810].
Ruben, Nov. 4, 1819.
Samuel, Dea., Jan. 1, 1810.

INGALS, Diana, w. Samuel, Dec. 3, 1833.

JILLSON (see Jilson), Albert Lyman, Sept. 23, 1831.
Lura, Apr. 29 [?27], 1833.
Nathan, July 17, 1827.
Otis C., Feb. 27, 1837.

JILSON (see Jillson), Susan, Nov. 10, 1843.

JOHNSON (see Johnston), Elizabeth, wid. Hugh, Jan. 9, 1827.
Mary, Jan. 13, 1831.
Rachel, Dec. 1, 1843.

JOHNSTON (see Johnson), Hugh, h. Elizabeth, June 8, 1806.
John, h. Lyda, Aug. 22, 1803.
Molly, July 7, 1807.
Thomas, h. Jean, Nov. 6, 1774.

JONES, Triphena, wid., b. Cumberland, R. I., old age, Jan. 12, 1848, a. 93.

JOSLIN, Joseph, Mar. 5, 1814.
Percies, d. Joseph and w., Oct. 4, 1810.

KENNEDY (see Cenedy).

KING, Cloe. d. Peter and Abigal, Feb. 6, 1802.
Isabel, d. Starlin and Mary, July 16, 1799.
Levi, s. Starlin and Mary, Mar. —, 1785.
Sally, May 24, 1800.

KING, Starlin, h. Mary, Jan. 7, 1799.
William, s. Robert [and Ja‡]nnet, Nov. 14, [177]4.
Will[ia]m, s. Starlin and Mary, Dec. 18, 1797.

KINGMAN, Anna, w. Henry, May 17, 1811.
Mary Augusta, d. Cyrus and Phebe, Mar. 10, 1829.
Sophia J., w. Francis, b. Belchertown, d. Asa Tomson and Ruth,
    consumption, Feb. 17, 1849, a. 19.

KNOX, Sarah, w. Adam, June 15, 1794.

LEE, Lavonia, ch. Ezra and Mary, May 2, 1826.
Maria, ch. Ezra and Mary, Aug. 19, 1825.
Mary, d. Ezra and Mary, Sept. 30, 1822.
Mary, w. Ezra, May 25, 1833.
Noah, s. Ezra and Mary, Apr. 30, 1824.

LINCOLN, Emerson M., s. Marshal T., Mar. 28, 1827.
Lydia J., w. Marshal T., Nov. 27, 1824.

LOVETT, John H., s. Sanford M. and Ann R., scalded, Dec. 29,
    [18]47, a. 3 y. 10 m.

MACUMBER, Esther, d. George and Anna, Oct. 17, 1828.

MANLEY, Hannah, w. Chandler (Manly), July 28, 1830.
Henry W., s. Chandler (Manly) and ———, Apr. 4, 1835.
Sanford, s. Chandler and Hannah, Feb. 21, 1831.

McCOLLAH (see McColloch, McColluch, McColluh), Alford, s.
    Hanery and Marthew, Jan. 5, 1800.
Robert, h. Sarah [dec'd], Oct. 3, 1800.
Sarah, w. Robert, May 28, 1798.
Sarah, w. Allex[ande]r, Dec. 10, 1804.

McCOLLOCH (see McCollah, McColluch, McColluh), George, s.
    Robert and Sarah, Dec. 2, 1757.
[Ja‡]mes, July 10, 1759.

McCOLLUCH (see McCollah, McColloch, McColluh), Allexander,
    h. Sarah, Feb. 21, 1781.

McCOLLUH (see McCollah, McColloch, McColluch), Malinday,
    d. John and Moly, Feb. 24, 1789.

McFALL, Elizabeth, w. William, May 13, 1807.
Judith, w. W[illia]m, Sept. 21, 1815.

‡ Torn in original record ; supplied from town copy.

McFALL, William, Oct. 7, 1815.

McKEE, Robert, h. Mary dec'd, Dec. 23, 1780.

McMULLEN [Jon]atham, s. Patrick and M[torn], Sept. 8, 1763.

MEKLEM, Andrew, s. John and Martha, Dec. [torn ; prob. 1776-7].
Elisabeth, w. Robert, Feb. 16, 1758.
[R‡]obert, h. [torn], Jan. 1, 1748.
Rob[er]t, s. Rob[er]t [torn], Dec. 17, 1754.
[torn]dw, s. Rob[er]t and [torn], Nov. 9, 1759.

MELLEN (see Millen, Millin), ———, ch. Patrick and Judith, Dec. 27, 1827.

MILLEN (see Mellen, Millin), Achsah, d. Will[ia]m and Jean, Sept. 9, 1803.
Hannah, w. David, June 18, 1809.
Nathen Freeman, s. Jonathen and Sally, Oct. 4, 1791.
Pattrick, Dea., h. Mary, May 18, 1797.
Patty, w. David, Apr. 2, 1816.
Polley, d. Jonathan and Salley, Mar. 30, 1811.
Sally, d. John and Mary, June 14, 1809.

MILLIN (see Mellen, Millen), Betsey Eliza, d. Pattrick and Lovina, Aug. 25, 1811.
Levi Smith, s. Rufus and Unice, Aug. 11, 1811.

MONTGOMERY, Jane, d. Thomas and Martha, Oct. 11, 1801.
Sarah, d. Thomas and Martha, Mar. 15, 1803.

MOOR, Isebal, "Wife to James Moor Late of londonderry Decased," Feb. 13 [torn ; abt. 1774].

MOWREY, ———, ch. Osborn and Eliza Ann, still born, Nov. 10, 1819.

NASH, Samuel, Apr. 20, 1808.

NEWALL (see Newell), David, July 14, 1810.
Zibe, Feb. 20, 1841.

NEWELL (see Newall), Charles Lyman, s. Lemuel H. and Charlotte C., July 28, 1839.
Hannah, Aug. 8, 1842, a. 2.

‡ Torn in original record ; supplied from town copy.

NEWELL, Oliver D., s. David and Huldah, disease of heart, Apr.
     12, 1847, a. 2 y. 2 m.
Rufus, July 29, 1842, a. 5.

OLIVER, Mairy Paul, d. W[illia]m and Mary, Sept. 2, 1811.

PACKARD (see Packord), Anna, w. Jonathan, Aug. 26, 1838.
Eliab, Jan. 21, 1828.
Jacob, Apr. 15, 1809.
Johnithan, July 8, 1842, a. 78.
Jonathen, s. Jonathen and Anne, Oct. 4, 1805.
Justin, s. Daniel and Nancy, Nov. 19, 1839.
Martha, w. Thomas, Aug. 22, 1810.
Sally, wid., ————, 1834.
Solamon, May 5, 1830.
Sophronia, w. Joel, June 9, 1838.
Thomas, Sept. 27, 1822.

PACKORD (see Packard), Ira, s. Jonathan, Oct. 15, 1814.

PARK, Jenney, d. Stewart James and Nancy, Feb. 2, 1802.
Nancy, w. James Stewart, Dec. 22, 1803.

PEBELS (see Peebels, Peebles), John, h. Mary, Jan. 1, 1780.
[torn]es, [torn] Oct. 3, 1752.

PECK, Anna, w. Jesse F., Nov. 8, 1818.
Jesse F., Nov. 26, 1822, in Rantham.
Lyman, Oct. 26, 1828.

PEEBELS (see Pebels, Peebles), John, [torn] and Anne, Apr.
     [torn; prob. 1777].

PEEBLES (see Pebels, Peebels), James, h. Rachel, Mar. 6,
     1787.
Mary, Nov. 28, 1809.
Polley, d. James and Rachel, Oct. 19, 1790.
Rob[er]t Young, s. James and Rachel, Feb. 15, 1791.

PEIRCE, Josiah Addison, s. Josiah, Feb. 10, 1819.

PETTESON, [torn]dam, h. Iseb[torn], Apr. 14, 1757.

PHILLIPS, John, Sept. 15, 1833.

POLLEY, James, Jan. 15, 1843, a. 4.

POTTER, Asa, s. Cristefor and Susannah, Apr. 20, —.

PRAT (see Pratt), Isaac, s. William and Betsey, Aug. 31, 1811.
Mary, d. W[illia]m and Betsey, Sept. 15, 1811.

PRATT (see Prat), Asenath, ch. Jonathan and Abigail, Sept. 18, 1824.
Calvin Dwight, s. Benjamin, May 17, 1838.
Hannah, ch. Jonathan and Abigail, Aug. 7, 1826.
Polly B., ch. Jonathan and Abigail, Sept. 19, 1830.

PRESHO, Zadoc Lyman, s. Zadoc and Betsy, Aug. 17, 1830.

RAMENT, Sally, " Town Paughfor," July 7, 1812.

RANDAL (see Randell), Henrietta, w. Elijah, Dec. 4, 1839.

RANDELL (see Randal), Lyman Willard, s. Warren and Asenath, Aug. 30, 1843.
Zeviah, Oct. 4, 1834.

RANKEN (see Rankin, Rinken), Cyntha, d. John (Rinken) and Mary, Mar. 30, 1795.

RANKIN (see Ranken, Rinken), Anna, w. John Esq., Feb. 21, 1829.
Austin H., s. John and Anna, Oct. 4, 1817.
James, July 11, 1823.
John H., Feb. 16, 1835.
John, Lt., Aug. 1, 1830.
Mary, w. John, Feb. 9, 1814.
Mary Caroline, d. John Esq., Apr. 23, 1829.
Patty Millen, d. John Esq., Aug. 1, 1829.
Polly, Feb. 6, 1823.
Polly, wid., Sept. 11, 1829.
Sally [dup. Salley], d. James and Sarah [dup. Salley], June 14 [dup. 16], 1810.
Sarah [dup. Salley], w. James, Feb. 18, 1811.
Silas, May 22, 1834.

RENIFF, Abisha, Mar. 28, 1838.
Ephraim Kimball, s. Ephrain and Betsey, Oct. 3, 1828.
Eunice, d. Abisha and Huldah, Sept. 12, 1808.
Eunice, d. Morey and Sally, Mar. 26, 1811.
Huldah, w. Abisha [dec'd], Mar. 30, 1838.

RHOADS, Abigal, d. Solomon and Elinor, Feb. 27, 1803.
Amos, s. Solomon and Elinor, Apr. 15, 1794.
Battsey, d. Solomon and Elinor, July 16, 1801.
James, s. Solomon and Elinor, Oct. —, 1795.

RICHARDSON, Rinaldo V. [dup. Rineldo V. Richerson], s. Wyat and Hannah, lung fever, July 6, 1842, a. 5.

RIDER, Isaac, s. Isaac and w., Jan. 5, 1811.
John, Aug. 20, 1839.

RINKEN (see Ranken, Rankin), Amos, s. John and Mary, May 1, 1790.
Melinda, d. James and Sarah, Nov. 9, 1802.
Polly, d. John and Mary, June 18, 1795.

ROBINSON, Ellen Stone, ch. Abiel and Maryan, July 29, 1830.
Sanford Mason, ch. Abiel and Maryan, July 18, 1830.
————, inf. Abiel and Maryann, Dec. 25, 1837.

RUGGLES, Dwight, s. Constant and Sairah, Aug. 21, 1811.

SALFRIDGE (see Selfridge), Elizabeth, w. Edward, May 8, 1800.

SAMPSON (see Samson), Ezra, s. Nathenal and Nancy, Sept. 13, 1800.
Huldah, d. Nath[anie]ll and Nancy, Jan. 19, 1802.

SAMSON (see Sampson), [H‡]anah, d. Nath[anie]l and Nany, Apr. 19, 1789.

SELFRIDGE (see Salfridge), Edward, h. Elisabeth, Oct. 15, 17 [torn].
[M‡]artha, d. [Ed‡]ward and Elisabeth, Jan. 30, 1763.
Rebekah, Jan. 3, 1815.

SHAW, James, Aug. 18, 1832.
Maria, d. Eunice, wid., Sept. 8, 1838.
Nancy, Oct. 10, 1834.
Stewart, m., b. Palmer, consumption, Apr. 1, 1846.

SIBLEY, Ebeneazer, Mar. 13, 1827.
Ebenezer, May 12, 1819.

SLOAN, Archa, s. Samul and Eunic, Oct. 16, 1794.
Elizibath, w. David, Sept. 24, 1811.
George Washington, Feb. 10, 1837.
James, h. Margret [dec'd], Mar. 17, 1786 [dup. 1776].
James Procter, s. Mary, wid., Aug. 5, 1838.
Margret, w. James, Feb. 8, 1780.
Polly, w. Gardner, Sept. 4, 1811.
Samuel, h. Eunice, Mar. 19, 1810.

‡ Torn in original record; supplied from town copy.

SMITH, Betsy, Jan. 3, 1843, a. 75.
David F., Nov 30, 1833.
Job [dup. h. Mehetable], Feb. 14, 1805, a. 28.
Mehitabel, wid., ——, 1835.
William, July 6, 1814, a. 34.

SMITT, ——, inf. Job and Polly, ——, 1833.

SOUTHWORTH, Solomon, s. Abiah and Kesiah, Nov. 17, 1801.
Solomon, s. Abiah and Kesiah, May 16, 1803.

STEPHENSON, Elizabeth, wid., Aug. 27, 1837.
John, Mar. 31, 1835.
Samuel, Feb. 4, 1814.

STRATON, Frances, Jan. 24, 1802, a. 85.

SWAN, Robert, Jan. 30, 1812.

TAYLOR, Abiah, w. John dec'd, Apr. 16, 1818.
Jam[e]s, h. Margr[torn], Mar. 28, 1755.
James, h. Abia, Mar. 24, 1798.

THOMPSEN (see Thompson, Tomson), Peleg, s. James and Matilda, Apr. 16, 1799.

THOMPSON (see Thompsen, Tomson), Alfred Taylor, s. Peleg P. and Permelia, Sept. 12, 1838.
Ambrose, s. Pamelia, wid., Apr. 13, 1839.
Daniel, Oct. 10, 1822, in Penn.
Dorcas, d. James and Mary, June 28, 1776.
Georg, s. John and [P‡]rudance, Mar. 17, 1784.
James, Nov. 24, 1821.
James, June 10, 1839.
John, Dea., July 14, 1809.
Levi, s. Tho[ma]s and Jean, Nov. 14, 1791.
Lucy, d. James and Mary, Mar. 22, 1800.
Margaret, Oct. 9, 1825.
Martha, w. James dec'd, Aug. 25, 1774 [this date has been crossed out].
Mary, d. John and Prudance, Mar. 8, 1759.
Mary, wid. James, Jan. 8, 1833, a. 91.
Mehitable, d. Daniel and Sarah, Feb. 20, 1811.
Melinda, d. James, Nov. 14, 1834.
Merrick Monroe, s. Isaac and Marcia, Aug. 5, 1830.

‡ Torn in original record ; supplied from town copy.

THOMPSON, Peleg Pierce, Apr. 9, 1839.
Sarah, June 25, 1836.
Silas B., Feb. 24. 1814.
[W‡]illiam, s. Joseph and Margret, June 13. 1779.

THURBER, Joanna, w. Ozias. Jan. 31, 1823.
Mary Maria, d. W[illia]m W., Jan. 11, 1838.

THURSTEN (see Thurston, Thuston), Susanna, w. James, Aug.
    22, 1825.

THURSTON (see Thursten, Thuston), Nancy, d. Paul and
    Mary, Aug. 28, 1829.
Paul, Oct. 12, 1829.
Susannah (d. wid. Thuston), Mar. 25, 1807.

THUSTON (see Thursten, Thurston), Paul. h. Mary. Mar. 10.
    1797.

TINKHAM, David, s. Joseph and Mary. May 10, 1791.
Hannah, d. Joseph and Mary, Oct. 22, 1792.

TOMSOM (see Thompsen, Thompson). Asa. b. Belchertown.
    s. Roswell and Anna, consumption, Dec. 21. 1847, a.
    45.
James, July 2, 1843, a. 26.
James T., s. Asa and Ruth, disentery, Aug. 1, 1844. a. 11 m.
    24 d.
Rachael, m., b. Ware, numb palsey, Dec. 17, [18]47, a. 71.
Roswell, widr., consumption, Mar. 22, [18]49, a. 73.

TORNER, [Wi‡]lliam, s. James and [torn], Jan. 26, 1761.

TURNER, Sunner, s. Miss Zilpha (Turnr), Nov. 6, 1832.

TYLOR, E[un]ice, d. Daniel and Molly, June 9, 1796.

WALLACE, Cloe. w. James. Aug. 24. 1840.

WASHBURN, Abraham, h. Mary, June 29. 1803.

WEDGE, Cyntha, w. Lemuel C., Nov. 10. 1841.
Cynthia, w. Naham. Nov. 15. 1811.

WESCOTT (see Westcott), Ruben, Jr., June 5, 1816, a. 14.
Walter, Mar. 17, 1841.
Walter D., s. J. T. and Ann, congestion of the lungs, Feb. 17,
    1849, a. 9 m. 10 d.

‡ Torn in original record; supplied from town copy.

WESTCOTT (see Wescott), Hannah, d. Ruben and Lucy, Nov. 24, 1828.
Lucy, w. Reuben, — 21, 1839.
Reuben Arratus, s. Walter and Harriet, Apr. 14, 1838.
Sally C., w. Jared T., Sept. 23, 1835.
Zoe Taft, d. Reuben and Lucy, Oct. 22, 1831, a. 21.
———, inf. Jared T. and Sally, Jan. 5, 1834.

WETHERBY, ———, inf. Varnum and Betsey, June 19, 1838.

WHEELER, Mariah Jane, d. Nathaniel [and] Faithfull, June 22, 1826.

WHIPPLE, Abigail, Dec. 23, 1841, a. 86.
Joseph, h. Azubah, Sept. 25, 1821.

WILDER, Rhoda, Miss, Apr. 27, 1839.

WILEY, Margarett, b. Wendell, w. George S., d. Levi Gates and Ann, May —, 1844, a. 19.

WILLAMS, (see Williams), Jasen, s. Silas (Williams) and Susannah, June 9, 1803.
Silas, s. Silas and Susannah, Sept. 3, 1803.

WILLIAMS (see Willams), Polly, d. Silas and Susannah, Oct. 6, 1800.

WOOD, Lydia, w. Jonathan, Sept. 29, 1839.

WOODS, George N., Jan. 27, 1836.
William, Mar. 9, 1838.

WRIGHT, Theodotia, w. Dea. Josiah of Pittsfield, Oct. 25, 1817, a. 73.

www.ingramcontent.com/pod-product-compliance
Lightning Source LLC
Chambersburg PA
CBHW061327220825